The HEALTHY HEART Cookbook

Oxmoor House®

Library of Congress Catalog Card Number: 92-80724
ISBN: 0-8487-0797-4

Manufactured in the United States of America
Eighth Printing 1994

Editor-in-Chief: Nancy J. Fitzpatrick
Executive Editor: Ann H. Harvey
Senior Foods Editor: Susan Carlisle Payne
Senior Editor, Editorial Services: Olivia Kindig Wells
Director of Manufacturing: Jerry R. Higdon
Art Director: James Boone

The Healthy Heart Cookbook

Editor: Lisa A. Hooper
Assistant Editor: Caroline A. Grant, R.D.
Associate Foods Editor: Cathy A. Wesler, R.D.
Copy Editor: Diane Lewis Swords
Editorial Assistant: Carole Cain
Director, Test Kitchens: Vanessa Taylor Johnson
Assistant Director, Test Kitchens: Gayle Hays Sadler
Test Kitchen Home Economists: L. Michele Brown, Elizabeth Luckett,
   Angie Neskaug Sinclair, Christina A. Pieroni, Kathleen Royal, Jan A. Smith
Senior Photographer: Jim Bathie
Photographer: Ralph Anderson
Senior Photo Stylist: Kay E. Clarke
Photo Stylist: Virginia R. Cravens
Designer: Carol Damsky
Associate Production Manager: Theresa L. Beste
Production Assistant: Pam Beasley Bullock
Text and Recipe Coordination: Helen Anne Dorrough, M.S., R.D.
Medical Consultant: Julius Linn, M.D., University of Alabama at
   Birmingham Medical Center

Cover: *Pork Medaillons with Sweet Peppers (page 176)*
Back Cover: *Chocolate-Crème de Menthe Pie (page 116)*
Frontispiece: *Elegant Peach Cups with Raspberry Sauce (page 114)*

CONTENTS

HEALTHY HEART Lifestyle

LIVING A HEALTHY LIFESTYLE

*Building a healthy lifestyle takes commitment. Habits learned throughout a
lifetime are hard to break, but with desire, determination, and patience change is possible.
The changes that last tend to come about in small increments. As you gradually build on them and
make them part of everyday life, they become habits. And while it is best to start healthy habits
early in life, adopting good habits at any age can have a positive impact on heart health.*

Using *The Healthy Heart Cookbook* can be
the first step toward making those positive
lifestyle changes because it shows you just how
delicious and satisfying nutritious eating can
be. It features strategies for reducing the risk of
heart disease and stroke, techniques for heart-
healthy cooking, and delicious recipes low in
fat, cholesterol, and sodium that everyone
can enjoy.

Of course, even with the healthiest of diets,
some of the risk factors for heart disease—age,
sex, heredity—cannot be changed. But living a
healthy lifestyle is a choice that can help you
beat the odds of developing heart disease and
increase your chances of living a longer, hap-
pier, healthier life.

Atherosclerosis

The underlying cause of coronary heart disease is atherosclerosis, or hardening of the
arteries, in which cholesterol, fat, and scar tissue are deposited in the walls of arteries. This
buildup, often referred to as plaque, narrows the
vessel, decreasing the amount of blood that can
reach organs or muscles normally supplied by
the affected vessel.

If a coronary artery—one of the arteries that
supply the heart muscle with oxygen and
nutrients—becomes sufficiently narrowed, the
heart muscle does not receive enough blood.
This causes angina, or chest pain, which usually
occurs during exertion when the heart must pump
harder than usual. If an artery is completely
blocked—usually by a blood clot forming in a
vessel narrowed by plaque buildup—the blockage prevents blood and oxygen from reaching a
portion of the heart muscle. The result is a
heart attack.

If one of the arteries in the neck that supply
blood to a portion of the brain becomes sufficiently narrowed, a stroke can occur. The consequences of the stroke depend on the location
of the blockage and the part of the body the
affected portion of the brain controls. Symp-
toms can range from transient confusion to
paralysis of one side of the body to loss of func-
tions such as speech and swallowing.

The actual causes of atherosclerosis are
unknown, but scientists do know that it is a
slowly progressive disease. Plaque buildup begins
in early childhood, particularly in countries
such as ours where people eat foods high in saturated fat and cholesterol.

Risk Factors for Coronary Heart Disease

There are some uncontrollable risk factors associated with coronary heart disease. Compared to women, men have a greater chance of developing heart disease—at least until women reach menopause. At menopause, a woman's risk of heart disease begins increasing dramatically. If your family has a history of heart disease before age 55, your risk for a heart attack is increased. And certainly the older you become, the greater your risk of heart disease.

However, there are several primary and secondary risk factors for coronary heart disease over which you do have some control, whether through diet, exercise, lifestyle, or medication.

Primary Risk Factors

Primary risk factors for heart disease are those circumstances that directly affect heart health, including blood cholesterol levels, high blood pressure, smoking, and physical inactivity.

High Blood Cholesterol Levels Cholesterol is a major component of plaque, and the rate that plaque forms is related to how much cholesterol is in the blood. The higher your total blood cholesterol level, the greater your risk of suffering a heart attack. In fact, blood cholesterol levels are thought by some to be the single most important correctable risk factor in the development of heart disease.

Blood cholesterol levels depend to an extent on the amount of cholesterol in your diet, but more importantly on the amount of saturated fat you eat. The liver uses saturated fat to manufacture cholesterol, which is essential for cell formation and hormone production. Cholesterol cannot move through the bloodstream on its own but must be carried by substances called lipoproteins, which is a combination of the words lipid (a medical term for fat) and protein.

Low-density lipoproteins (LDL), the "bad guys" in the cholesterol-coronary heart disease story, are the most abundant lipoproteins, carrying 65 percent of the cholesterol circulating in the blood. LDL got its reputation because it carries cholesterol to cells and deposits excess cholesterol in artery walls. Thus, high levels of LDL-cholesterol increase the buildup of plaque in artery walls, raising the risk of heart disease.

On the other hand, high-density lipoproteins (HDL) carry only small amounts of cholesterol, but their role is a vital one. HDL carries cholesterol away from artery walls, decreasing plaque buildup. Hence, high levels of HDL decrease the risk of developing coronary artery disease. While the type of food you eat does not increase HDL-cholesterol levels, exercising consistently, losing weight, and stopping smoking will.

Lowering High Blood Cholesterol

The National Cholesterol Education Program guidelines will help you lower your blood cholesterol:

- Eat fewer high-fat foods, especially those high in saturated fats.
- Replace part of the saturated fats in your diet with unsaturated fats.
- Eat fewer high-cholesterol foods.
- Choose foods high in complex carbohydrates.
- Reduce your weight if you are overweight.

When you go for a blood cholesterol test, you should ask not only for a total cholesterol measurement but also for an HDL-cholesterol measurement, according to a recently convened National Institutes of Health panel of experts. An HDL level below 35 mg/dl, even when total cholesterol is in the 200 mg/dl desirable range, puts you in a high-risk category for coronary heart disease. A ratio of total cholesterol to HDL-cholesterol lower than 4.5 puts you in a below-average risk category. An easy way to remember it is that your total cholesterol should be no more than about four times higher than your HDL.

High Blood Pressure   Blood pressure, the measure of the force of blood against arterial walls, is recorded in units that reflect how many millimeters the pressure can raise a column of mercury. Hence, blood pressure is reported in terms of millimeters (mm) of mercury (Hg).

Each time the heart beats, blood is pumped out and creates a surge of pressure called the systolic pressure—the top number in a blood pressure reading. The pressure in the arteries between heartbeats is the diastolic pressure, the bottom number. People with high blood pressure (hypertension) also have narrowed, or tightened, vessels. Therefore, the heart must work harder to pump blood through the body. This strains the heart muscle and, over time, causes it to enlarge and weaken. Research also indicates that high blood pressure damages the walls of arteries, which increases the chances of developing atherosclerosis.

A blood pressure greater than 140 mm Hg systolic or 90 mm Hg diastolic needs treatment. It is best to keep blood pressure around 120/80 mm Hg. Lowering blood pressure lowers the risk of heart disease and stroke.

Blood pressure tends to increase with age. A young person with a normal blood pressure may develop high blood pressure later in life. Men are more likely to have high blood pressure than women up to about age 50. After that, high blood pressure is more common in women.

The cause of most cases of high blood pressure is not known; however, medical experts agree that changes in lifestyle can help lower blood pressure. These lifestyle changes include exercising regularly, losing extra pounds, reducing alcohol intake, and stopping smoking. For some, limiting sodium intake proves effective. For those who still have high blood pressure despite lifestyle changes, medications can bring it into the normal range.

Cigarette Smoking   Of all the habits that can damage health, none has been as clearly documented as smoking. It contributes to atherosclerosis by damaging arteries and making it easier for plaque to build up and block the arteries, including those that supply blood to the heart. Smoking can raise total blood cholesterol levels, lower protective HDL-cholesterol levels, and increase the stickiness of blood platelets, making a blood clot more likely to form.

Carbon monoxide in smoke reduces the amount of oxygen the blood can carry, while nicotine causes the heart to beat faster and use more oxygen. Smoking may also constrict coronary arteries, interfering with the supply of oxygen to the heart muscle during physical exertion. And smoking raises blood pressure. All of these are conditions for a heart attack.

Physical Inactivity   There is a significant relationship between coronary artery disease and physical inactivity. Those who exercise regularly have fewer fatal heart attacks than those who are sedentary, and stand a better chance of surviving a heart attack if one occurs.

Regular physical activity is one of the few things known to raise levels of protective HDL-cholesterol. At the same time, it lowers potentially harmful LDL-cholesterol and triglycerides, which are fats circulating in the blood that may contribute to atherosclerosis.

Exercise helps strengthen the heart and improves its overall fitness. A strong heart doesn't have to work as hard to circulate blood through the body because it can pump more efficiently with each beat. Exercise also improves the ability of other muscles to efficiently use the available blood and oxygen they receive, and it may widen coronary arteries so more blood can flow to the heart muscle.

The American Heart Association (AHA) recommends 30 to 60 minutes of aerobic activity—the kind that makes the heart beat faster—three to four times a week. Aerobic activities include running, swimming, biking, hiking, climbing stairs, jumping rope, cross-country skiing, brisk walking, raking leaves, and mowing grass. If you're over 40 or have any risk factors for heart disease, check with your doctor before beginning an exercise program.

Secondary Risk Factors

Secondary risk factors for heart disease are those factors that indirectly affect heart health, such as diabetes mellitus, obesity, and stress.

Diabetes Mellitus The condition called diabetes mellitus is the inability of the body to metabolize glucose properly. It occurs as Type I (insulin-dependent), which usually begins in childhood, or Type II (noninsulin-dependent), previously called adult-onset diabetes.

Type II accounts for at least 90 percent of the cases and usually is associated with obesity. The pivotal treatment is loss of excess weight. Diabetes, whatever the type, causes an increase in lipid (blood fat) abnormalities, an increase in cholesterol levels, and damage to artery walls that greatly accelerates the process of atherosclerosis and heart disease. Today, heart disease is the major cause of death in people with diabetes.

Obesity Excess weight strains the heart, increasing the risk of high blood pressure, diabetes, and high blood cholesterol. People who are more than 30 percent over ideal body weight are more likely to develop heart disease and suffer strokes, even if they have no other risk factors.

Weight can be reduced by eating fewer calories and increasing physical activity on a regular basis. Doctors and nutritionists recommend a diet of nutritious, low-fat foods such as whole grains, lean meats, poultry, fish, fruits, vegetables, and low-fat dairy products. Also, watching portion size is an important part of losing weight while eating a balanced diet.

Stress The relationship between stress and coronary heart disease has not been proved. However, stressful behavior can affect heart health in many ways. For example, stress may prevent an individual from living a heart-healthy lifestyle that includes eating right, exercising regularly, and stopping smoking. People under great stress may feel these lifestyle changes are too difficult and time consuming.

Nutrition and a Healthy Heart

The AHA recently revised its dietary guidelines for the prevention of coronary heart disease. The following guidelines are considered safe and prudent for all healthy American adults. Immediately following the AHA guidelines you will find more detailed information on each of the components including fat, cholesterol, carbohydrate, protein, and sodium intake as well as alcohol consumption, calorie intake, and food variety.

American Heart Association Dietary Guidelines

1. Total fat intake should be less than 30 percent of calories.
2. Saturated fat intake should be less than 10 percent of calories.
3. Polyunsaturated fat intake should not exceed 10 percent of calories.
4. Cholesterol intake should not exceed 300 milligrams a day.
5. Carbohydrate intake should make up 50 percent or more of calories, with emphasis on complex carbohydrates.
6. Protein intake should provide the remainder of calories.
7. Sodium intake should not exceed 3 grams (3,000 milligrams) a day.
8. Alcohol consumption should not exceed 1 to 2 ounces a day. Two ounces of 100-proof whiskey, 8 ounces of wine, or 24 ounces of beer each contain 2 ounces of ethanol.
9. Total calories should be sufficient to maintain an individual's recommended body weight.
10. A wide variety of foods should be consumed.

Fat Intake

Most Americans consume at least 10 percent more fat than they should each day. Trimming down from 40 percent of calories from fat to 30 percent is a significant reduction. At first, the confusing part may be figuring out how much fat is allowed in the diet each day.

How much fat is 30 percent of calories? For a male who consumes about 2200 calories a day, 30 percent of calories would be 660 calories (2200 x .30). Divide that amount by 9 (there are 9 calories in a gram of fat) and that tells you that 30 percent of his total calories is about 75 grams of fat. Since most product labels show the amount of fat in grams, it seems easier to know how many grams of fat you can have rather than how many calories from fat.

What's Your Fat Limit?

Calories Per Day	30 Percent of Calories	Grams of Fat
1,200	360	40
1,500	450	50
1,800	540	60
2,000	600	66
2,200	660	73
2,500	750	83
2,800	840	93

There are two major types of fat—saturated and unsaturated. Unsaturated fats are further classified as polyunsaturated or monounsaturated. Together they comprise total fat intake.

Saturated Fat Saturated fats are found in animal products and a few vegetable products; they are usually solid at room temperature.

Animal products such as high-fat meats, lard, poultry skin, and whole-milk dairy products contain large amounts of saturated fat. Tropical oils—coconut, palm, palm kernel, and cocoa butter—are saturated fats that come from plants. Tropical oils are used in many convenience products and confectioneries. Saturated fats can raise your blood cholesterol levels more than anything else in your diet and should be limited to less than 10 percent of calories. Even if almost no cholesterol is eaten, blood cholesterol levels may remain high if saturated fats are not limited in the diet.

Unsaturated Fat Unsaturated fats are usually liquid at room temperature and are classified as either monounsaturated or polyunsaturated fats.

Polyunsaturated fats help lower blood cholesterol. Polyunsaturated fats are found mainly in vegetable oils such as safflower, sunflower, corn, soybean, sesame, and cottonseed oils, and should account for no more than 10 percent of total calories.

Monounsaturated fats may be even more effective in reducing blood cholesterol levels. Canola, olive, avocado, and peanut oils as well as most nuts and oils from nuts are monounsaturated fats, which should account for no more than 10 percent of total calories.

Hydrogenation Vegetable oils are changed from their natural liquid state to a more solid form by a process called hydrogenation. During hydrogenation, air is rapidly incorporated into the oil, filling all the empty spaces on the molecules with hydrogen. This causes the liquid to take on a more solid form and become a more saturated fat with the potential of raising blood cholesterol levels.

Completely hydrogenated oils, such as vegetable shortening, resemble saturated fats in their cholesterol-raising ability. Partially hydrogenated oils, such as margarine, are acceptable if they contain twice as much polyunsaturated as saturated fat. This breakdown is often listed on the label.

Children and Fat Intake Because heart disease begins early in life, children two years of age and older, like their parents, should consume no more than 30 percent of calories as fat, and no more than 10 percent of calories should come from saturated fat. This age group should also consume no more than 300 milligrams of dietary cholesterol per day. Children under two years of age should not be placed on any type of fat restriction. Fat is needed during the formative years to ensure proper development of the brain, bones, and muscles.

Comparison of Fats

	Saturated Fatty Acids	Monounsaturated Fatty Acids	Polyunsaturated Fatty Acids

Food			
Canola oil	7%	58%	35%
Safflower oil	10%	13%	77%
Sunflower oil	11%	20%	69%
Corn oil	13%	25%	62%
Olive oil	14%	77%	9%
Soybean oil	15%	24%	61%
Peanut oil	18%	49%	33%
Margarine	19%	49%	32%
Vegetable Shortening	28%	44%	28%
Lard	41%	47%	12%
Beef fat	52%	44%	4%
Butter	66%	30%	4%

Source: *Composition of Foods, Agriculture Handbook No. 8-4.* Washington, D.C.: USDA, 1990.

Cholesterol Intake

Cholesterol is a soft, waxy, fat-like substance. You get cholesterol from the body producing what little it needs and from eating animal products.

Cholesterol is an essential substance found in all cell walls where its function is to help waterproof the skin and slow down the evaporation of water from the body, as well as aid in the formation of certain hormones and serve as insulation around nerves. Many people fail to distinguish between this type of cholesterol that the body manufactures and dietary cholesterol, which comes from the foods you eat.

Because the body automatically produces most of the cholesterol it needs, dietary cholesterol isn't necessary. If too much cholesterol gets into the bloodstream, it can build up on blood vessel walls, clog the vessels, and lead to coronary heart disease. The AHA recommends that dietary cholesterol intake should not exceed 300 milligrams per day for a healthy heart.

Eating foods high in saturated fats and dietary cholesterol may increase total blood cholesterol and LDL-cholesterol levels. For this reason, a diet low in cholesterol and saturated fat is the first line of defense against high blood cholesterol levels. The type of food you eat does not influence HDL-cholesterol levels, however. (For further explanation, see page 9.)

Some foods that are high in dietary cholesterol, such as shrimp and oysters, are actually low in saturated fat. Compare the saturated fat content and cholesterol content of the foods in the chart below to help you make the healthiest choices.

Saturated Fat vs. Cholesterol

Food (3 ounces cooked)	Saturated Fat (grams)	Cholesterol (milligrams)
Chicken, light meat, skinned	1.1	73
Turkey, light meat, skinned	0.3	74
Turkey frankfurters (2)	5.0	92
Top round beef	1.9	72
T-bone steak	8.7	72
Ham, cured, extra lean	1.2	39
Pork tenderloin	1.4	80
Lobster	0.1	62
Oysters	1.1	93
Shrimp	0.2	167

Blood Cholesterol Levels

	Total Cholesterol	LDL Level	HDL Level
Desirable	Less than 200 mg/dl	130 mg/dl	More than 45 mg/dl
Borderline High	200-239 mg/dl	130-159 mg/dl	
High	240 mg/dl	160 mg/dl	Less than 35 mg/dl

The National Cholesterol Education Program states that people should aim for cholesterol levels of 200 mg/dl or less. At this level there is a relatively low risk for heart disease, but that doesn't necessarily mean "no" risk. As previously mentioned, a low HDL-cholesterol level increases the risk of coronary heart disease even with a desirable cholesterol level. A blood cholesterol level in the 200 to 239 mg/dl range is considered borderline high; people with a blood cholesterol level in this range have twice the risk of heart disease as those with levels below 200. Levels of 240 mg/dl or greater are considered high and carry over twice the risk of heart disease than do blood cholesterol levels of 200 mg/dl or less.

Carbohydrate Intake

There are two types of carbohydrates: simple (sugars) and complex (starch and fiber). Both types are found naturally in fruits, vegetables, whole grains, and milk. Simple carbohydrates may be either fruit sugars or concentrated sugars such as table sugar, corn syrup, and honey. Complex carbohydrates are found in whole grain breads and cereals, pastas, legumes, vegetables, and fruits.

Complex carbohydrates are an excellent substitute for foods high in saturated fat and cholesterol. Not only are these foods lower in calories, but they also contain vitamins, minerals, and fiber. Carbohydrates have 4 calories per gram while fat has 9 calories per gram. Exchanging complex carbohydrates for fat is an easy way to cut calories, and you are more likely to help lower blood cholesterol, reduce the risk of heart disease, and lose weight.

Americans get 47 percent of their calories from carbohydrates. The AHA recommends that 50 to 60 percent of daily calorie intake come from carbohydrates. According to U.S. Dietary Guidelines, adults should consume at least six servings of breads, grains, and cereals and at least five servings of fruits and vegetables each day.

Complex carbohydrates are the main sources for dietary fiber. The dietary fiber found in complex carbohydrates is an important part of a healthy diet because it can help lower blood cholesterol levels; in addition, it may also reduce the risk of colon cancer. There are two types of dietary fiber: water-insoluble and water-soluble. Foods typically contain a mixture of both types of fiber but are often more concentrated in one type.

Although insoluble fiber is less important in fighting heart disease, this fiber is necessary for overall health. Insoluble fiber is found mainly in whole grains, wheat bran, fruits, and vegetables.

Soluble fiber (gums and pectin) helps lower blood cholesterol. It has also been shown to stabilize blood sugar levels, an important factor for people with diabetes. Soluble fiber is found in fruits, vegetables, legumes, oats, oat bran, barley, brown rice, and seeds.

Carbohydrate Benefits

Complex carbohydrates can offer health benefits in the following ways:

- Help lower blood cholesterol.
- Decrease risk of some types of cancer.
- Help reduce risk of heart disease.
- Aid in weight loss and control of diabetes.
- Provide B-vitamins and iron.
- Supply soluble and insoluble fiber.

Protein Intake

Proteins consist of amino acids that are linked together. The body manufactures some amino acids, referred to as nonessential amino acids. Dietary protein provides the essential amino acids that cannot be made by the body. Protein contains 4 calories per gram and is necessary for building and repairing body tissue and manufacturing enzymes. It takes very little protein to meet these needs. According to the AHA guidelines, only about 20 percent of total daily calories should be made up of protein. The average American diet contains more than enough protein.

It is easy to get enough protein from a mixture of vegetables alone. Good sources of vegetable protein include bean curd (tofu), peas, and beans. Yet most people are not willing to give up meat. The way to fit meat into a heart-healthy diet is to simply decrease the amount of meat eaten and to choose the leanest cuts.

Sodium Intake

The human body requires only 250 milligrams (⅛ teaspoon) of sodium a day, yet present consumption in the U.S. has been estimated at 4,000 to 6,000 milligrams (4 to 6 grams or 2 to 3 teaspoons) per day. The AHA recommends decreasing sodium intake to less than 3,000 milligrams (3 grams or 1½ teaspoons) per day. Cutting back on sodium may help lower blood pressure in some individuals.

Alcohol Consumption

Alcohol consumption in America has increased over the last three decades. The ill effects of drinking too much alcohol are well established—increased incidence of accidental death, liver disease, high blood pressure, and stroke, in addition to a disrupted social life.

Some studies have shown that modest alcohol consumption may raise HDL-cholesterol levels and lower the incidence of coronary heart disease. However, this is still being studied, and the AHA does not advise the use of alcohol in hopes of preventing heart disease.

Calories

The number of calories consumed is often greater than the actual amount needed for the body to function. In short, Americans are putting on weight. Studies have shown that even a moderate weight increase of 10 to 30 percent over ideal weight is a risk factor for heart disease. Calories taken in and not expended immediately are converted to triglycerides and stored in fat cells. Triglycerides, a type of fat found in food and fatty tissues in the body, provide the body with energy and a way to store excess calories. A high triglyceride level generally goes hand-in-hand with the high LDL- and low HDL-cholesterol levels that increase the risk of heart disease. Excess body weight is also linked to high blood pressure, elevated blood cholesterol levels, and diabetes.

Variety of Foods

Choosing a wide variety of foods is like taking out an insurance policy to make sure you have adequate nutrient coverage. The vitamins and minerals obtained from eating many different foods eliminate the need for a supplement. In addition, variety in flavor, color, and texture also adds palatability and interest to menus.

Sample Nutrition Label

**Vanilla Swirl Frozen Yogurt
Nutrition Information Per Serving**

Serving size........................3 fl oz
Servings per container...........2.3
Calories.................................95
Protein....................................2g
Carbohydrate.......................15g
Fat..3g
Cholesterol...........................5mg
Sodium................................50mg

New labeling laws propose that labels list a serving size "customarily consumed by an average person over the age of four, and it must appear in common household and metric measures, such as 1 cup (240 milliliters)." This law should eliminate any adjusting of serving size.

Protein, carbohydrate, and fat are listed in grams (see Sample Nutrition Label above). Protein and carbohydrate each supply 4 calories per gram. Fat, which has the most calories, supplies 9 calories per gram. To figure the number of calories that comes from each nutrient, multiply the grams per serving by the number of calories in a gram (see Calculating Calories per Gram chart below).

Then, to determine the percent of calories from protein, carbohydrate, or fat, simply divide the number of calories each nutrient yields by the total number of calories per serving, in this case 95. For example, 27 calories from fat ÷ 95 total calories = 28 percent fat per serving (28 percent of total calories per serving derived from fat).

Calculating Calories per Gram

	Grams Per Serving		Calories Per Gram		Total
Protein	2	x	4	=	8
Carbohydrate	15	x	4	=	60
Fat	3	x	9	=	27

At present, few foods list the number of calories from fat. Yet knowing these numbers helps put the fat content of a food into perspective, particularly when foods are advertised as being a certain percentage fat free. New labeling proposals will require the number of calories derived from fat to be listed on the nutrition label, though listing the percent of calories from fat will be optional.

Listing cholesterol content on a food label is currently optional unless a claim is made about it. Under new labeling proposals, foods that have been reduced in cholesterol by 25 percent or more can claim they are low cholesterol. If a product claims it is reduced-cholesterol, then the label must explain what the reduction is and the reduction must be more than 20 milligrams per serving. The FDA currently allows the following cholesterol terminology to be used on food products:

Cholesterol free—2 milligrams or less of cholesterol per serving.

Low cholesterol—20 milligrams or less of cholesterol per serving.

Reduced cholesterol—75 percent or more reduction in the amount of cholesterol from the original food; both original and reduced amount must be shown.

All foods making a nutritional claim must list the sodium content. Terms that can be used when referring to sodium content include:

Sodium-free or salt-free—5 milligrams or less of sodium per serving.

Very low sodium—35 milligrams or less of sodium per serving.

Low sodium—140 milligrams or less of sodium per serving.

Reduced sodium—75 percent less sodium than the regular product.

Lower or less salt—25 percent less sodium than the regular product.

No-salt-added, unsalted, without added salt—no salt added during processing to a food usually processed with salt.

The second part of a nutrition information label—Percentage of U.S. Recommended Daily Allowances (U.S. RDA)—currently must list protein, vitamins A and C, thiamine, riboflavin, niacin, calcium, and iron. Listing of other nutrients is optional unless they have been added to a product or a claim is made about them. New labeling laws would make the listing of thiamine, riboflavin, and niacin (the B vitamins) optional because people no longer suffer from diseases related to B-vitamin deficiencies.

Ingredient Label

A list of ingredients is required for all processed foods except those that are made by "standard" recipes. Ice cream, bread, jam, macaroni, fruit cocktail, mayonnaise, and catsup fall into this category because makers of these products use standard ingredients specified by the FDA. However, new labeling laws will require an ingredient list on standardized foods because many consumers don't know the contents of these foods.

Ingredients must be listed in descending order according to weight—that is, the ingredient of largest quantity down to the one of smallest quantity. This listing doesn't show the exact amount of the ingredients, but knowing the order of ingredients is helpful in determining the healthfulness of a product. Keep in mind, however, that because the list shows only the order of ingredients without giving actual amounts, a food such as a cereal, with sugar as the second ingredient, can still be low in sugar on a percentage basis.

Often the only way to determine the source of fat and the type of fat (saturated or unsaturated) used in a product is by reading the ingredient list. A food that lists any fat as one of the first ingredients is going to be high in total fat. Less obvious sources of fat, such as nuts, cream cheese, whole milk, cheese, and poultry skin, can also run up the fat count. Carefully read labels and check how many different fats and fat-containing ingredients a food has and where they fall in the listing.

If the following ingredients appear toward the beginning of an ingredient list, the product is high in saturated fat—the kind that can raise blood cholesterol levels:

beef tallow	palm kernel oil
butter	palm oil
cocoa butter	partially hydrogenated
coconut oil	vegetable oil
cream	poultry fat
lard	shortening
meat fat	suet

The sodium content of a food product can also be judged by reading the ingredient list. Look for the following sodium-containing ingredients when reading labels:

baking powder	salt
baking soda	seasoned salt
bouillon	sodium caseinate
brine	sodium citrate
disodium inosinate	sodium nitrate
meat tenderizer	sodium phosphate
monosodium glutamate	sodium saccharin

Some products, especially cereals, provide an extra nutrition label for carbohydrate information. Most food manufacturers break down this information into starch and related carbohydrates, sucrose and other sugars, and dietary fiber. This information can be used to compare cereals, particularly where sugar and fiber are concerned. When adopted, new labeling laws will require all sweeteners to be listed together in descending order by weight. This will allow you to determine at a glance whether or not a product is high in sugar.

When the labeling laws go into effect, it will be easier to read food labels. The FDA has proposed an easy-to-read chart to be placed on about 90 percent of foods sold in supermarkets. The chart will show total calories per serving and percent of calories from fat, as well as protein, saturated fat, cholesterol, total carbohydrates, complex carbohydrates, sugars, dietary fiber, protein, sodium, vitamins A and C, calcium, and iron. Supermarkets will be asked to voluntarily label raw fruits and vegetables, seafood, meats, and poultry; if they don't, regulations will be written to make compliance mandatory. In the meantime, the information presented here will help you make healthy decisions when shopping. And when the new labels appear, many of these strategies will still apply.

Healthy Selections At the Supermarket

The number of food items offered in the supermarket is staggering. Reading the nutrition and ingredient labels and choosing the best and healthiest foods for the money will take a little extra time at first, but once you have chosen some of your staples and often-purchased items, the task becomes easier.

Don't try to read all the labels in the whole supermarket on one trip. Concentrate on items on your shopping list and if you have extra time, read the labels on the products found on one aisle or in one section of the store. By breaking the supermarket down into small sections, you'll make this huge task manageable.

The information contained on the next nine pages will guide you through the supermarket, providing you with helpful information for making healthy selections.

Fresh Produce

Fresh produce has always been considered the best nutritional buy. Fresh fruits and vegetables are naturally low in fat, calories, and sodium (except for avocados, nuts, and coconuts), and high in fiber, nutrients, and flavor.

Harvesting produce and eating it on the same day is ideal. However, most people shop at supermarkets where the produce may sit several days before it is purchased, not to mention the time it took to get the produce to the store. Though some nutrients are lost during transport, fresh fruits and vegetables are still a good source of important vitamins and minerals. To get the most nutrition from produce, shop frequently and use it as soon as possible.

Dairy Products

Shop for dairy products that are labeled skim, low-fat, or nonfat when these items appear on your grocery list.

Milk Milk and milk products run the gamut when it comes to fat, calorie, and sodium content. Nutrition labeling found on most products allows you to figure the percent of calories that comes from fat. When comparing similar products, make sure serving sizes are the same.

Lower fat milks are described by the amount of fat they contain by weight—2 percent, 1½ percent, 1 percent, and skim. Two percent milk is 35 percent fat, which makes it too high in fat to be considered a low-fat food (see chart, facing page). One percent milk and skim milk are the best choices for heart-healthy eating.

Chocolate milk, a favorite of children, is generally made from whole milk. Some local dairies now make 1 percent chocolate milk, which is a better choice for children over two years of age as well as adults.

Cheese With as much as 70 percent of calories from fat, all types of cheese have been crossed off the shopping list of many fat-conscious consumers. Cheesemakers have responded to consumer demand for good tasting, lower fat products. Still, many low-fat cheeses are over 50 percent fat.

Nutrition labeling is not required on cheese made from whole milk, but processed cheese products and reduced-fat cheeses are labeled, making it possible to calculate the fat content. Cheeses such as Brie, Monterey Jack, and Cheddar tend to be highest in fat. Part-skim cheeses such as mozzarella and ricotta contain less fat than their whole milk counterparts but not much less.

With the recent arrival of healthier cheese products—fat-free pasteurized process cheese slices, nonfat cottage cheese, and fat-free cream cheese— comes hope that a wide variety of reduced-fat and fat-free cheeses are in the making.

Yogurt   Yogurt is simply milk that has been curdled by adding bacteria. The amount of fat in yogurt depends on the amount of fat in the milk it's made from. Some yogurts are made with whole milk, but the majority are from low-fat or nonfat sources, which are the healthier choices.

Eggs and Egg Substitutes   To help keep cholesterol intake down, four eggs a week are the limit suggested by the AHA. All of the cholesterol in an egg is found in the yolk. A large yolk has about 213 milligrams of cholesterol, which is more than half the recommended amount of cholesterol for one day.

A variety of commercial egg substitutes containing no cholesterol are available. Most egg substitutes start with egg whites as the main ingredient, and most add oil, sodium, coloring, and preservatives so that the product will taste and perform like whole eggs.

Two egg whites can be used in place of a whole egg in many recipes with good results. While some recipes work fine with egg whites, others do not, so keep both egg whites and egg substitutes on hand.

Tips for Buying Eggs and Egg Substitutes:
- Buy large-size whole eggs when buying eggs for their whites; two large whole eggs yield ¼ cup egg white.
- Examine eggs before buying to make sure they are not cracked or dirty; cracked eggs may be contaminated with salmonella bacteria, and should not be used.
- Avoid buying eggs stored at room temperature.
- Remember that egg substitutes found in the freezer section should be frozen solid; if there is evidence of sweating on the carton, choose another carton.

Canned and Packaged Foods

Canned and packaged foods were, at one time, the most-used convenience items until the frozen food revolution. They are still a part of most diets because they're easy to prepare and have a long shelf life.

Tips for Buying Canned and Packaged Foods:
- Read labels and look for "packed in its own juice," "no sugar added," "water-packed," and "no-salt-added" references.
- Select canned soups or dry soup mixes that have 5 grams of fat or less per serving and are low in sodium. Several brands of canned soups have a healthy line of products.
- Look for pasta sauces that contain less than 6 grams of fat and no added salt or less than 500 milligrams of sodium per ½-cup serving.
- Choose canned fruit juices without added sugar or corn syrup.
- Buy peanut butter with oil on the top (often called natural); most brands are made with hydrogenated shortening to prevent separation and have sugar and salt added.

Comparison of Milk and Milk Products

Milk or Milk Product	Calories	Percent fat	Fat(g)	Cholesterol(mg)
2 percent milk, 1 cup	122	35	4.7	20
1 percent milk, 1 cup	102	22	2.5	10
Skim milk, 1 cup	86	4	0.4	5
Evaporated whole milk, 1 cup	338	51	19.0	73
Evaporated skimmed milk, 1 cup	200	2	0.5	10
Sweetened condensed milk, 1 cup	982	24	26.3	104
Buttermilk, 1 cup	98	19	2.1	10
Nonfat buttermilk, 1 cup	90	1	1.0	0
Chocolate milk (whole), 1 cup	208	37	8.5	30
Chocolate milk (1 percent), 1 cup	158	14	2.5	8

Grains, Legumes, and Pastas

For a nutritious main dish or side dish, grains, legumes, and pastas are hard to beat. They're rich in complex carbohydrates, protein, fiber, vitamins, and minerals and are low in fat, calories, and sodium. But beware—cooking these items with butter or topping them with a high-fat sauce can turn a healthy dish into a fat-laden one.

Grains   A wide variety of grains are often overlooked as potential main or side dishes. Amaranth, barley, bulgur (cracked wheat), hominy, grits, millet, oats, triticale, and wheat berries are such grains. All are low in fat and high in complex carbohydrates, fiber, protein, and other nutrients.

Rice is the main food for more than half the world's population, which speaks well of its nutritional content. Rice contains only a trace of fat and no cholesterol; in addition, studies have shown that rice bran—a by-product of the milling of brown rice into white rice—has cholesterol-lowering effects.

Brown rice is a better nutritional choice than white rice because it contains more fiber. Specialty rices such as basmati, texmati, wehani, and wild rice add variety and flavor to meals without adding fat or cholesterol.

Preseasoned mixes for tabbouleh, whole grain pilafs, and other whole grain dishes are beginning to appear in the supermarket. As with rice mixes, most will be equally as tasty when made with half the fat called for; thus, serving homemade side dishes made from grains, legumes, and pastas is the best way to keep fat and sodium to a minimum.

Legumes   Legumes are plants that produce pods with edible seeds such as kidney beans, pinto beans, soybeans, garbanzo beans (chickpeas), lentils, and peas (split and whole, yellow and green). They are a good source of soluble fiber (the kind that lowers blood cholesterol levels), complex carbohydrates, protein, vitamins, and minerals.

Some supermarkets offer no-salt-added versions of canned black beans, chili beans, pinto beans, kidney beans, and garbanzo beans. If you are unable to find a no-salt-added version, simply rinse canned beans of their salty liquid before using.

Pastas   Made in a seemingly endless variety of shapes, colors, and flavors, pasta is a favorite high-carbohydrate, low-fat food.

The choice of a topping for pasta can turn it from a low-fat dish into a high-fat one. Read nutrition labels to determine which pasta sauces are lowest in fat and sodium. There are several commercial tomato-based sauces that qualify as good nutrition choices. Creamy sauces, such as alfredo and clam sauce, and oil-based pesto sauce can increase the fat in a pasta dish far above a healthy level.

Breads and Cereals

Most breads and cereals are low in fat and are a good source of complex carbohydrates. The more nutritious breads and cereals are the ones that are the least refined because they contain more fiber, vitamins, and minerals.

Breads   Whole-grain breads made with liquid oil—not hydrogenated shortening—are the best choices for heart health, but figuring out which breads are whole grain can be tricky. A bread with wheat flour listed as its first ingredient is not a fiber-rich whole wheat bread. And a brown or dark-colored bread isn't necessarily whole wheat because some bread makers use caramel coloring and raisin juice to make white breads look like whole wheat.

Make sure you're getting a true whole wheat bread by choosing one that lists one of the following first on the ingredient label:

100 percent whole wheat
Stone ground whole wheat flour
Whole grain
Rye
Multigrain
Cracked wheat

Commercial biscuits, cornbreads, muffins, and quick breads are higher in fat, particularly saturated fat, than plain breads. Reading labels is important in the evaluation of these products. However, many products are not labeled. One way to make sure a quick bread meets healthy guidelines is to make it from scratch using less fat (preferably a liquid oil), less sugar, and egg whites or an egg substitute.

Italian and French breads and rolls are often made without fat and may come in whole-grain varieties, which makes them a good low-fat choice. Other nutritious bread choices include whole grain bagels, whole wheat pita rounds, breadsticks, whole grain English muffins, corn tortillas, flour tortillas made with oil, and sourdough bread and rolls.

Cereals Ready-to-eat cereals can be as sweet as candy or as salty as pretzels and contain up to 2 teaspoons of fat per ¼-cup serving, or they can be a nutritious way to start the day. The key to choosing a healthy cereal is understanding the information on the nutrition label.

Tips for Buying Cereal:
• Check the ingredient list; the first item should be a grain. The shorter the list, the less refined (and more nutritious) the cereal.
• Look for whole-grain cereals. The word "whole" must appear unless it is an oat-based cereal; then it can say rolled oats or whole oat flour—not oat flour.
• Choose a cereal with at least 2 grams of dietary fiber per serving.
• Check the nutrition label for grams of fat and select cereals that have no more than 1 or 2 grams per serving. Examine the ingredient list for the kind of fat used and avoid those with coconut, palm, or palm kernel oils; these are saturated fats. Granolas are guilty of being high in fat and often contain saturated fats.
• Keep in mind that most ready-to-eat cereals have 200 to 300 milligrams of sodium per serving. If you are trying to cut down on sodium, select a cereal that has little or no added sodium such as shredded wheat, puffed rice, or puffed wheat.
• Consider that among the hot cereals, regular and quick-cooking types are usually lower in salt and sugar than the instant varieties. Check the nutrition labels of hot cereals, keeping in mind the guidelines for purchasing ready-to-eat cereals.

Vegetable Oils and Margarines

All vegetable oils and margarines are a combination of polyunsaturated, monounsaturated, and saturated fats. Monounsaturated and polyunsaturated fats help lower blood cholesterol levels and, therefore, reduce the risk of heart disease. Saturated fat, on the other hand, can cause blood cholesterol levels to increase.

Vegetable Oils Selecting an oil that is totally free of saturated fat is impossible because all oils contain some saturated fat, though some have less than others. The key is finding one that has a higher percentage of monounsaturated and polyunsaturated fats than saturated fats.

Vegetable oils high in monounsaturated fats should be your first choice because monounsaturated fats can lower artery-clogging LDL-cholesterol levels. Canola, olive, and peanut oils are the three vegetable oils highest in monounsaturated fats. The best choices for oils high in polyunsaturated fats are safflower, sunflower, corn, and soybean oils.

Remember that no matter what kind of vegetable oil you choose, it's going to be 100 percent fat, so choose wisely and use sparingly. The chart on page 13 shows the amount of polyunsaturated, monounsaturated, and saturated fat found in various oils.

Margarines Choose a margarine that lists water or an acceptable liquid vegetable oil such as canola, safflower, sunflower, corn, or soybean oil as the first ingredient. Make sure that the amount of saturated fat is 2 grams or less per tablespoon.

The first ingredient in reduced-calorie and diet margarines is water. By whipping water into margarine, the volume is increased without adding calories, making diet margarine a good choice. Soft margarines such as those found in squeeze bottles and tubs are less saturated than stick margarines.

Another good margarine choice is one with at least twice as much polyunsaturated or monounsaturated fat as saturated (grams of polyunsaturated and saturated fat appear on the label; monounsaturated fat may or may not be listed). This ratio of polyunsaturated fat to saturated fat is called the P/S ratio, and the higher the ratio the better.

Meats and Poultry

Purchasing lean, heart-healthy meats is simple if you choose the leanest cuts possible, and trim any excess fat. Remove any skin and excess fat from poultry before cooking.

Beef   Because beef is a source of saturated fat and cholesterol, the recommended serving size is 3 ounces of cooked meat. Beef easily fits into a heart-healthy eating plan when attention is paid to the grade and cut of the meat.

The U.S. Department of Agriculture (USDA) divides beef into three grades: prime, choice, and select. Prime beef contains the most fat, which makes it tender but adds fat and saturated fat. Choice beef is the grade most often found in the supermarket. Flecks of fat are evident in naturally fatty cuts of choice beef, but naturally lean choice cuts can be low in fat. Examples of these lean cuts include top round, eye of round, sirloin tip, round tip, and tenderloin.

Select beef is the leanest beef with approximately 20 percent less fat than choice, and nearly 40 percent less fat than prime beef. Because select cuts are low in fat, they are much less tender and need special attention.

Veal   Veal is the meat of one- to four-month-old calves. Though it is higher in cholesterol than other lean cuts of meat, veal is lower in saturated fat. For that reason, lean cuts of veal such as a cutlet, sirloin, loin chop, and shoulder roast can be included in a heart-healthy diet.

Lamb   As with the producers of other meats, sheep producers have made strides in breeding leaner animals. And the distinctive taste of lamb offers variety and flavor to menus. Choose the leg, shoulder, and loin for the leanest cuts, trimming all visible fat before cooking.

Pork   Lean cuts of pork such as the tenderloin, center loin, and fresh pork leg or reduced-fat low-salt ham fit into a heart-healthy eating plan when limited to a 3-ounce portion of cooked meat. The amount of saturated fat found in lean pork is less than the amount found in lean beef.

Processed pork products are almost always high in fat and cholesterol. Regular bacon, sausage, cold cuts, and hot dogs contain too much saturated fat and cholesterol to be included in a program of healthy eating. As leaner versions of these items become available, be sure to calculate the percent of calories from fat per serving to make sure the products are as low in fat as they claim to be. If sodium is a concern, avoid all cured and processed pork products.

Poultry   For versatility, it's hard to beat naturally lean poultry. A 3-ounce serving of skinned, boned cooked chicken or turkey breast has about one-third fewer grams of fat than the same amount of lean beef.

Lean poultry is often turned into a high-fat food by the cooking method used to prepare it. For example, a cooked 3-ounce serving of skinless chicken breast has 140 calories and 3 grams of fat. If that same portion is battered and fried with skin intact, the calories soar to 221 and fat measures 11 grams.

Here's a general rule for choosing the leanest chicken. Small chickens such as fryers and broilers are leaner than roasters, and roasters are leaner than hens and capons.

Comparing Fat Content of Meats and Poultry

Higher Fat Content

Marbling, the white streaks of fat found in beef, acts as a built-in tenderizer but also adds fat, especially saturated fat.

Excess fat should be trimmed from lean cuts of pork. Pork sausage is high in fat; use sparingly, if at all, in a heart-healthy diet.

Remove skin from poultry before cooking to keep it healthy. Keep in mind that large hens are higher in fat than smaller fryers and broilers.

Lower Fat Content

Leaner cuts of beef have less marbling. They are also less tender and require methods such as marinating or braising to tenderize them.

A 3-ounce serving of cooked lean pork fits into a healthy eating program. To reduce fat, make your own sausage using lean ground pork.

Skinned, boned poultry may be purchased for convenience. Ground poultry is a lower fat alternative to ground beef.

Turkey breast meat is one of the leanest meats available. When buying a whole turkey, avoid the self-basting ones because the basting solution contains mostly fat. Instead, baste the turkey yourself with fat-free chicken broth or stock.

Ground turkey and chicken are available in many supermarkets. Commercially packaged ground turkey may contain as much as 15 percent fat. If the supermarket grinds its own turkey or chicken, ask the butcher if he uses dark meat in the mixture and whether he adds skin or fat. To get the leanest product possible, ask the butcher to grind fresh turkey breast or chicken breast for you without the skin or added fat.

When cooking turkey or chicken that has been ground without the skin or added fat, you will notice that the skillet in which the poultry is browned will be very dry. This is a good indication that the poultry is very lean and low in fat.

It's best to eat duck only on special occasions since it contains the most fat of any poultry. Wild duck generally has less fat than domestic duck, but it's still higher in fat than most poultry and should not be eaten on a regular basis.

Tips for Buying Meats and Poultry:

- Examine meats for trimmable fat and marbling (the thin white streaks of fat that appear in the meat), and choose the cut with the least amount of fat.
- Check the "sell by" date on all meats and poultry, and purchase the freshest product possible.
- If possible, buy poultry that has not been frozen. Poultry that has thawed in the meat case should not be refrozen.
- Look for the USDA "Grade A" marking on poultry for assurance that it meets government standards.
- Make sure that the meat or poultry looks and smells fresh.
- Remember that chicken with yellow skin is no more nutritious than chicken with pale skin. The skin color is due to the type of feed the chicken is given.

Meats and Poultry
Comparison of Nutritional Content

3 ounces, cooked	Calories	Fat (g)	Sat. Fat (g)	Cholesterol (mg)
Beef				
Eye of round	156	5.5	2.1	59
Top round	162	5.3	1.8	71
Round tip	162	6.4	2.3	69
Top loin	173	7.6	3.0	65
Sirloin	177	7.4	3.0	76
Tenderloin	173	7.9	3.1	71
Ground beef	244	17.8	7.0	74
Ground chuck	228	15.6	6.1	66
Ground round	213	13.7	5.4	70
Veal				
Shoulder	145	5.6	2.1	97
Sirloin	143	5.3	2.1	88
Leg, cutlets, breaded	175	5.3	1.4	96
Loin	149	5.9	2.2	90
Lamb				
Leg	162	6.6	2.4	76
Shoulder	173	9.2	3.5	74
Loin	184	8.3	3.0	81
Pork				
Tenderloin	141	4.1	1.4	79
Center loin	196	8.9	3.1	83
Leg (fresh ham)	188	9.0	3.1	82
Shoulder	208	12.7	4.4	82
Chicken				
Breast, without skin	140	3.0	0.9	72
Breast, with skin	168	6.6	1.9	71
Leg, without skin	146	4.8	1.3	79
Leg, with skin	184	9.5	2.6	77
Turkey				
Breast, without skin	115	0.6	0.1	71
Breast, with skin	161	6.3	1.7	63
Dark meat, without skin	159	6.1	2.1	72
Dark meat, with skin	188	9.8	3.0	76
Ground, light and dark meat	195	11.7	3.2	59

Fish and Shellfish

There is a wide variety of fresh, frozen, and canned fish and shellfish available in most supermarkets, so deciding which one to cook for dinner may be difficult.

Fish   By choosing fish as an entrée two or three times a week, you decrease saturated fat and cholesterol in your diet and increase omega-3 fatty acids that protect against heart disease. In addition, you'll find fish is relatively low in calories and a good source of protein. As far as being low in saturated fat and cholesterol, all fish are good choices.

Darker-flesh fish generally contain more oil and omega-3 fatty acids than those with lighter flesh. These fish tend to come from deep, cold waters where they need oil for insulation. Tuna, salmon, mackerel, anchovies, and sardines are examples of fish that are high in omega-3 fatty acids. (See chart on page 132 for more information on omega-3 fatty acids.)

Before fresh and quick-frozen fish were readily available, canned fish was a staple. If packed in water, canned tuna, salmon, and sardines offer the same lower fat benefits as other seafood.

Shellfish   At one time, mollusks (oysters, scallops, mussels, and clams) and crustaceans (shrimp, crab, crayfish, and lobster) were thought to be a significant source of cholesterol. However, new technology for testing the amount of cholesterol in foods has revealed that most shellfish is actually low in cholesterol. Add this to the fact that shellfish is naturally low in saturated fat and it becomes a healthy addition to any menu.

Shrimp and lobster are the exceptions to the rule when it comes to cholesterol content. They have more cholesterol than any other shellfish—and even more than lean beef. On the other hand, shrimp and lobster are very low in saturated fat. For that reason, the AHA approves a 3-ounce serving once a week. Be sure to prepare shrimp and lobster without extra fat to keep them as lean as possible.

Tips for Buying Fish and Shellfish:

- Whole fresh fish should have clear, bulging eyes and rosy pink gills.
- Fresh fish should not smell fishy—if it does, it's old.
- Fish steaks and fillets should be firm and moist with no dry edges and the skin should be shiny. If liquid has accumulated in the package, look for a fresher one.
- Frozen fish and shellfish should be frozen solid, have little or no odor, and be free of brown spots and freezer burn (indicated by white, dry patches around the edges of the fish). The packaging should be intact, not torn or opened.
- Fresh shrimp and lobster should have a firm texture and a mild odor.
- Live crabs and lobsters should move their legs when prodded. Live oysters, clams, and mussels should have tightly closed shells. If the shells are not closed, they should close immediately when tapped; if they don't, discard them.

Frozen Foods

Frozen foods have become a staple of many American diets, whether in the form of an entrée, side dish, dessert, or complete dinner. Although some prepared frozen foods are high in fat and sodium, there are many healthy selections to choose from.

Frozen Dinners and Entrées   For a quick and easy meal, it's hard to beat frozen dinners or entrées. When chosen carefully, they can be a part of heart-healthy eating.

Look for products that have less than 30 percent of calories from fat—that's 10 grams or less fat per 300-calorie serving. Many products labeled "light" or "healthy" easily meet this goal. However, just because several items of one brand meet healthy guidelines doesn't mean all of them will. Sodium content should be less than 850 milligrams for a frozen dinner—about one-third of the recommended daily allowance for most people.

Cholesterol content may not be listed on the nutrition label since it is not currently required, but by checking the amount of meat or chicken in the dinner you can figure if it is high. Three ounces of cooked meat or chicken have about 25 percent of the RDA for cholesterol.

Make a complete dinner by adding a slice of whole-grain bread, skim milk, and a salad or fruit. Most frozen dinners are deficient in vitamins A and C and fiber, so these additions will add nutrients and make the meal more filling.

Frozen Desserts There are many frozen desserts on the market that are nutritious alternatives to ice cream. Frozen nonfat and low-fat yogurts (without added nuts), sherbets, sorbets, fruit ices, most ice milks, and frozen fruit and juice bars are all good choices for frozen desserts.

Snack Foods

America is a snacking nation. Whether salty, crunchy, or sweet, snacks are a part of our food style. Most commercial snacks, even many "light" ones, are unhealthy because they are loaded with fat and saturated fat, cholesterol, calories, sugar, and salt. However, some good choices can be found.

Cookies Most cookies get 40 to 60 percent of their calories from fat. When searching for a healthy cookie, look for one that has less fat than the average cookie (less than 30 percent of calories from fat is best), and make sure the type of fat it contains is acceptable. Be on the lookout for products containing coconut oil, palm oil, butter, and animal fats, in particular. Softer cookies have a higher fat content than crisp ones because fat softens the texture of baked goods.

Healthier choices for cookies include vanilla wafers, animal crackers, gingersnaps, graham crackers, and fig, apple, raspberry, cherry, or blueberry newtons.

Pretzels Unsalted or lightly salted pretzels are a great low-fat snack. Pretzels are mainly flour and water, and they're baked, not fried. Most have less than 20 percent of calories from fat, but check the labels carefully before you buy because brands vary.

Popcorn Microwave popcorn is generally high in salt and fat, but some brands are better than others. Check the labels for low-fat versions and you may be surprised that some fit a heart-healthy eating plan.

When making popcorn at home, use a hot-air popper or a special microwave popper and little or no oil. Both of these methods will keep calories from fat well below 30 percent.

Specialty chips Most commercial bagel chips and pita chips are 45 to 50 percent fat because they are fried. Baking can reduce the fat to less than 30 percent of calories in commercial products and less than 5 percent for homemade. Whether you choose commercial or homemade bagel and pita chips, baked versions are the healthy way to go.

Condiments

As with other processed products, sodium and fat are the main nutritional concerns with commercial condiments. Always choose low-sodium or reduced-sodium versions of a condiment. Soy sauce, catsup, mustard, Worcestershire sauce, and teriyaki sauce all have lower sodium counterparts.

The main concern with mayonnaise and salad dressings is the amount of fat, cholesterol, and sodium in these products. The best choice for mayonnaise is the fat-free mayonnaise dressing followed by "light," "diet," or imitation mayonnaise products that have one-half to two-thirds the calories of regular mayonnaise and less than half the fat.

Select commercial salad dressings with monounsaturated or polyunsaturated oils listed on the ingredient label. Avoid salad dressings made with cheese, egg yolks, and cream. There are as many low-fat and nonfat versions to choose from as there are high-fat ones, so finding one to your liking shouldn't be a problem.

Heart-Healthy Cooking

After making wise choices at the supermarket, preparing those foods in a healthy manner is the next step. Using low-fat cooking techniques and equipment that promote heart-healthy cooking will ensure that the finished product is as nutritious as possible.

Cooking Techniques

Some cooking methods are better than others for cutting cholesterol, fat, and calories while enhancing the flavor and nutritional value of foods. As you prepare the recipes in this book, you'll see that many of the following cooking techniques are used.

Baking This method cooks food in an oven with dry heat. Essentially the same as roasting, baking is most often used when referring to cooking fish, soufflés, breads, and casseroles. Oven-frying is a low-fat baking technique in which food bakes on a rack (so all sides will be equally exposed to the heat) to yield a crisp coating that imitates deep-fat frying. Oven-frying is ideal for lean pork chops or fish.

Braising Particularly good for tenderizing lean cuts of meat which are less tender, braising can be done in the oven or the stove. Braising involves browning food, usually large cuts of meat, and then cooking, tightly covered, in a small amount of liquid at low heat for a long period of time. The long, slow cooking process tenderizes the meat by breaking down fibers.

Use vegetable cooking spray or a small amount of vegetable oil to coat the pan when browning the meat, and refrigerate braised meat and poultry overnight to allow the fat that cooks out to congeal on the surface. Remove congealed fat before reheating.

Broiling With this technique, food is cooked directly under the heat source, usually in an oven. Cooking temperatures are regulated by the distance between the food and the heat source.

Grilling Except for the heat source being below the food, grilling is similar to broiling. Food is placed on a metal or ceramic grid above the heat source, and fat drips away from the food onto the heat source, creating an aromatic smoke which helps flavor the food.

Poaching Poached foods cook in water or other liquid that is held just below the boiling point. Poaching keeps foods moist and tender without adding fat. Using such liquids as broth or wine can impart flavor to the food.

Roasting Roasting refers to baking at a constant moderate temperature (about 300° to 350°F) to produce a well-browned exterior and moist interior. Reasonably tender cuts of meat and poultry can be roasted with good results. Meats and poultry should be placed on a rack so they don't cook in their own drippings, and to assure that heat penetrates all sides.

Sautéing Cooking food quickly in a small amount of fat in a skillet or sauté pan over direct heat is the trademark of this technique. Nonstick skillets or sauté pans make this cooking technique virtually foolproof. Coating skillets with vegetable cooking spray or sautéing food in a small amount of broth, wine, or water is a low-fat option to adding vegetable oil.

Steaming Steamed foods cook over, not in, boiling water, making this cooking method one of the most nutritious. The aroma from herbs and spices added to the water will infuse the food. Added fat is not necessary when foods are steamed.

Stir-frying Frequently associated with oriental cooking and the wok, stir-frying cooks small pieces of food over high heat while constantly moving the food to prevent sticking. Similar to sautéing, this method requires a minimum amount of fat and yields crisp-tender foods. If a wok is not available, a large heavy skillet may be used.

Cooking Equipment

In addition to cooking techniques that promote healthy cooking, there are several pieces of cooking equipment that help chip away at the fat in recipes. The following items are by no means essential. Evaluate your eating and cooking style; then gradually add the equipment to your kitchen that would benefit you most.

Food processor or blender   These helpful appliances come in many sizes and make quick work of chopping, slicing, mincing, shredding, and pureeing. Food processors and blenders are ideal for making fresh fruit beverages and pureeing vegetables for soups and sauces.

Broiler pan   The top rack on a broiler pan allows fat to drip away from meat and poultry. For easy cleanup, coat the bottom pan with vegetable cooking spray or pour water in the pan to cover the bottom.

Gravy skimmer or fat-separating cup   The opening from the cup to the spout is at the bottom of the cup so that the liquid can be poured off while the fat remains behind.

Fat-off ladle   This gadget works on the same principle as the gravy skimmer. Fat rises to the top and can be poured off, leaving the low-fat liquid behind.

Loafpan with drain holes   Used mainly for meat loaf, this pan has a liner with holes that allows fat to drain into the outer pan away from the meat.

Nonstick baking pans and muffin pans   These pans allow baked products to be prepared without heavy greasing, which adds extra fat. Paper muffin liners can accomplish the same result when preparing muffins.

Nonstick skillet   Now available in a variety of sizes and weights, nonstick skillets allow foods to be cooked with little or no added fat.

Modifying Recipes Without Sacrificing Taste

Many recipes in this book will become regulars in your menus, but you will also want to modify some longtime favorites. The techniques for lowering fat in these recipes can be used as a reference when you begin to experiment with your own recipes, but it's helpful to have some guidelines.

There are two basic ways to modify a recipe: change the cooking technique or change an ingredient. We have already discussed several low-fat cooking techniques such as oven-frying and roasting on a rack to allow fat to drip away from meat.

Making an ingredient change is a little more complicated. Each recipe must be studied to see where modifications can be made without changing the basic structure of the finished product. Only certain ingredients can be changed without altering the basic nature of the recipe. To get started, ask the following questions about your recipe:

- Do any of the ingredients come in a nonfat, lower fat, lower calorie, or lower sodium version?
- Will the recipe work if high-fat ingredients are reduced?
- Are all the ingredients—particularly those that are high in fat—essential?
- Can this dish be prepared by a method that reduces fat?
- If there is a topping, is it necessary? If it is, can it be decreased or changed to incorporate lower fat ingredients?

There are three ways to modify an ingredient: reduce it, eliminate it, or substitute it. Paying attention to the source of fat in a recipe and reducing, eliminating, or changing it is the key to keeping recipes light and nutritious.

Let's look at several categories of foods and examine some modifications that can be made to help lower fat, cholesterol, sodium, and calories in your favorite recipes.

Dairy Products

It can be difficult to get the calcium your body needs without eating foods from the dairy group. Fortunately, many dairy products come in low-fat and skim versions.

Milk   When a recipe calls for cream or whole milk, substitute skim milk. And if the recipe doesn't look creamy enough, try adding nonfat dry milk. Soups in particular benefit from the addition of nonfat dry milk.

Cheese   The variety of low-fat cheeses is steadily increasing. However, many of these are over 50 percent fat. When cooking with cheese, use the following tips for decreasing the amount used in recipes:
- Shred or grate cheese to make it go further.
- Decrease the amount of cheese used by one-third to one-half, and substitute a strong-flavored cheese to achieve a full flavor.
- Choose nonfat or low-fat cottage cheese and part-skim ricotta cheese.
- Substitute reduced-fat Monterey Jack or Swiss cheeses for their higher-fat counterparts.
- Choose light cream cheese products for use in recipes.

Sour Cream and Yogurt   If nonfat sour cream is available in your supermarket, substitute it for its higher fat counterpart. If not, substitute plain nonfat yogurt or low-fat sour cream. When cooking with yogurt, however, be aware that it reacts differently than sour cream. Use the following recommendations for best results when cooking with yogurt:
- When adding yogurt to other ingredients, fold rather than stir it in to prevent thinning.
- Bring yogurt to room temperature before adding to hot foods; blend a little of the hot food into the yogurt first to prevent curdling.
- When cooking with yogurt, keep temperature low and heating time short to prevent separation.

Eggs and Egg Substitutes   Thirty-five percent of the cholesterol in American diets comes from egg yolks, with half of that from "visible" eggs—scrambled eggs, omelets, poached eggs, and boiled eggs. The other half is from "invisible" eggs, such as those in pancakes. By substituting two egg whites or ¼ cup egg substitute for a whole egg, the cholesterol content of baked products can be lowered.

When substituting egg whites and egg substitutes, be sure to cook them slowly over low heat; they are lower in fat than whole eggs and can be tough and dry if cooked over high heat.

Meats, Poultry, Fish, and Shellfish

Although you are eating healthier, meats don't have to be sacrificed totally. Learning to choose lean cuts or substituting poultry is a step many are taking to control fat intake. And fish and shellfish are excellent entrée choices.

Meats   Meats contribute fat, saturated fat, and cholesterol to the diet. To minimize these, trim all visible fat from meats and choose the leanest cuts.

One of the biggest complaints about lean cuts of meat is that they are tough and dry. Because lean meat cooks more quickly than fatty meat, it is often overcooked. Some suggestions for cooking lean meats are:
- Use a meat thermometer when cooking lean meats, and cook the cuts rare to medium.
- Marinate lean meat in an acid-based marinade to make it more tender. Acid-based marinades may contain lemon or lime juice, vinegar, or tomato products.
- Braise large cuts of lean meats to make them tender and juicy.

Poultry   Skinning chicken and turkey eliminates half the fat but often contributes to dryness. To prevent dryness in skinned, boned chicken breast halves, reduce heat and cook just until done.

Substituting white meat for dark meat will further reduce the amount of fat in recipes. And substituting poultry for red meat will substantially decrease the amount of saturated fat and cholesterol in recipes.

Fish and Shellfish Substituting fish and poultry for red meat is a way to meet the AHA goals of heart-healthy eating. Except for a few types that are high in omega-3 fatty acids, fish is naturally low in fat. The way fish is prepared makes it a high-fat main dish or a healthy one. Deep-frying doubles the fat content in fish while oven-frying changes it little.

The cholesterol content of shrimp and lobster has relegated them to a once-a-week food under AHA dietary guidelines, while other shellfish can be eaten as often as desired. For recipes in which shrimp is the main ingredient, try substituting scallops for half the shrimp—the amount of cholesterol in the dish will be decreased by half.

Grains, Fruits, and Vegetables

Eaten in their natural state, grains, breads, pastas, fruits, and vegetables are some of the healthiest foods you can eat. However, the way in which they are cooked and served can make a big difference in their nutritional value. Rice with gravy, freshly baked bread spread with butter, broccoli with cheese sauce, and baked potatoes topped with butter, sour cream or bacon bits are all examples of healthy foods turned into fat-laden ones.

Pasta, rice, grains, and green and starchy vegetables should be cooked with little or no added fat. And choose commercial breads and rolls made with monounsaturated or polyunsaturated oils or margarines.

Steaming, sautéing, and stir-frying are the best cooking methods for vegetables because they require a minimum of fat while preserving nutrients. Other cooking methods may keep fat low, but the nutrients lost in the cooking method used may be greater because water-soluble vitamins leech into the cooking liquid.

Sugars and Fats

Sugars and fats are necessary ingredients in many recipes, especially those for baked goods. Granulated, brown, and powdered sugars, as well as margarines and vegetable oils, act as tenderizers while helping to provide the crisp brown crust desired in many baked products.

Sugars and fats should be used as sparingly as possible while still achieving satisfactory results.

Sugars Though sugars don't play a direct role in the development of heart disease, they may contribute to obesity, one of the secondary risk factors for heart disease. When preparing recipes that contain sugar, try cutting the amount of sugar by one-third to one-half, and substituting brown sugar or honey for white sugar. Brown sugar and honey taste sweeter than white sugar, so less is needed to achieve the same sweetness.

When decreasing sugar in recipes, enhance the flavor of the recipe with spices such as cinnamon, nutmeg, or cloves, and extracts such as vanilla, almond, or lemon. Raisins, dates, ripe bananas, applesauce, and dried apricots add a natural sweetness to recipes.

Fats Switching from butter to margarine or vegetable oil cuts cholesterol and saturated fat, but doesn't cut calories. Butter, margarine, and vegetable oil all have 100 to 120 calories per tablespoon. However, margarine and vegetable oil are the healthier choices.

Decreasing the fat in cooking can be as simple as eliminating added fat, decreasing the amount of fat called for in a recipe, or sautéing in a nonstick skillet using vegetable cooking spray. Reduce the amount of fat in recipes for baked goods by one-fourth to one-third, and swap monounsaturated or polyunsaturated fats for saturated ones.

When fat is decreased, you may need to add a liquid such as water, fruit juice, or skim milk to make up for some of the moisture loss. Be careful when substituting reduced-calorie margarine for regular margarine in baked goods; the water that's whipped into reduced-calorie margarine may cause sogginess.

Mayonnaise is an emulsion of oil and eggs, which makes it very high in fat. Substitute fat-free mayonnaise, reduced-calorie mayonnaise, or low-cholesterol mayonnaise for the higher fat version.

Healthy Ingredient Substitutions

Recipe calls for:	Use:
Whole or 2% milk	Skim milk, 1% milk, or evaporated skimmed milk diluted equally with water
Whipping cream	Chilled evaporated skimmed milk, whipped
Cheddar, American, Swiss, and Monterey Jack cheese	Cheeses with 5 grams of fat or less per ounce
Mozzarella cheese	Part-skim mozzarella cheese
Cream cheese	Light cream cheese products, or Neufchâtel cheese
Creamed cottage cheese	Nonfat or 1% fat cottage cheese, or farmer's cheese
Ricotta cheese	Nonfat, lite, or part-skim ricotta cheese
Sour cream	Nonfat or low-fat sour cream, or nonfat or low-fat yogurt
Whole egg	2 egg whites or ¼ cup egg substitute
Baking chocolate, 1-ounce square	3 tablespoons cocoa plus 1 tablespoon monounsaturated or polyunsaturated vegetable oil or margarine
Fudge sauce	Chocolate syrup
White flour, 1 cup	½ cup whole wheat flour plus ½ cup white flour, or ⅔ cup white flour plus ⅓ cup oat bran
Sugar	Reduce amount by ⅓ to ½; substitute brown sugar or honey when flavor will not be affected

Recipe calls for:	Use:
Salt	Reduce by ½ or eliminate
Margarine	Reduce amount, using a margarine made from monounsaturated or polyunsaturated oil, or use reduced-calorie margarine
Vegetable oil	Reduce amount, using a monounsaturated or polyunsaturated oil
Mayonnaise	Fat-free, reduced-calorie, or low-cholesterol mayonnaise
Gravy	Gravy made with bouillon granules or broth and thickened with flour or cornstarch
Condensed cream of mushroom soup	99% fat-free condensed cream of mushroom soup
Egg noodles	Noodles made without egg yolks
White rice	Brown or wild rice
Pecans, walnuts	Reduce by ⅓ to ½
Beef, pork, veal, or lamb	Lean cuts of red meat trimmed of all visible fat, or substitute with chicken or turkey
Ground beef	Ground turkey or lean ground round
Bacon strips	Turkey bacon or Canadian bacon
Poultry	Skinned poultry
Self-basting turkey	Baste turkey with fat-free chicken broth
Tuna packed in oil	Tuna packed in spring water

Healthy Heart Recipe Makeover

With some ingredient substitutions, your family's favorite recipes can be made healthier. For example, something as basic as macaroni and cheese becomes more nutritious with a few simple substitutions. When you replace the butter, cheese, and whole milk in the traditional recipe with margarine, reduced-fat cheeses, and skim milk, you drastically reduce the calories, fat, saturated fat, cholesterol, and sodium. What remains the same is all the rich goodness you've come to expect from old-fashioned baked macaroni and cheese.

Healthy Heart Macaroni and Cheese

1½ tablespoons margarine
¼ cup all-purpose flour
¾ teaspoon dry mustard
⅛ teaspoon ground red pepper
3 cups skim milk
1¼ cups (5 ounces) shredded reduced-fat
  sharp Cheddar cheese, divided
¼ cup (1 ounce) shredded reduced-fat Swiss
  cheese
¼ teaspoon salt
⅛ teaspoon pepper
5 cups cooked elbow macaroni
  (cooked without salt or fat)

Serves 8 (223 calories and 27% fat per serving)

Protein 13.1 / Fat 6.8 (Saturated Fat 2.9) / Carbohydrate 26.7
Fiber 1.2 / Cholesterol 16 / Sodium 177

Traditional Macaroni and Cheese

¼ cup butter or margarine
¼ cup all-purpose flour
¾ teaspoon dry mustard
⅛ teaspoon ground red pepper
2 cups milk
2 cups (8 ounces) shredded sharp Cheddar
  cheese
½ teaspoon salt
1 egg, beaten
1 (8-ounce) package elbow macaroni
½ cup soft breadcrumbs
2 tablespoons butter or margarine,
  melted

Serves 8 (364 calories and 53% fat per serving)

Protein 14.2 / Fat 21.3 (Saturated Fat 12.9) / Carbohydrate 28.7
Fiber 0.8 / Cholesterol 89 / Sodium 464

A Healthy Heart Guide To Dining Out

Dining out is no longer reserved for special occasions—it has become part of everyday life. Choosing nutritious foods from restaurant menus is not impossible. In fact, many restaurants feature menu items low in fat, cholesterol, and sodium, and those that don't will often have something on the menu that can easily be substituted. It's up to you to make the best choice for your particular eating pattern.

Listed below are some helpful suggestions to guide you in choosing the most nutritious foods when dining out:

- Order entrées or appetizers that are broiled, steamed, roasted, poached, or stir-fried.
- Watch portion sizes; if it's more than you should eat, ask for a "doggy bag."
- Choose vegetable, bean, or tomato-based soups over creamed soups.
- Ask for low-fat or reduced-calorie salad dressing, and ask that the salad dressing be served on the side.
- Choose whole wheat or rye bread and rolls; avoid croissants and buttered rolls.
- Avoid sandwiches made with high-fat meats such as corned beef, bologna, meatballs, pastrami, sausage, luncheon meats, and meat loaf. Order a turkey or a chicken breast sandwich instead, and go easy on the mayonnaise and cheese.
- Order a main course comprised of healthy appetizers to keep portion sizes manageable.
- Select a low-fat appetizer to take the edge off your appetite.
- Choose fresh fruit, fruit ices, low-fat frozen yogurt, sorbet, or angel food cake for a low-fat dessert.
- Choose entrées made with vegetables and grains. Order side dishes such as curries, pilafs, or a stir-fry; avoid fried rice.
- Learn to recognize words on the menu that indicate when low-fat preparation techniques have been used. Such techniques include steaming, grilling, broiling, and poaching.

Eating in Specialty Restaurants

You will discover that many restaurants, even specialty restaurants, are catering to a health-conscious public. As you become adept at reading menus, learn to look for key words and phrases that indicate heart-healthy, low-fat foods.

Chinese   Order steamed, stir-fried, or broiled chicken and fish dishes that include vegetables and rice. Request steamed rice instead of fried rice as an accompaniment, and ask that the dishes be prepared without monosodium glutamate.

French   Order dishes prepared with wine sauces such as bordelaise rather than those prepared with butter, cream, and egg yolks. Avoid "au gratin" dishes, patés, and duck. Choose seafood, poached fish, stock-based soups, chicken in wine sauce, steamed vegetables, and French bread.

Italian   Pastas topped with red clam sauce, mussel sauce, or marinara sauce are good choices. Other healthy selections for entrées include pasta primavera, minestrone, chicken or shrimp cacciatore, shrimp in wine sauce, and chicken or veal picatta. And try Italian ice for a virtually fat-free dessert.

Japanese   Avoid fried foods such as tempuras, fried dumplings, and deep-fried chicken and pork. Order broth-based soups, fish or chicken teriyaki, sukiyaki, and stir-fried Japanese vegetables.

Mexican   For starters, try black bean soup or gazpacho. Chicken fajitas, chicken tacos or tostadas, burritos or enchiladas (made with chicken, beans, or seafood), rice, black beans, and corn tortillas are all good choices. Avoid enchiladas, burritos, tostadas, and tacos made with beef and cheese, chimichangas, chorizo (sausage), con queso, nachos, tortilla chips, and refried beans.

The Healthy Heart Cookbook Menu Plans

These menus for seven days of calorie- and fat-controlled meals provide a nutritious approach to heart-healthy eating. The plans were developed according to the American Heart Association dietary guidelines for the prevention of coronary heart disease; they contain 30 percent or less of the total calories per day from fat and 10 percent or less from saturated fat.

Although weight reduction is not the primary focus of these menu plans, keeping fat intake 30 percent or less per day and consuming approximately 1500 calories for women and 1800 calories for men may allow safe, gradual weight loss. A weight reduction diet for women generally contains 1200 to 1600 calories, while men may consume 1600 to 2000 calories. Combine a low-fat diet with regular exercise, and the weight will stay off.

The menu items marked with an asterisk are included in the menu or recipe sections and can be located in the Recipe Index. When planning your own menus, remember that of the total calories consumed, at least 50 percent of calories should come from carbohydrate, 20 percent from protein, and 30 percent or less from fat.

1500 Calories		Day 2	1800 Calories	
		BREAKFAST		
1 (8-ounce) carton	225	Peach-flavored low-fat yogurt	1 (8-ounce) carton	225
½ cup	77	Raisin bran cereal	1 cup	154
¾ cup	65	Skim milk	1 cup	86
	367			465
		LUNCH		
1 serving	336	*Chili-Stuffed Baked Potatoes	1 serving	336
1 cup	17	Mixed salad greens	1½ cups	26
1½ tablespoons	17	*Thousand Island Dressing	3 tablespoons	33
½ cup	41	Fresh blueberries	1 cup	82
	411			477
		DINNER		
1 serving	167	*Halibut Steaks with Tangy Mustard Sauce	1 serving	167
½ cup	100	*Barley and Mushroom Bake	¾ cup	150
1 serving	63	*Roasted Pepper, Onion, and Broccoli Salad	1 serving	63
1 each	81	*Honey-Wheat Crescents	2 each	162
½ cup	67	*Pear-Lemon Sorbet	½ cup	67
	478			609
		SNACK		
1 each	159	*Oatmeal-Date Bars	1 each	159
1 cup	86	Skim milk	1 cup	86
Total	1501 calories (14% from fat)		Total	1796 calories (12% from fat)

1500 Calories		Day 1	1800 Calories	
		BREAKFAST		
1 serving	118	*Spiced French Toast	1 serving	118
1 each	75	*Peppered Turkey Sausage	1 each	75
1¼ cups	145	*Strawberry-Orange Shake	1¼ cups	145
	338			338
		LUNCH		
1 serving	386	*Sesame Pork Sandwiches	1 serving	386
½ cup	88	*Colorful Corn Salad	½ cup	88
1 each	73	*Oatmeal-Molasses Cookies	1 each	73
—		*Tutti-Frutti Punch	1 cup	74
	547			621
		DINNER		
1 serving	24	*Sweet Red Pepper Dip with Polenta Chips	2 servings	48
1 serving	316	*Creamy Seafood Casserole	1 serving	316
1 serving	41	*Spinach and Fruit Salad with Honey-Lime Dressing	1 serving	41
1 each	72	Whole wheat roll	1 each	72
2 teaspoons	40	Reduced-calorie margarine	2 teaspoons	40
—		*Chocolate-Crème de Menthe Pie	1 serving	197
	493			714
		SNACK		
½ cup	119	*Blackberry Frozen Yogurt	½ cup	119
Total	1497 calories (23% from fat)		Total	1792 calories (22% from fat)

1500 Calories		Day 3	1800 Calories	
		BREAKFAST		
2 each	92	*Buttermilk-Buckwheat Pancakes	3 each	138
¼ cup	60	*Blueberry Syrup	¼ cup	60
1 cup	86	Skim milk	1 cup	86
½ cup	56	Orange juice	½ cup	56
	294			340
		LUNCH		
1 cup	55	*Fresh Tomato Soup with Basil	1 cup	55
1 serving	266	*Roast Beef and Swiss Sandwiches	1 serving	266
½ cup	83	*Zesty Potato Salad	½ cup	83
1 serving	157	*Cranberry and Pear Crisp	1 serving	157
	561			561
		DINNER		
1 serving	283	*Vegetable Lasagna	1 serving	283
1 serving	33	*Tossed Greens with Country-Style Dressing	1 serving	33
1 each	81	*Herbed Dinner Rolls	1 each	81
1 each	139	*Peppermint Brownies	2 each	278
	536			675
		SNACK		
10 each	25	Thin pretzel sticks	30 each	75
1 cup	92	*Fruit Juice Spritzer	1½ cups	138
Total	1508 calories (16% from fat)		Total	1789 calories (17% from fat)

Day 4

1500 Calories			1800 Calories	
BREAKFAST				
1 cup	60	Fresh cantaloupe	1 cup	60
1 each	150	*Raisin-Applesauce Bran Muffins	2 each	300
1 teaspoon	20	Reduced-calorie margarine	1 teaspoon	20
1 cup	86	Skim milk	1 cup	86
	316			466
LUNCH				
1 cup	63	*Savory Carrot Soup	1½ cups	94
1½ cups	226	*Chinese Chicken Salad	2 cups	301
3 each	114	*Peppered Cheese Biscuits	4 each	152
1 serving	94	*Strawberries in Raspberry Sauce	1 serving	94
	497			641
DINNER				
1 serving	294	*Grilled Beef Kabobs	1 serving	294
1 cup	160	*Couscous Toss	1 cup	160
1 cup	17	Mixed salad greens	1 cup	17
2 tablespoons	22	*Creamy Pepper Dressing	2 tablespoons	22
¼ cup	72	*Watermelon Ice	¼ cup	72
	565			565
SNACK				
3 servings	126	*Grilled Quesadillas with Yogurt Salsa	3 servings	126
Total	1504 calories (21% from fat)		Total	1798 calories (20% from fat)

Day 5

1500 Calories			1800 Calories	
BREAKFAST				
1 serving	202	*Fresh Apple Coffee Cake	1 serving	202
1 ounce	37	Lean cooked ham	2 ounces	74
½ medium	38	Grapefruit	½ medium	38
1 cup	86	Skim milk	1 cup	86
	363			400
LUNCH				
1 cup	93	*Scarlet Sipper	1 cup	93
1 serving	128	*Southwestern Crabmeat Salad	1 serving	128
½ cup	20	*Fresh Mushroom Salad	1 cup	40
1 (½-inch) slice	54	*Peppered Parmesan Twist	2 (½-inch) slices	108
		*Honeyed Banana Sauté	1 serving	158
	295			527
DINNER				
1 serving	269	*Crunchy Oven-Fried Chicken	1 serving	269
3 wedges	129	*Rosemary-Roasted Potato Wedges	3 wedges	129
1 serving	25	*Lemon Broccoli	1½ servings	38
1 each	83	*Cornmeal Crescent Rolls	1 each	83
		Reduced-calorie margarine	1 teaspoon	20
1 serving	177	*Favorite Apple Pie	1 serving	177
	683			716
SNACK				
1 cup	152	*Chocolate-Banana Shake	1 cup	152
Total	1493 calories (16% from fat)		Total	1795 calories (18% from fat)

Day 6

1500 Calories			1800 Calories	
BREAKFAST				
1 each	256	*Breakfast Pita Sandwiches	1 each	256
1 cup	86	Skim milk	1 cup	86
½ cup	63	Fresh fruit cup	1 cup	126
	405			468
LUNCH				
1 serving	169	*Honey-Mustard Chicken Nuggets	1 serving	169
½ cup	85	*American Fries	¾ cup	128
2 slices	3	Sliced tomatoes	2 slices	3
1 each	73	*Whole Wheat Yeast Biscuits	1 each	73
1 serving	147	*Chocolate-Cherry Squares	1 serving	147
	477			520
DINNER				
1 serving	164	*Oriental Shrimp Stir-Fry	1 serving	164
½ cup	128	Cooked rice	1 cup	256
½ cup	55	*Spiced Cabbage and Apple Slaw	¾ cup	83
½ cup	111	*Peach Sherbet	½ cup	111
	462			622
SNACK				
2 each	66	*Old-Fashioned Hermits	3 each	99
1 cup	86	Skim milk	1 cup	86
Total	1492 calories (13% from fat)		Total	1787 calories (13% from fat)

Day 7

1500 Calories			1800 Calories	
BREAKFAST				
1 each	111	*Oatmeal Biscuits	2 each	222
1 ounce	45	Canadian bacon	1 ounce	45
2 teaspoons	19	Low-sugar raspberry spread	1 tablespoon	29
1 cup	86	Skim milk	1 cup	86
¾ cup	36	Low-sodium tomato juice	¾ cup	36
	297			418
LUNCH				
1 cup	217	*Hearty Hamburger Stew	1⅓ cups	289
1 each	103	*Buttermilk Corn Muffins	2 each	206
¾ cup	73	*Marinated Confetti Coleslaw	¾ cup	73
1 each	43	Frozen fruit juice bar	1 each	43
	436			611
DINNER				
1 cup	143	*Mock Margaritas	1 cup	143
1 serving	232	*Turkey Tostadas	1 serving	232
1 serving	66	*Southwestern Hominy	1 serving	66
1 serving	77	*Orange-Jicama Salad	1 serving	77
1 serving	120	*Individual Caramel Custards	1 serving	120
	638			638
SNACK				
1 medium	78	Apple wedges	1 medium	78
¼ cup	52	*Quick Fruit Dip	¼ cup	52
Total	1501 calories (17% from fat)		Total	1797 calories (10% from fat)

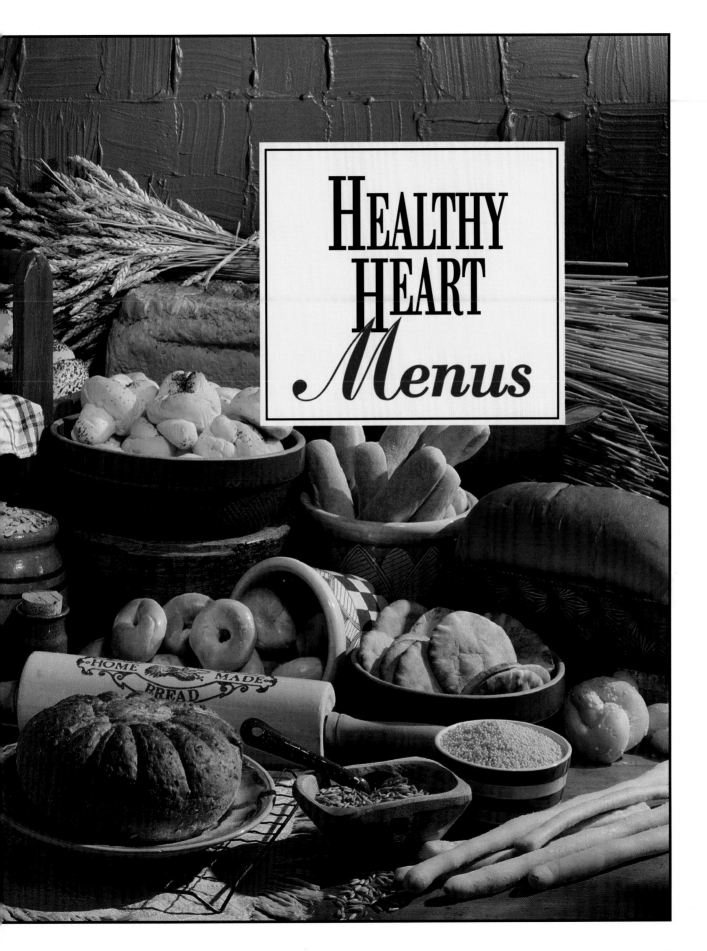

HEALTHY HEART Menus

The American Heart Association (AHA) has established guidelines for grouping recipes into menus for healthy eating. *The Healthy Heart Cookbook* applied that criteria to the following menus so you can enjoy heart-healthy meals without having to calculate nutrients. For your convenience, the total calories and the percent of calories from fat for each serving have been calculated in every menu. All the menus meet or exceed the AHA goals of no more than 30 percent of total calories from fat, less than 10 percent of fat from saturated fat, 50 percent or more of calories from carbohydrate, and the remainder of calories from protein. Whether you want quick ideas for every day or an impressive meal for your supper club, you can rely on these menus to fit your needs and be healthy, too.

Breakfasts and Brunches Starting the day with a nutritious breakfast is a big step toward living a healthy lifestyle. Tempt family members dashing out the door to school or work with Breakfast on the Run. For more leisurely dining, serve Brunch on the Veranda, or enjoy a Country Breakfast. And a special occasion such as a christening or morning wedding calls for a Celebration Brunch.

Summer Suppers Summertime seems ideal for casual get-togethers with friends, neighbors, and family. A Backyard Barbecue is perfect for weeknight or weekend entertaining, and catfish lovers will enjoy a healthy Mississippi Fish "Fry." And whether you grow your own vegetables or stop by a farmer's market, Supper from the Garden features favorite vegetable dishes that are sure to please. For a casual get-together, fire up the grill for Steak with a Flair.

Ethnic Favorites Viva variety! Ethnic foods add color and an abundance of flavor to all types of menus. A Mexican Fiesta will certainly please those who enjoy the traditional tastes of the Southwest, while Creole food lovers will savor the Down-Home Louisiana Dinner. The rich colors and vibrant of flavors in the Mediterranean Magic and Middle Eastern Feast menus provide an imaginative theme for a dinner party.

Holiday Celebrations Health-conscious people will appreciate an invitation to a holiday celebration such as a New Year's Day Buffet. A Family Easter Dinner signals the arrival of spring, while the Fourth of July Celebration features a menu that may be either a bit casual or a little more formal. The year ends with a traditional Holiday Dinner that includes healthy versions of favorites such as cornbread-stuffed turkey and sweet potato casserole. There's even ambrosia and pumpkin pie for dessert.

Treat calorie-conscious guests to a menu that includes Broccoli-Rice Quiche and Tomato Wedges with Basil Dressing— with only 444 calories.

BREAKFASTS & BRUNCHES

41

Breakfast Pita Sandwiches, Oatmeal-Date Bars, and Strawberry-Orange Shake provide a nutritionally balanced, no-rush meal.

BREAKFAST ON THE RUN

If breakfast at your house is a hurried event, tempt your busy family with this nutritious menu that can be eaten at the table or in the car during rush hour. This quick breakfast menu accounts for about one-third of the day's calories and supplies essential complex carbohydrates, protein, vitamins, and minerals.

Breakfast Pita Sandwiches consist of heart-healthy ingredients neatly tucked in whole

Breakfast Pita Sandwiches
Oatmeal-Date Bars
Strawberry-Orange Shake

Serves 4

560 calories and 15% fat per serving

wheat pitas. Prepare Oatmeal-Date Bars the night before, and serve 1 bar to each person for breakfast or as a healthy mid-morning snack with a glass of skim milk.

Strawberry-Orange Shake boasts two sources of vitamin C and only 5 percent fat per serving. For a special touch to the meal, add a fresh fruit garnish of orange slices and strawberries to the plate.

Breakfast Pita Sandwiches

Vegetable cooking spray
1 cup thinly sliced fresh mushrooms
½ cup chopped onion
½ cup finely chopped sweet red pepper
2 cups frozen egg substitute, thawed
½ cup 1% low-fat cottage cheese
¼ teaspoon pepper
½ cup (2 ounces) shredded reduced-fat
   Cheddar cheese
2 (6-inch) whole wheat pita bread rounds,
   cut in half crosswise

Coat a medium nonstick skillet with cooking spray; place over medium-high heat until hot. Add mushrooms, onion, and red pepper; sauté 4 to 5 minutes or until vegetables are tender.

Combine egg substitute, cottage cheese, and pepper in a small bowl; stir well, and pour over vegetables. Cook mixture over medium heat, stirring frequently, until mixture is firm but still moist. Add Cheddar cheese, stirring just until cheese melts.

Spoon mixture evenly into pita halves. Serve immediately. Yield: 4 servings (256 calories and 15% fat per serving).

Protein 22.5 / Fat 4.2 (Saturated Fat 1.8) / Carbohydrate 28.6
Fiber 4.9 / Cholesterol 10 / Sodium 508

Oatmeal-Date Bars

1½ cups pitted whole dates, chopped
¾ cup water
2½ tablespoons lemon juice
⅓ cup margarine, softened
⅔ cup firmly packed brown sugar
1 teaspoon vanilla extract
1 cup regular oats, uncooked
¾ cup all-purpose flour
¼ cup whole wheat flour
½ teaspoon baking soda
⅛ teaspoon salt
Vegetable cooking spray

Combine dates, water, and lemon juice in a medium saucepan. Bring to a boil; reduce heat, and simmer, uncovered, 5 minutes or until mixture thickens, stirring frequently. Set aside.

Cream margarine; gradually add brown sugar, beating well at medium speed of an electric mixer until light and fluffy. Add vanilla, beating well. Combine oats and next 4 ingredients; add to creamed mixture, stirring until mixture resembles coarse meal.

Press 2 cups oat mixture evenly into a 9-inch square baking pan coated with cooking spray; set remaining oat mixture aside. Bake at 375° for 5 minutes or until crust looks puffed.

Spread date mixture over prepared crust, and top with remaining oat mixture. Bake at 375° for 20 minutes or until golden. Cool in pan on a wire rack. Cut into bars. Yield: 16 bars (159 calories and 24% fat each).

Protein 2.0 / Fat 4.3 (Saturated Fat 0.8) / Carbohydrate 29.7
Fiber 2.3 / Cholesterol 0 / Sodium 92

Strawberry-Orange Shake

2 cups unsweetened frozen strawberries
1 cup unsweetened orange juice, chilled
1 cup skim milk
1 (8-ounce) carton strawberry low-fat
   yogurt

Place frozen strawberries, orange juice, and skim milk in container of an electric blender; top with cover, and process just until strawberry mixture is blended. Add strawberry yogurt, and process just until blended.

Pour strawberry mixture into chilled glasses; serve immediately. Yield: 5 cups (145 calories and 6% fat per 1¼-cup serving).

Protein 5.2 / Fat 0.9 (Saturated Fat 0.5) / Carbohydrate 30.6
Fiber 1.1 / Cholesterol 3 / Sodium 65

Country Breakfast

For most health-conscious people, the old-fashioned country breakfast is a thing of the past. Laden with calories, fat, cholesterol, and sodium, a breakfast of eggs, spicy sausage, buttered grits or hash browns, and homemade biscuits has too many adverse nutritional consequences.

This menu offers healthier versions of these favorites including ½ cup orange juice, ½ cup cooked grits, and 1 tablespoon Blackberry Spread for each person. At less than 40 milligrams of cholesterol per serving, this breakfast could become a healthy weekend tradition.

Orange juice
Peppered Turkey Sausage
Creamy Breakfast Scramble
Piping hot grits
Oatmeal Biscuits
Blackberry Spread
Serves 4
421 calories and 17% fat per serving

Peppered Turkey Sausage

½ pound freshly ground raw turkey
¼ cup chopped green pepper
¼ cup chopped sweet red pepper
1½ teaspoons low-sodium soy sauce
½ teaspoon pepper
¼ teaspoon rubbed sage
⅛ teaspoon salt
2 to 3 feet pork sausage casing
Vegetable cooking spray

Position knife blade in food processor bowl; add first 7 ingredients. Process until well blended; set aside.

Rinse pork casing thoroughly with warm water; drain. Tie one end of casing securely with cotton string. Insert a large, wide-mouth tip into a large pastry bag. Fill bag with sausage mixture. Slip open end of casing over tip of bag. Pipe sausage mixture into casing, using hand to force mixture evenly into casing. Tie open end of casing to close. Twist sausage into 4 equal lengths; tie between lengths with string. Cut sausage into links.

Place links in a large skillet; add water to a depth of 1 inch. Bring to a boil; cover, reduce heat to medium, and cook 20 minutes or until sausage is done, turning occasionally. Drain links on paper towels. Wipe skillet dry with a paper towel. Coat skillet with cooking spray. Return links to skillet, and cook over medium heat until browned, turning occasionally. Yield: 4 (4-inch) links (75 calories and 23% fat each).

Protein 12.5 / Fat 1.9 (Saturated Fat 0.6) / Carbohydrate 1.3
Fiber 0.4 / Cholesterol 37 / Sodium 162

Creamy Breakfast Scramble

½ cup 1% low-fat cottage cheese
1 tablespoon reduced-calorie margarine
1½ tablespoons all-purpose flour
½ cup skim milk
Vegetable cooking spray
1 cup frozen egg substitute, thawed
1 tablespoon minced fresh chives
⅛ teaspoon pepper

Place cottage cheese in container of an electric blender or food processor; top with cover, and process until smooth. Set aside.

Melt margarine in a small, heavy saucepan over low heat; add flour, stirring until smooth. Cook 1 minute, stirring constantly. Gradually add milk, stirring constantly. Cook over medium heat, stirring constantly, until thickened and bubbly. Remove from heat; set aside.

Coat a large nonstick skillet with cooking spray; place over medium-low heat until hot. Add egg substitute; cook, stirring frequently, until softly set. Gently stir in cottage cheese, white sauce, chives, and pepper. Cook until mixture is firm but still moist, stirring frequently. Yield: 4 servings (88 calories and 25% fat per serving).

Protein 10.8 / Fat 2.4 (Saturated Fat 0.5) / Carbohydrate 5.4
Fiber 0.1 / Cholesterol 2 / Sodium 248

This lighter version of a traditional country-style breakfast ends on a sweet note with Oatmeal Biscuits and Blackberry Spread.

Oatmeal Biscuits

¼ cup regular oats, uncooked
½ cup all-purpose flour
¾ teaspoon baking powder
¼ teaspoon baking soda
Dash of salt
1 teaspoon brown sugar
1½ tablespoons reduced-calorie margarine
⅓ cup nonfat buttermilk
2 teaspoons all-purpose flour
Vegetable cooking spray

Place oats in container of an electric blender. Top with cover; process until oats are ground.

Combine ground oats, ½ cup flour, and next 4 ingredients. Cut in margarine with a pastry blender until mixture resembles coarse meal. Add buttermilk; stir until dry ingredients are moistened.

Sprinkle 2 teaspoons flour over work surface. Turn dough out onto floured surface; knead 10 to 12 times. Roll to ½-inch thickness; cut into rounds with a 2-inch cutter. Place on a baking sheet coated with cooking spray. Bake at 400° for 10 minutes or until lightly browned. Yield: 4 biscuits (111 calories and 28% fat each).

Protein 3.2 / Fat 3.5 (Saturated Fat 0.5) / Carbohydrate 17.1
Fiber 0.9 / Cholesterol 0 / Sodium 208

Blackberry Spread

3 cups fresh blackberries, crushed
¼ cup sugar
1 (1¾-ounce) package powdered pectin
1 tablespoon unsweetened orange juice

Combine all ingredients in a medium saucepan. Bring to a boil; boil 1 minute, stirring constantly. Remove from heat; stir 3 minutes.

Immediately pour spread into freezer containers, leaving ½-inch headspace; cover at once with lids. Cool to room temperature; freeze. To serve, thaw spread. Yield: 2 cups (18 calories and 0% fat per tablespoon).

Protein 0.1 / Fat 0 (Saturated Fat 0) / Carbohydrate 4.6
Fiber 1.1 / Cholesterol 0 / Sodium 0

CELEBRATION BRUNCH

Whether the occasion is an anniversary, christening, birthday, or wedding, make it special with this Celebration Brunch menu.

Broccoli-Rice Quiche is a hearty vegetable-cheese creation surrounded by a rice crust that is pressed into the pieplate. Serve Tomato Wedges with Basil Dressing as an appropriate complement to the quiche. A bowl of seasonal fresh fruit served with the meal lends sweetness

---

Fresh fruit bowl
Broccoli-Rice Quiche
Tomato Wedges with Basil Dressing
Fresh Apple Coffee Cake
Coffee or tea
Serves 12

444 calories and 21% fat per serving

---

while boosting complex carbohydrates. The menu calories reflect a ½-cup serving of fresh fruit for each guest.

End this heart-healthy celebration on a festive note with Fresh Apple Coffee Cake. Chopped apple tops the cake instead of pecans, lowering the fat content. Serve each person one slice of this moist, rich-tasting cake for dessert, and reserve the remainder of the cake for another meal.

Broccoli-Rice Quiche

2 cups water
2 (10-ounce) packages frozen chopped broccoli
½ cup chopped onion
3 cups cooked long-grain rice (cooked without salt or fat)
1½ cups (6 ounces) shredded reduced-fat sharp Cheddar cheese, divided
1½ cups frozen egg substitute, thawed and divided
¾ teaspoon salt, divided
Vegetable cooking spray
½ teaspoon pepper
½ cup skim milk
2 (2½-ounce) jars sliced mushrooms, drained

Bring water to a boil in a medium saucepan. Add broccoli and onion; cover, reduce heat, and simmer 8 to 10 minutes or until vegetables are tender. Drain well; set aside.

Combine rice, ½ cup cheese, ½ cup egg substitute, and ¼ teaspoon salt. Press evenly over bottoms and up sides of two 9-inch quiche dishes or pieplates coated with cooking spray.

Combine remaining 1 cup egg substitute, remaining ½ teaspoon salt, pepper, milk, mushrooms, and broccoli mixture in a bowl; stir well. Pour mixture evenly into prepared dishes.

Bake at 375° for 20 minutes. Remove from oven, and sprinkle evenly with remaining 1 cup cheese; bake an additional 10 minutes or until cheese melts. Let stand 5 minutes before serving. Yield: 12 servings (145 calories and 19% fat per serving).

Protein 10.5 / Fat 3.1 (Saturated Fat 1.6) / Carbohydrate 19.0
Fiber 1.7 / Cholesterol 10 / Sodium 328

Tomato Wedges with Basil Dressing

½ cup plain nonfat yogurt
¼ cup fat-free mayonnaise
2¼ teaspoons malt vinegar
½ teaspoon dried whole basil
⅛ teaspoon dry mustard
6 medium tomatoes, each cut into 6 wedges
Curly leaf lettuce (optional)

Combine first 5 ingredients; cover and chill. Place lettuce leaves on each serving plate, if desired. Place 3 tomato wedges on lettuce on each plate; top with dressing. Yield: 12 servings (39 calories and 12% fat per serving).

Protein 1.8 / Fat 0.5 (Saturated Fat 0.1) / Carbohydrate 8.4
Fiber 1.9 / Cholesterol 0 / Sodium 83

Bring brunch to a sweet conclusion with Fresh Apple Coffee Cake.

Fresh Apple Coffee Cake

4 cups finely chopped cooking apple
½ cup unsweetened orange juice,
   divided
1½ teaspoons ground cinnamon
¼ cup skim milk
½ cup margarine, softened
1 cup sugar
1 (8-ounce) carton frozen egg substitute,
   thawed
2½ teaspoons vanilla extract
3 cups sifted cake flour
2 teaspoons baking powder
¼ teaspoon salt
Vegetable cooking spray
2 tablespoons brown sugar

Combine apple, ¼ cup orange juice, and cinnamon in a medium bowl; stir well, and set aside. Combine remaining ¼ cup orange juice and milk; stir well, and set aside.

Cream margarine; gradually add 1 cup sugar, beating at medium speed of an electric mixer until light and fluffy. Add egg substitute and vanilla; beat well.

Combine flour, baking powder, and salt, stirring well. Gradually add flour mixture to creamed mixture alternately with milk mixture, beginning and ending with flour mixture.

Pour half of batter into a 10-inch tube pan coated with cooking spray; top with half of apple mixture. Pour remaining batter into pan; top with remaining apple mixture, and sprinkle with brown sugar.

Bake at 350° for 1 hour and 10 minutes or until cake springs back when lightly touched. Cool in pan on a wire rack 10 minutes; remove from pan, and cool on a wire rack. Yield: 16 servings (202 calories and 27% fat per serving).

Protein 3.2 / Fat 6.0 (Saturated Fat 1.0) / Carbohydrate 34.1
Fiber 1.0 / Cholesterol 0 / Sodium 165

Guests will appreciate a festive brunch of Crabmeat Crêpes, Lemon-Blueberry Muffins (page 50), and Mint Lover's Tea (page 50).

BRUNCH ON THE VERANDA

A sunny veranda provides the perfect setting for a spring brunch. And a simple yet elegant menu creates an atmosphere that welcomes guests and celebrates the season.

Sit back, relax, and sip a glass of refreshing Mint Lover's Tea. The fresh mint adds a flavorful twist to iced tea.

Fresh lump crabmeat, mushrooms, and herbs fill Crabmeat Crêpes. A melon ball salad of honeydew, cantaloupe, and watermelon accompanies the crêpes. For an attractive presentation, serve each guest 1 cup of salad on a lettuce leaf.

Full of juicy blueberries, Lemon-Blueberry Muffins are sweet enough to serve as dessert. Menu calories include 1 muffin per serving.

Crabmeat Crêpes
Melon ball salad
Lemon-Blueberry Muffins
Mint Lover's Tea
Serves 8
428 calories and 18% fat per serving

Crabmeat Crêpes

Vegetable cooking spray
2 teaspoons reduced-calorie margarine
1⅓ cups sliced fresh mushrooms
1 cup chopped green onions
1 teaspoon dried whole thyme
1 tablespoon all-purpose flour
1 cup skim milk
1 pound fresh lump crabmeat, drained
2 tablespoons chopped fresh parsley
2 teaspoons lemon juice
¼ teaspoon salt
¼ teaspoon dry mustard
⅛ teaspoon ground red pepper
Light Crêpes
Fresh thyme sprigs (optional)

Coat a large nonstick skillet with cooking spray; add margarine. Place over medium-high heat until margarine melts. Add mushrooms, green onions, and 1 teaspoon thyme; sauté 2 to 3 minutes or until vegetables are tender. Reduce heat to low; stir in flour. Cook 1 minute, stirring constantly. Gradually add milk. Cook over medium heat, stirring constantly, until thickened and bubbly. Remove from heat; stir in crabmeat and next 5 ingredients.

Spoon 3 tablespoons crabmeat mixture down center of each Light Crêpe; roll up crêpes, and place seam side down in two 13- x 9- x 2-inch baking dishes coated with cooking spray. Cover and bake at 350° for 15 to 18 minutes or until thoroughly heated. Remove cover; broil crêpes 5½ inches from heat 1 minute or until golden. To serve, place 2 crêpes on each serving plate; garnish with thyme sprigs, if desired. Yield: 8 servings (144 calories and 16% fat per serving).

Light Crêpes

½ cup plus 2 tablespoons all-purpose flour
1⅓ cups skim milk
4 egg whites
Vegetable cooking spray

Combine flour, milk, and egg whites in container of an electric blender or food processor; top with cover, and process 30 seconds. Scrape sides of container; process an additional 30 seconds. Refrigerate batter at least 1 hour. (This allows flour particles to swell and soften so that crêpes are light in texture.)

Coat a 6-inch nonstick crêpe pan or skillet with cooking spray. Place over medium heat until just hot, but not smoking. Pour 2 tablespoons batter into pan; quickly tilt pan in all directions so batter covers bottom of pan in a thin film. Cook 1 minute or until lightly browned.

Lift edge of crêpe to test for doneness. Crêpe is ready for flipping when it can be shaken loose from pan. Flip crêpe, and cook about 30 seconds. (This side is usually spotty brown and is the side on which filling is placed.)

Place crêpes on a towel to cool. Stack crêpes between layers of wax paper to prevent sticking. Repeat procedure until all batter is used. Yield: 16 (6-inch) crêpes.

Protein 17.1 / Fat 2.5 (Saturated Fat 0.4) / Carbohydrate 12.6
Fiber 0.7 / Cholesterol 58 / Sodium 307

Lemon-Blueberry Muffins

2 tablespoons sugar
1 tablespoon lemon juice
2½ cups all-purpose flour
2 teaspoons baking powder
½ teaspoon baking soda
¼ teaspoon salt
¼ cup sugar
1½ cups nonfat buttermilk
¼ cup vegetable oil
¼ cup frozen egg substitute, thawed
1 tablespoon grated lemon rind
1 teaspoon vanilla extract
1½ cups frozen unsweetened blueberries, thawed
Vegetable cooking spray

Combine 2 tablespoons sugar and lemon juice; stir well, and set aside.

Combine flour and next 4 ingredients in a large bowl, stirring well; make a well in center of mixture.

Combine buttermilk, oil, egg substitute, lemon rind, and vanilla; add to flour mixture, stirring just until dry ingredients are moistened. Gently fold in blueberries.

Spoon batter into large (2¾-inch) muffin pans coated with cooking spray, filling three-fourths full. Bake at 375° for 20 minutes.

Remove pans from oven. Brush hot muffins with lemon juice mixture. Bake an additional 6 to 8 minutes or until muffins are golden. Remove from pans immediately. Let cool on wire racks. Yield: 1 dozen (181 calories and 27% fat each).

Protein 4.2 / Fat 5.4 (Saturated Fat 0.9) / Carbohydrate 29.1
Fiber 1.3 / Cholesterol 0 / Sodium 142

Mint Lover's Tea

8 cups water
1½ cups loosely packed fresh mint leaves, minced
3 tablespoons loose gunpowder tea
5 mint herb tea bags
¼ cup plus 1 tablespoon lime juice
¼ cup plus 1 tablespoon honey
Mint Ice Cubes
Fresh mint sprigs (optional)

Bring water to a boil; pour over mint leaves, loose tea, and tea bags. Cover and steep 10 minutes. Strain mixture, discarding mint leaves, loose tea, and tea bags.

Add lime juice and honey to tea; stir mixture well. Cover and chill thoroughly. Serve tea over Mint Ice Cubes. Garnish each serving

with fresh mint sprigs, if desired. Yield: 8 cups (45 calories and 0% fat per 1-cup serving).

Mint Ice Cubes

4 cups water
2 cups loosely packed fresh mint leaves, crushed

Bring water to a boil, and pour over mint leaves. Cover and let stand 10 minutes. Strain mixture, discarding mint leaves. Let cool completely. Pour liquid into each of 28 ice cube tray compartments; freeze until firm. Yield: 28 ice cubes.

Protein 0.1 / Fat 0 (Saturated Fat 0) / Carbohydrate 12.5
Fiber 0 / Cholesterol 0 / Sodium 8

Healthy entertaining is simple when you serve Grilled Sirloin with Sweet Red Pepper Sauce, Hot and Spicy Marinated Vegetables, and Herbed Corn-on-the-Cob. (Menu begins on page 54.)

Lemon Green Beans and Country Corncakes showcase an abundant summer harvest.

SUPPER FROM THE GARDEN

In the summer, backyard gardens and roadside vegetable stands offer an abundance of fresh fruits and vegetables. Take advantage of these nutritious foods of the season with this menu that boasts only 8 percent fat.

Summer Squash Casserole is high enough in protein to be considered the main dish of the menu. Onion, green pepper, pimiento, and 40% less-fat Cheddar cheese are combined with

Summer Squash Casserole
Lemon Green Beans
Boiled new potatoes
Country Corncakes
Fresh berries

Serves 4

662 calories and 8% fat per serving

the squash to give this casserole a savory flavor, while the breadcrumb topping gives a crunchy texture.

Add to this garden sampler a serving of colorful Lemon Green Beans, 3 boiled new potatoes, and 3 Country Corncakes per person to boost complex carbohydrates.

A 1-cup serving of fresh-picked raspberries and blackberries is a cool, sweet dessert that is easy on the waistline.

Summer Squash Casserole

2 pounds yellow squash, sliced
⅔ cup chopped onion
¼ cup plus 2 tablespoons chopped green
   pepper
⅔ cup (2.6 ounces) shredded 40% less-fat
   Cheddar cheese
½ cup frozen egg substitute, thawed
1 (4-ounce) jar diced pimiento, drained
¼ teaspoon salt
¼ teaspoon pepper
Vegetable cooking spray
3 tablespoons fine, dry breadcrumbs
2 tablespoons chopped fresh parsley
⅛ teaspoon paprika

Place squash, onion, and green pepper in a vegetable steamer over boiling water; cover and steam 10 to 12 minutes or until vegetables are crisp-tender. Combine steamed vegetables, cheese, and next 4 ingredients in a medium bowl; stir gently. Spoon mixture into a 2-quart casserole coated with cooking spray.

Combine breadcrumbs, parsley, and paprika, stirring well; sprinkle over squash mixture. Bake at 350° for 25 to 30 minutes or until thoroughly heated. Yield: 4 servings (144 calories and 22% fat per 1-cup serving).

Protein 10.2 / Fat 3.5 (Saturated Fat 1.2) / Carbohydrate 21.8
Fiber 4.8 / Cholesterol 13 / Sodium 366

Lemon Green Beans

½ pound fresh green beans
½ small sweet red pepper, cut crosswise
   into rings
¼ cup water
¼ teaspoon dried whole basil
1 tablespoon lemon rind strips
1 tablespoon lemon juice
1 teaspoon sesame seeds, toasted

Wash beans; trim ends, and remove strings. Cut beans into 2-inch pieces. Combine beans,

pepper rings, water, and basil in a medium saucepan with a small amount of water. Bring to a boil; cover, reduce heat, and simmer 12 to 15 minutes or until vegetables are tender. Drain well. Transfer mixture to a serving bowl. Add lemon rind, lemon juice, and sesame seeds; toss well. Yield: 4 servings (25 calories and 18% fat per ½-cup serving).

Protein 1.3 / Fat 0.5 (Saturated Fat 0.1) / Carbohydrate 5.2
Fiber 1.3 / Cholesterol 0 / Sodium 4

Country Corncakes

1 cup fresh corn cut from the cob (about
   2 ears)
½ cup yellow cornmeal
1 cup boiling water
2 teaspoons honey
¼ teaspoon salt
2 egg whites
Vegetable cooking spray

Cook corn, covered, in boiling water to cover 8 to 10 minutes or until tender; drain and set aside to cool.

Combine corn and next 4 ingredients in a medium bowl; stir well.

Beat egg whites at high speed of an electric mixer until stiff peaks form. (Do not overbeat.) Fold egg whites into corn mixture.

For corncakes, pour ¼ cup batter onto a hot griddle coated with cooking spray. Cook 3 minutes on each side or until brown. Yield: 12 (3½-inch) corncakes (40 calories and 7% fat each).

Protein 1.5 / Fat 0.3 (Saturated Fat 0) / Carbohydrate 8.2
Fiber 0.6 / Cholesterol 0 / Sodium 59

STEAK WITH A FLAIR

On summer evenings, the aroma of steak on the grill is like no other—especially if it's coming from your neighbor's yard.

Your steaks can be extra special, though, when topped with this colorful sauce and pepper strips. Serve the steaks with corn and marinated vegetables and a 1-ounce slice of commercial French bread.

Chocolate Angel Food Cake is a virtually fat-free dessert that can be prepared ahead. The calories reflect 1 slice per person.

Grilled Sirloin with Sweet Red
Pepper Sauce
Herbed Corn-on-the-Cob
Hot and Spicy Marinated Vegetables
French bread
Chocolate Angel Food Cake

Serves 4

556 calories and 20% fat per serving

Grilled Sirloin with Sweet Red Pepper Sauce

1 (1-pound) lean boneless beef top
  sirloin steak
½ cup commercial oil-free Italian dressing
½ cup red wine vinegar
4 medium-size sweet red peppers, divided
⅓ cup chopped green onions
¼ cup water
2 tablespoons Chablis or other dry
  white wine
¾ teaspoon beef-flavored bouillon granules
Vegetable cooking spray

Trim fat from steak; cut steak into 4 equal portions. Place in a large shallow dish. Combine dressing and vinegar; pour over steaks. Cover and marinate in refrigerator at least 8 hours, turning occasionally. Remove steaks from marinade; discard marinade.

Cut 1 pepper into thin strips; set aside. Seed and chop remaining peppers. Combine chopped pepper and next 4 ingredients in a nonstick skillet; bring to a boil. Cover, reduce heat, and simmer 15 minutes. Cool slightly. Place chopped pepper mixture in container of an electric blender; top with cover, and process until smooth. Strain mixture, and set aside.

Coat a grill rack with cooking spray; place on grill over medium-hot coals. Place steaks on rack, and cook 5 minutes on each side or to desired degree of doneness. Set aside; keep warm.

Coat skillet with cooking spray; place over medium-high heat until hot. Add pepper strips; sauté until tender. Remove from skillet; set aside. Add red pepper sauce to skillet; cook over low heat until thoroughly heated.

Place steaks on individual serving plates; spoon sauce evenly over steaks. Top evenly with pepper strips. Yield: 4 servings (215 calories and 31% fat per serving).

Protein 14.6 / Fat 7.5 (Saturated Fat 5.2) / Carbohydrate 7.9
Fiber 2.0 / Cholesterol 80 / Sodium 364

Herbed Corn-on-the-Cob

4 ears fresh corn
1 tablespoon dried whole dillweed
1 tablespoon dried whole thyme
1 tablespoon water
1 teaspoon vegetable oil
1 clove garlic, minced

Remove husks and silk from corn; set aside.

Combine dillweed and remaining ingredients in a small bowl, stirring well. Rub herb mixture evenly over corn; place each ear on a piece of heavy-duty aluminum foil. Roll foil lengthwise around each ear; twist foil at each end to seal.

Grill corn over medium-hot coals 15 to 20 minutes or until corn is tender, turning every 5 minutes. Yield: 4 servings (81 calories and 22% fat per serving).

Protein 2.2 / Fat 2.0 (Saturated Fat 0.4) / Carbohydrate 16.4
Fiber 2.5 / Cholesterol 0 / Sodium 13

You can afford to indulge in dessert when it's Chocolate Angel Food Cake. Garnish each slice with a strawberry fan.

Hot and Spicy Marinated Vegetables

½ cup fresh cauliflower flowerets
½ cup fresh broccoli flowerets
½ cup thinly sliced yellow squash
¼ cup thinly sliced zucchini
¼ cup diagonally sliced carrot
¼ cup white wine vinegar
½ teaspoon garlic powder
¾ teaspoon chili oil
½ teaspoon vegetable oil

Combine first 5 ingredients; set aside.

Combine vinegar, garlic powder, and oils; stir well. Pour vinegar mixture over vegetables; toss gently to coat. Cover and marinate in refrigerator at least 8 hours, tossing occasionally. Serve with a slotted spoon. Yield: 4 servings (30 calories and 45% fat per ½-cup serving).

Protein 1.0 / Fat 1.5 (Saturated Fat 0.4) / Carbohydrate 3.4
Fiber 1.3 / Cholesterol 0 / Sodium 10

Chocolate Angel Food Cake

1 (14½-ounce) package angel food cake mix
¼ cup unsweetened cocoa
¼ teaspoon chocolate flavoring
1 tablespoon powdered sugar
Fresh strawberries (optional)

Combine flour packet from cake mix and cocoa. Stir well with a wire whisk.

Prepare cake according to package directions; fold chocolate flavoring into batter. Bake according to package directions.

Sprinkle cooled cake with powdered sugar; garnish with strawberries, if desired. Yield: 16 servings (107 calories and 2% fat per serving).

Protein 2.5 / Fat 0.2 (Saturated Fat 0.1) / Carbohydrate 23.9
Fiber 0 / Cholesterol 0 / Sodium 49

Mississippi Fish "Fry"

A drive through Mississippi leaves no doubt that catfish is a favorite food in that state. Neon signs announce scores of all-you-can-eat catfish houses where fried catfish, hush puppies, french fries, creamy coleslaw, and an array of desserts are served. Here is a menu that gives this favorite Southern supper a healthy twist.

Oven-Fried Catfish and Baked Hush Puppies keep fat low without sacrificing flavor, with each person enjoying a whole catfish and 3 hush puppies with their meal.

Marinated Confetti Coleslaw gets its flavor from a vinegar-based dressing, and so omits the fat found in mayonnaise versions. The coleslaw and thick slices of home-grown tomato accompany the catfish and hush puppies in this traditional Southern meal. Serving chilled watermelon wedges makes dessert preparation easy; menu calories include the equivalent of 1 cup watermelon per person.

Oven-Fried Catfish
Marinated Confetti Coleslaw
Sliced tomatoes
Baked Hush Puppies
Watermelon wedges
Iced tea

Serves 8

420 calories and 25% fat per serving

Oven-Fried Catfish, Marinated Confetti Coleslaw, and Baked Hush Puppies offer a healthy twist to some Southern favorites.

Oven-Fried Catfish

6 (1-inch) slices French bread,
  cubed
¼ cup fat-free mayonnaise
1 tablespoon plus 1 teaspoon water
8 (6-ounce) dressed catfish
Vegetable cooking spray
Lemon wedges (optional)
Fresh parsley sprigs (optional)

Position knife blade in food processor bowl; add bread cubes. Process 30 seconds or until breadcrumbs are fine. Sprinkle breadcrumbs onto an ungreased baking sheet; bake at 350°

for 5 to 7 minutes or until lightly browned. Place breadcrumbs in a shallow bowl; set aside.

Combine mayonnaise and water; stir well. Dip fish in mayonnaise mixture; dredge in breadcrumbs. Place fish on a baking sheet coated with cooking spray. Bake at 450° for 15 to 17 minutes or until fish flakes easily when tested with a fork. Transfer fish to individual serving plates. If desired, garnish with lemon wedges and fresh parsley sprigs. Yield: 8 servings (197 calories and 24% fat per serving).

Protein 22.0 / Fat 5.2 (Saturated Fat 1.2) / Carbohydrate 13.3
Fiber 0.5 / Cholesterol 65 / Sodium 298

Marinated Confetti Coleslaw

3½ cups coarsely shredded cabbage
1¼ cups coarsely shredded red cabbage
1 cup coarsely shredded carrot
1 cup diced celery
½ cup chopped onion
¾ cup cider vinegar
¼ cup sugar
1½ tablespoons vegetable oil
¾ teaspoon dry mustard
½ teaspoon ground turmeric
½ teaspoon celery seeds
Small red cabbage leaves (optional)

Combine first 5 ingredients in a large bowl; toss mixture gently, and set aside.

Combine vinegar, sugar, oil, mustard, turmeric, and celery seeds in a small saucepan; bring to a boil over medium heat. Cook until sugar dissolves, stirring occasionally. Pour vinegar mixture over cabbage mixture; toss gently to coat. Cover and marinate in refrigerator at least 8 hours, stirring occasionally.

To serve, place a cabbage leaf on each individual serving plate, if desired. Toss coleslaw; using a slotted spoon, place ¾ cup coleslaw onto each cabbage leaf. Yield: 8 servings (73 calories and 36% fat per ¾-cup serving).

Protein 0.9 / Fat 2.9 (Saturated Fat 0.5) / Carbohydrate 12.5
Fiber 1.7 / Cholesterol 0 / Sodium 26

Baked Hush Puppies

⅔ cup yellow cornmeal
⅓ cup all-purpose flour
1 teaspoon baking powder
½ teaspoon salt
½ cup minced onion
⅓ cup skim milk
¼ cup frozen egg substitute, thawed
1 tablespoon vegetable oil
⅛ teaspoon pepper
Vegetable cooking spray

Combine first 5 ingredients in a medium bowl; make a well in center of mixture.

Combine milk, egg substitute, oil, and pepper in a small bowl; stir well. Add to cornmeal mixture, stirring just until dry ingredients are moistened.

Spoon batter into miniature (1¾-inch) muffin pans coated with cooking spray, filling three-fourths full. Bake at 450° for 12 to 15 minutes or until hush puppies are lightly browned. Remove from pans immediately. Serve hush puppies warm. Yield: 2 dozen (31 calories and 26% fat each).

Protein 0.9 / Fat 0.9 (Saturated Fat 0.2) / Carbohydrate 4.8
Fiber 0.3 / Cholesterol 0 / Sodium 67

BACKYARD BARBECUE

Warm summer evenings set the stage for leisurely outdoor entertaining. Start with an appetizer of Tabbouleh with Pita Chips, a flavor-packed source of complex carbohydrates and fiber. The pita chips may be served anytime you want a low-fat chip to serve with dips or spreads.

Quick Sesame-Ginger Chicken is hard to beat for an easy entrée. Simply baste the chicken with a flavorful mixture of honey, soy sauce, and gingerroot as it grills. Corn-Stuffed Tomatoes is a perfect accompaniment for this menu, taking advantage of fresh summertime ingredients. For added convenience, the stuffed tomatoes cook on the grill alongside the chicken.

Round out the main course with 1 cup of a favorite tossed green salad served with 1 tablespoon oil-free dressing, and a commercial dinner roll for each person.

For a cool, sweet finale, scoop homemade Strawberry Frozen Yogurt into pretty little dessert dishes. It's an easy make-ahead treat that will leave the hostess some extra time to visit with friends and family.

Tabbouleh with Pita Chips
Quick Sesame-Ginger Chicken
Corn-Stuffed Tomatoes
Green salad
Dinner rolls
Strawberry Frozen Yogurt

Serves 6

669 calories and 13% fat per serving

Tabbouleh with Pita Chips

2 cups boiling water
⅓ cup plus 1 tablespoon bulgur wheat, uncooked
1¾ cups diced tomato
¾ cup minced fresh parsley
½ cup sliced green onions
1 tablespoon minced fresh mint
1 tablespoon minced celery
1 tablespoon minced green pepper
1 tablespoon minced ripe olives
2 tablespoons lemon juice
1½ teaspoons olive oil
¼ teaspoon salt
⅛ teaspoon pepper
Pita Chips

Pour water over bulgur in a large bowl; cover and let stand 1 hour. Drain thoroughly. Add diced tomato and next 10 ingredients; stir well. Cover and chill at least 2 hours, stirring occasionally. Serve with Pita Chips. Yield: 6 appetizer servings (151 calories and 14% fat per ½ cup tabbouleh and 8 pita chips).

Pita Chips

3 (6-inch) whole wheat pita bread rounds

Separate each pita bread into 2 rounds; cut each round into 8 wedges. Place wedges on an ungreased baking sheet; bake at 350° for 10 to 12 minutes or until lightly browned. Remove chips from baking sheet; let cool completely on a wire rack. Yield: 4 dozen pita chips.

Protein 3.8 / Fat 2.4 (Saturated Fat 0.2) / Carbohydrate 27.6
Fiber 4.8 / Cholesterol 0 / Sodium 130

Invite the neighbors for a backyard barbecue that includes Quick Sesame-Ginger Chicken (page 60) and Corn-Stuffed Tomatoes (page 60).

Quick Sesame-Ginger Chicken

1½ tablespoons sesame seeds, toasted
1 tablespoon grated fresh gingerroot
3 tablespoons honey
3 tablespoons low-sodium soy sauce
6 (4-ounce) skinned, boned chicken breast halves
Vegetable cooking spray

Combine first 4 ingredients; set aside.
Place chicken between 2 sheets of heavy-duty plastic wrap, and flatten to ¼-inch thickness, using a meat mallet or rolling pin. Brush half of soy sauce mixture over chicken, coating both sides.

Coat grill rack with cooking spray; place on grill over medium-hot coals. Place chicken on rack, and cook 8 to 10 minutes or until chicken is tender, turning and basting frequently with remaining soy sauce mixture. Yield: 6 servings (187 calories and 21% fat per serving).

Protein 26.3 / Fat 4.3 (Saturated Fat 1.0) / Carbohydrate 9.1
Fiber 0.1 / Cholesterol 70 / Sodium 258

Corn-Stuffed Tomatoes

6 medium tomatoes
2 cups fresh corn cut from cob (about 4 ears)
½ cup water
¼ cup chopped green onions
Vegetable cooking spray
1 tablespoon chopped fresh basil or 1 teaspoon dried whole basil
2 teaspoons minced fresh parsley
¼ teaspoon freshly ground pepper
Fresh basil sprigs (optional)

Cut top off each tomato; discard tops. Scoop out pulp, leaving shells intact. Invert tomato shells on paper towels to drain. Chop pulp. Set aside ½ cup chopped pulp; reserve remaining pulp for other uses.

Combine corn, water, and green onions in a medium skillet coated with cooking spray. Cook, uncovered, over medium heat 8 to 10 minutes or until water is absorbed. Remove from heat; stir in ½ cup chopped pulp, chopped basil, parsley, and pepper. Spoon mixture evenly into tomato shells; wrap each tomato in heavy-duty aluminum foil.

Coat grill rack with cooking spray; place on grill over medium-hot coals. Place foil-wrapped tomatoes on rack; cook 5 to 7 minutes or until thoroughly heated. Unwrap tomatoes, and place on a serving platter. Garnish with fresh basil sprigs, if desired. Yield: 6 servings (77 calories and 14% fat per serving).

Protein 3.0 / Fat 1.2 (Saturated Fat 0.2) / Carbohydrate 16.9
Fiber 3.6 / Cholesterol 0 / Sodium 22

Strawberry Frozen Yogurt

1 pint fresh strawberries, hulled
¾ cup sugar
½ teaspoon grated lemon rind
1¼ cups plain nonfat yogurt
¼ cup skim milk

Combine first 3 ingredients in container of an electric blender or food processor; top with cover, and process until smooth. Add yogurt and milk; process 30 seconds. Pour mixture into freezer can of a 2-quart hand-turned or electric freezer. Freeze according to manufacturer's instructions. Let ripen 1 hour, if desired.

Scoop yogurt into individual dessert bowls, and serve immediately. Yield: 4 cups (141 calories and 2% fat per ⅔-cup serving).

Protein 3.4 / Fat 0.3 (Saturated Fat 0.1) / Carbohydrate 32.5
Fiber 1.3 / Cholesterol 1 / Sodium 42

For dining elegance at its nutritional best, serve Grecian Snapper with Feta Cheese and Orzo Milanese. (Menu begins on page 66.)

MIDDLE EAST FEAST

Inspired by the variety of foods of the Middle East, this menu offers a rich sampling of colors, textures, and flavors.

Marinated cubes of lamb are skewered with eggplant and cherry tomatoes for Mideastern-Style Lamb Kabobs. And Couscous with Vegetables offers a good source of complex carbohydrates and dietary fiber.

Spinach-Orange Salad adds a sweet-and-sour note to the meal. For authenticity, serve commercial whole wheat pita bread rounds (1 per person). Frozen Pineapple Yogurt with Raspberries is a cool finale for this spicy meal.

Fresh ingredients and an assortment of spices take the spotlight in Couscous with Vegetables.

Mideastern-Style Lamb Kabobs
Couscous with Vegetables
Spinach-Orange Salad
Whole wheat pita bread
Frozen Pineapple Yogurt with Raspberries
Serves 8

651 calories and 17% fat per serving

Mideastern-Style Lamb Kabobs

2 pounds lean boneless lamb
⅔ cup unsweetened white grape juice
½ cup chopped fresh parsley
2 teaspoons grated lime rind
½ cup fresh lime juice
2 teaspoons chopped fresh rosemary
1 teaspoon ground cinnamon
2 large cloves garlic, minced
2 medium eggplants (about 1½ pounds)
32 cherry tomatoes
Vegetable cooking spray

Trim fat from lamb; cut lamb into 48 (1-inch) cubes. Combine grape juice and next 6 ingredients in a large zip-top heavy-duty plastic bag; add lamb cubes. Seal and marinate in refrigerator at least 8 hours, turning bag occasionally.

Cut eggplants lengthwise into quarters; cut each quarter into 6 pieces. Arrange in a vegetable steamer over boiling water; cover and steam 5 minutes or until crisp-tender. Drain; set aside.

Remove lamb from marinade. Place marinade in a small saucepan. Bring to a boil; cover, reduce heat, and simmer 5 minutes. Set marinade aside.

Thread lamb, eggplant, and cherry tomatoes alternately on 16 (12-inch) skewers. Coat grill rack with cooking spray; place on grill over medium-hot coals. Place kabobs on rack, and cook 12 to 14 minutes or to desired degree of doneness, turning and basting frequently with marinade. Yield: 8 servings (222 calories and 29% fat per serving).

Protein 25.9 / Fat 7.1 (Saturated Fat 2.4) / Carbohydrate 14.5
Fiber 2.5 / Cholesterol 76 / Sodium 70

Couscous with Vegetables

½ pound fresh asparagus spears
¼ pound carrots, scraped and cut into
   julienne strips
1 cup fresh snow pea pods, trimmed
¾ cup diagonally sliced zucchini
¼ cup golden raisins
1 teaspoon reduced-calorie margarine,
   melted
½ teaspoon curry powder
¼ teaspoon dried whole thyme
¼ teaspoon ground cinnamon
2 cups water
2 teaspoons reduced-calorie margarine
¼ teaspoon salt
1¼ cups couscous, uncooked

Snap off tough ends of asparagus. Remove scales from stalks with a knife or vegetable peeler, if desired. Cut asparagus into 1-inch pieces; set aside.

Arrange carrot in a vegetable steamer over boiling water; cover and steam 3 minutes. Add asparagus; cover and steam an additional 2 minutes. Add snow peas and zucchini; toss vegetables gently. Cover and steam an additional 1 to 2 minutes or until vegetables are crisp-tender.

Transfer vegetables to a large bowl; add raisins and next 4 ingredients, and toss well. Set aside, and keep warm.

Combine water, 2 teaspoons margarine, and salt in a medium saucepan; bring to a boil. Remove from heat. Add couscous; cover and let stand 5 minutes or until couscous is tender and liquid is absorbed.

Transfer couscous to a serving platter. Top with vegetable mixture. Yield: 8 servings (149 calories and 7% fat per serving).

Protein 5.2 / Fat 1.1 (Saturated Fat 0.2) / Carbohydrate 30.2
Fiber 2.8 / Cholesterol 0 / Sodium 93

Spinach-Orange Salad

7 cups torn fresh spinach
1⅓ cups chopped purple onion
1 large navel orange, peeled and coarsely
   chopped
2½ tablespoons red wine vinegar
1½ tablespoons water
1½ tablespoons vegetable oil
1½ tablespoons honey
½ teaspoon beef-flavored bouillon granules

Combine first 3 ingredients in a large bowl; toss gently, and set aside.

Combine vinegar and remaining ingredients; stir with a wire whisk until bouillon granules dissolve. Pour over spinach mixture, and toss gently. Yield: 8 servings (58 calories and 42% fat per 1-cup serving).

Protein 1.0 / Fat 2.7 (Saturated Fat 0.5) / Carbohydrate 8.3
Fiber 2.0 / Cholesterol 0 / Sodium 74

Frozen Pineapple Yogurt with Raspberries

2 (20-ounce) cans pineapple chunks in
   juice, drained
1 cup plain nonfat yogurt
¼ cup sifted powdered sugar
2 tablespoons lemon juice
2 cups fresh raspberries
Fresh mint sprigs (optional)

Arrange pineapple on a baking sheet; freeze 2 hours or until firm.

Combine yogurt, sugar, and lemon juice in container of an electric blender; top with cover,

and process until blended. Add pineapple; process until smooth. Pour mixture into a 13- x 9- x 2-inch baking dish. Cover and freeze 2 to 3 hours or until firm.

Scoop ½ cup yogurt into each individual dessert bowl; top each serving with ¼ cup raspberries. Garnish with fresh mint sprigs, if desired. Serve immediately. Yield: 8 servings (100 calories and 2% fat per serving).

Protein 1.9 / Fat 0.2 (Saturated Fat 0) / Carbohydrate 22.9
Fiber 3.6 / Cholesterol 1 / Sodium 22

DOWN-HOME CREOLE DINNER

When you think of Louisiana, Creole food naturally comes to mind. A healthy alternative to one of the traditional Creole favorites is Chicken and Sausage Jambalaya. Lean turkey sausage is substituted for pork sausage to keep the fat content low.

A salad of Tossed Greens with Country-Style Dressing is a simple accompaniment to the myriad flavors in the jambalaya.

Chicken and Sausage Jambalaya
Tossed Greens with
Country-Style Dressing
Bread Pudding with Whiskey Sauce
Iced tea

Serves 6

616 calories and 15% fat per serving

Chicken and Sausage Jambalaya

4 (4-ounce) skinned, boned chicken breast
  halves
¼ teaspoon ground red pepper
¼ teaspoon ground black pepper
Vegetable cooking spray
¾ pound lean turkey sausage
2¼ cups chopped onion
2 cups chopped celery
1½ cups sliced green onions
½ cup chopped green pepper
½ cup chopped sweet red pepper
2 cloves garlic, minced
2½ cups water
1 teaspoon chicken-flavored bouillon
  granules
½ teaspoon browning-and-seasoning sauce
1¼ cups long-grain rice, uncooked
Green onion fans (optional)

Cut chicken into bite-size pieces; sprinkle with ground red and black pepper. Coat an electric skillet with cooking spray; heat to medium-high (325°). Add chicken; cook 3 to 5 minutes or until lightly browned, stirring frequently. Remove chicken from skillet; drain and pat dry with paper towels. Wipe drippings from skillet with a paper towel.

Reduce heat to medium (300°). Add sausage, and cook until meat is browned, stirring to crumble. Remove sausage from skillet. Drain and pat dry with paper towels. Wipe drippings from skillet with a paper towel.

Coat skillet with cooking spray; heat to medium-high (325°). Add onion and next 5 ingredients; sauté until tender. Add chicken; cover, reduce heat, and cook 10 minutes or until thoroughly heated.

Combine water, bouillon granules, and browning-and-seasoning sauce, stirring well; add to chicken mixture. Bring to a boil; stir in sausage and rice. Cover, reduce heat, and simmer 20 minutes or until rice is tender and liquid is absorbed. Spoon jambalaya into individual bowls; garnish with green onion fans, if desired. Yield: 6 servings (371 calories and 21% fat per 1½-cup serving).

Protein 31.5 / Fat 8.7 (Saturated Fat 0.7) / Carbohydrate 40.7
Fiber 3.2 / Cholesterol 83 / Sodium 523

Tossed Greens with Country-Style Dressing

⅓ cup nonfat sour cream
2 tablespoons sugar
3 tablespoons white wine vinegar
⅛ teaspoon dried whole dillweed
2 cups torn romaine lettuce
2 cups torn iceberg lettuce
2 cups torn red leaf lettuce
1 cup halved cherry tomatoes

Combine first four ingredients; stir well with a wire whisk until smooth. Combine lettuce and tomatoes in a large bowl. Pour dressing over greens; toss gently. Yield: 6 servings (33 calories and 3% fat per 1-cup serving).

Protein 1.3 / Fat 0.1 (Saturated Fat 0) / Carbohydrate 6.4
Fiber 0.5 / Cholesterol 0 / Sodium 13

Chicken and Sausage Jambalaya and Tossed Greens with Country-Style Dressing provide plenty of flavor but very little fat.

Bread Pudding with Whiskey Sauce

2 cups skim milk
½ cup frozen egg substitute, thawed
⅓ cup firmly packed brown sugar
1¼ teaspoons ground cinnamon
¾ teaspoon ground nutmeg
1½ teaspoons vanilla extract
5 cups (½-inch) French bread cubes
⅓ cup raisins
Butter-flavored vegetable cooking spray
Whiskey Sauce

Combine first 6 ingredients in a large bowl; stir well with a wire whisk. Add bread cubes and raisins; stir well. Spoon mixture into 6 (6-ounce) ovenproof ramekins or custard cups coated with cooking spray. Place ramekins in a 13- x 9- x 2-inch baking dish; add hot water to pan to a depth of 1 inch. Bake at 350° for 25 minutes or until knife inserted in center comes out clean. Remove ramekins from water. Spoon 2 tablespoons Whiskey Sauce over each serving. Yield: 6 servings (212 calories and 8% fat per serving).

Whiskey Sauce

½ cup plus 1 tablespoon water
1 tablespoon plus 1 teaspoon sugar
2 tablespoons whiskey
2 teaspoons cornstarch
2 teaspoons reduced-calorie margarine

Combine all ingredients in a small saucepan. Cook over medium heat, stirring constantly, until mixture comes to a boil; cook, stirring constantly, 1 minute or until thickened. Serve sauce warm. Yield: ¾ cup.

Protein 7.4 / Fat 1.8 (Saturated Fat 0.5) / Carbohydrate 41.1
Fiber 1.2 / Cholesterol 2 / Sodium 240

Bold colors and flavors are trademarks of Chicken-Chile Rolls (page 70), Southwestern Hominy (page 70), and Mock Sangría.

MEXICAN FIESTA

Mexican food by its very nature is festive and adventurous. It offers a wonderful array of colors and exciting combinations of flavors and textures.

Begin the meal with Mexicali Bean Dip served with toasted corn tortilla wedges and a glass of refreshing Mock Sangría. The dip is easy to prepare using canned pinto beans; all the ingredients are quickly blended in a food processor, which gives the dip a smooth consistency. Serve the dip immediately or refrigerate for an hour or two, allowing the flavors to mingle.

Mock Sangría
Mexicali Bean Dip
Chicken-Chile Rolls
Southwestern Hominy
Cinnamon Crisps

Serves 12

619 calories and 15% fat per serving

Flavorful green chiles are a common ingredient in Mexican cooking. Canned whole green chiles give Chicken-Chile Rolls an authentic south-of-the-border flavor. Slice the cheese-filled rolls, or serve them whole on a bed of shredded lettuce; add traditional toppings like picante sauce and nonfat sour cream for extra flavor.

Flour tortillas are baked into Cinnamon Crisps in just a few easy steps. Serve each person a whole tortilla to break apart and eat for a fun way to end the meal.

Mock Sangría

5¾ cups sparkling pink Catawba
4½ cups cranberry-apple juice cocktail
1½ cups club soda
¼ cup lime juice
1½ tablespoons instant powdered tea
Orange slices (optional)
Lime slices (optional)
Lemon slices (optional)

Combine first 5 ingredients in a large pitcher; stir until well blended. Chill thoroughly. If desired, garnish sangría with orange, lime, and lemon slices. Serve over ice. Yield: 12 cups (135 calories and 1% fat per 1-cup serving).

Protein 0.2 / Fat 0 (Saturated Fat 0) / Carbohydrate 34.8
Fiber 0 / Cholesterol 0 / Sodium 13

Mexicali Bean Dip

9 (6-inch) corn tortillas
½ cup plus 1 tablespoon chopped sweet
  red pepper
½ cup plus 1 tablespoon chopped green
  pepper
1 large green onion, cut into ½-inch pieces
1½ tablespoons chopped fresh cilantro
1 (16-ounce) can pinto beans, drained
1 tablespoon cider vinegar
1 teaspoon lime juice
½ teaspoon vegetable oil
⅛ teaspoon salt
⅛ teaspoon ground cumin
⅛ teaspoon ground red pepper

Cut each tortilla into 8 wedges; place tortilla wedges on ungreased baking sheets. Bake at 350° for 15 to 18 minutes or until crisp. Set aside.

Position knife blade in food processor bowl; add sweet red and green pepper, onion, and cilantro. Process until finely chopped. Add beans and remaining ingredients; process until well blended.

Serve dip with tortilla wedges. Yield: 12 appetizer servings (77 calories and 15% fat per 2 tablespoons dip and 6 tortilla wedges).

Protein 2.8 / Fat 1.3 (Saturated Fat 0.1) / Carbohydrate 14.2
Fiber 2.6 / Cholesterol 0 / Sodium 53

Chicken-Chile Rolls

12 (4-ounce) skinned, boned chicken
  breast halves
6 canned whole green chiles, halved
  and seeded
4 ounces reduced-fat Monterey Jack
  cheese, cut into 12 strips
¾ cup fine, dry breadcrumbs
1½ tablespoons chili powder
2¼ teaspoons ground cumin
¼ teaspoon salt
¼ teaspoon garlic powder
⅓ cup skim milk
Vegetable cooking spray
6 cups shredded iceberg lettuce
¾ cup commercial no-salt-added
  picante sauce
⅓ cup nonfat sour cream

Place chicken between 2 sheets of heavy-duty plastic wrap, and flatten to ¼-inch thickness, using a meat mallet or rolling pin.

Place a green chile half and 1 cheese strip in center of each breast half. Roll up lengthwise; tuck ends under. Secure with wooden picks.

Combine breadcrumbs and next 4 ingredients. Dip rolls in milk; dredge in breadcrumb mixture.

Place chicken in a 13- x 9- x 2-inch baking dish coated with cooking spray. Bake, uncovered, at 400° for 30 minutes or until tender. Place ½ cup lettuce on each serving plate. Slice rolls, if desired; place on lettuce. Serve with picante sauce and sour cream. Yield: 12 servings (205 calories and 17% fat per serving).

Protein 31.5 / Fat 3.9 (Saturated Fat 1.6) / Carbohydrate 9.4
Fiber 1.2 / Cholesterol 72 / Sodium 386

Southwestern Hominy

Vegetable cooking spray
4 cups peeled, seeded, and chopped tomato
2 cups chopped onion
2 (15½-ounce) cans golden hominy,
  drained
1 teaspoon chili powder
¼ teaspoon garlic powder
¼ teaspoon salt
¼ teaspoon pepper
½ cup (2 ounces) shredded reduced-fat
  Monterey Jack cheese

Coat a nonstick skillet with cooking spray; place over medium-high heat until hot. Add tomato and onion; sauté until onion is tender. Stir in hominy and next 4 ingredients.

Spoon into a 2-quart baking dish coated with cooking spray. Bake, uncovered, at 350° for 25 minutes. Sprinkle with cheese; bake 5 minutes or until cheese melts. Yield: 12 servings (66 calories and 19% fat per ½-cup serving).

Protein 2.7 / Fat 1.4 (Saturated Fat 0.6) / Carbohydrate 11.2
Fiber 1.3 / Cholesterol 3 / Sodium 146

Cinnamon Crisps

3 tablespoons hot water
1½ teaspoons vanilla extract
¼ cup plus 1 tablespoon sugar
1 tablespoon ground cinnamon
12 (6-inch) flour tortillas
Vegetable cooking spray

Combine water and vanilla. Combine sugar and cinnamon. Lightly coat both sides of 3 tortillas with cooking spray. Lightly brush each

side with water mixture, and sprinkle each side with about ¾ teaspoon sugar mixture. Place on a wire rack in a 15- x 10- x 1-inch jellyroll pan. Bake at 400° for 8 minutes or until lightly browned. Repeat procedure with remaining tortillas, water mixture, and sugar mixture. Yield: 12 servings (136 calories and 18% fat per serving).

Protein 2.4 / Fat 2.7 (Saturated Fat 0.6) / Carbohydrate 27.7
Fiber 1.0 / Cholesterol 0 / Sodium 0

Welcome Easter with a menu of Apple-Glazed Leg of Lamb, Asparagus Vinaigrette, and Hot Cross Buns. (Menu begins on page 75.)

Ring in the new year with a scrumptious, low-fat feast starring Honey-Dijon Pork Tenderloin.

NEW YEAR'S DAY BUFFET

New Year's Day offers an occasion to reflect on the past year and plan for the future. Invite friends to join you for a buffet that's sure to get the new year off to a lucky start.

When ready to serve, slice Honey-Dijon Pork Tenderloin into medaillons, and arrange them in a spiral pattern on a festive platter. A sprig of fresh rosemary as a garnish hints at the source of the tenderloin's unique flavor.

For good luck, serve Spicy Black-Eyed Peas seasoned with tomatoes, herbs, spices, and a little liquid smoke to keep flavor high and the fat and sodium content low.

Cornmeal Crescent Rolls may be prepared ahead and refrigerated. All you have to do is bake them at the last minute. One roll and a 1-cup serving of spinach salad (minus the egg and bacon) with 1 tablespoon commercial oil-free dressing for each person are appropriate accompaniments. Delight your guests with an old-fashioned Cranberry and Pear Crisp that takes advantage of the fruits of the season.

Scarlet Sipper
Honey-Dijon Pork Tenderloin
Spicy Black-Eyed Peas
Spinach salad
Cornmeal Crescent Rolls
Cranberry and Pear Crisp
Serves 12
526 calories and 22% fat per serving

Scarlet Sipper

1 (48-ounce) bottle cranberry-apple juice
  cocktail
1⅔ cups unsweetened orange juice
¼ cup lemon juice
3 (11-ounce) bottles sparkling mineral
  water, chilled

Combine first 3 ingredients in a large pitcher; stir well. Chill thoroughly. Stir in mineral water just before serving. Yield: 12 cups (93 calories and 0% fat per 1-cup serving).

Protein 0.4 / Fat 0 (Saturated Fat 0) / Carbohydrate 23.5
Fiber 0.1 / Cholesterol 0 / Sodium 19

Honey-Dijon Pork Tenderloin

4 (¾-pound) pork tenderloins
½ teaspoon salt
¼ teaspoon pepper
Vegetable cooking spray
1 tablespoon olive oil
½ cup balsamic vinegar
1 tablespoon minced fresh rosemary
3 tablespoons honey
1 tablespoon Dijon mustard
Fresh rosemary sprigs (optional)

Trim fat from tenderloins; sprinkle tenderloins with salt and pepper. Coat a large nonstick skillet with cooking spray; add oil. Place over medium-high heat until hot. Add 2 tenderloins; cook 10 minutes or until browned, turning occasionally. Remove from skillet, and keep warm. Repeat procedure with remaining 2 tenderloins.

Place tenderloins on a rack in a roasting pan coated with cooking spray. Combine vinegar, rosemary, honey, and mustard in a small bowl, stirring well; brush over tenderloins. Insert a meat thermometer into thickest part of tenderloin, if desired.

Bake at 400° for 25 to 30 minutes or until meat thermometer registers 160°, basting frequently with vinegar mixture. Let stand 10 minutes; cut into thin slices. Transfer to a serving platter; garnish with fresh rosemary sprigs, if desired. Yield: 12 servings (160 calories and 28% fat per serving).

Protein 22.6 / Fat 5.0 (Saturated Fat 1.5) / Carbohydrate 5.1
Fiber 0 / Cholesterol 73 / Sodium 188

Spicy Black-Eyed Peas

3¾ cups frozen black-eyed peas
2½ cups water
Vegetable cooking spray
1¼ cups chopped onion
1¼ cups chopped green pepper
2 (14½-ounce) cans no-salt-added stewed
  tomatoes, undrained and chopped
2 tablespoons low-sodium soy sauce
2 teaspoons dry mustard
1 teaspoon chili powder
1 teaspoon pepper
2 teaspoons liquid smoke
¼ teaspoon ground red pepper
2 tablespoons minced fresh parsley

Combine black-eyed peas and water in a saucepan. Bring to a boil; cover, reduce heat, and simmer 20 minutes. Drain; set aside.

Coat a nonstick skillet with cooking spray; place over medium heat until hot. Add onion and green pepper; sauté until crisp-tender. Add peas, tomato, and next 6 ingredients. Bring to a boil; reduce heat, and simmer 20 minutes or until peas are tender, stirring occasionally. Transfer to a serving dish; sprinkle with parsley. Serve with a slotted spoon. Yield: 12 servings (99 calories and 5% fat per ¾-cup serving).

Protein 5.4 / Fat 0.6 (Saturated Fat 0.1) / Carbohydrate 18.8
Fiber 1.4 / Cholesterol 0 / Sodium 83

Cornmeal Crescent Rolls

1 package dry yeast
⅛ teaspoon sugar
½ cup warm water (105° to 115°)
1 cup whole wheat flour
⅓ cup yellow cornmeal
3 tablespoons instant nonfat dry milk
  powder
½ cup plain nonfat yogurt
¼ cup vegetable oil
2 tablespoons molasses
½ teaspoon salt
1¼ cups plus 3 tablespoons bread flour,
  divided
Vegetable cooking spray
1 egg white, lightly beaten
1 teaspoon water

Dissolve yeast and sugar in warm water in a large bowl; let stand 5 minutes. Add whole wheat flour and next 6 ingredients; beat at medium speed of an electric mixer until well blended. Stir in enough of the 1¼ cups bread flour to make a soft dough.

Sprinkle 1 tablespoon bread flour evenly over work surface. Turn dough out onto floured surface, and knead until smooth and elastic (8 to 10 minutes). Place dough in a large bowl coated with cooking spray, turning to coat top. Cover and let rise in a warm place (85°), free from drafts, 1 hour or until doubled in bulk.

Sprinkle 1 tablespoon bread flour evenly over work surface. Punch dough down, and divide in half. Roll one portion of dough to a 12-inch circle; lightly coat top of dough with cooking spray. Cut circle into 12 wedges. Roll up wedges, beginning at wide end; seal points. Place rolls, point side down, 2 inches apart on baking sheets coated with cooking spray. Curve rolls into crescents. Repeat rolling and shaping procedure with remaining 1 tablespoon flour and remaining dough. Cover with plastic wrap, and chill 2 to 24 hours.

Combine egg white and 1 teaspoon water in a small bowl, stirring well. Uncover dough, and brush egg white mixture evenly over tops of rolls. Bake at 375° for 10 to 12 minutes or until rolls are golden. Yield: 2 dozen (83 calories and 28% fat each).

Protein 2.6 / Fat 2.6 (Saturated Fat 0.5) / Carbohydrate 12.6
Fiber 0.8 / Cholesterol 0 / Sodium 61

Cranberry and Pear Crisp

⅓ cup sugar
1½ tablespoons cornstarch
1¼ teaspoons ground cinnamon
¾ teaspoon ground ginger
¾ cup unsweetened orange juice
2¼ cups fresh cranberries
3 medium-size ripe pears, peeled, cored and
  thinly sliced
1½ teaspoons grated orange rind
Vegetable cooking spray
¾ cup quick-cooking oats, uncooked
⅓ cup all-purpose flour
⅓ cup firmly packed brown sugar
¼ cup margarine

Combine first 4 ingredients in a large saucepan; stir well. Gradually add orange juice, stirring constantly. Add cranberries, pears, and orange rind. Bring to a boil, stirring constantly. Reduce heat, and simmer 10 minutes or until cranberries pop and mixture thickens, stirring constantly. Remove from heat; spoon mixture into an 11- x 7- x 2-inch baking dish coated with cooking spray.

Combine oats, flour, and brown sugar in a small bowl; cut in margarine with a pastry blender until mixture resembles coarse meal. Sprinkle oat mixture evenly over fruit mixture. Bake at 375° for 20 to 25 minutes or until pears are tender. To serve, spoon into individual dessert bowls. Yield: 12 servings (157 calories and 25% fat per ½-cup serving).

Protein 1.5 / Fat 4.4 (Saturated Fat 0.8) / Carbohydrate 29.4
Fiber 2.1 / Cholesterol 0 / Sodium 47

Serve Strawberries in Raspberry Sauce whenever you are short on time. It's a simple make-ahead dessert.

FAMILY EASTER DINNER

Celebrate Easter with this colorful menu that is full of the fresh flavors of spring. Apple-Glazed Leg of Lamb marinates in a mixture of apple juice, vinegar, honey, soy sauce, and rosemary and is served on a bed of fresh spinach leaves surrounded by julienne strips of carrots and turnips.

Asparagus Vinaigrette is the perfect springtime accompaniment because the delicate stalks of asparagus are at their peak flavor and tender best. It's a make-ahead side dish that works equally well as an appetizer or

Apple-Glazed Leg of Lamb
Wild rice
Asparagus Vinaigrette
Hot Cross Buns
Strawberries in Raspberry Sauce
Sparkling mineral water

Serves 16

541 calories and 21% fat per serving

salad. Serve each person ½ cup of wild rice cooked without salt or fat to add complex carbohydrates to the menu. And don't forget Hot Cross Buns, a traditional Easter bread. Menu calories reflect 1 bun per person.

Strawberries in Raspberry Sauce takes advantage of naturally sweet ruby-red strawberries and complements them with a sauce. Prepare the colorful dessert a few hours before the dinner for convenience. Sprinkle with toasted sliced almonds, and garnish with a fresh mint sprig.

Apple-Glazed Leg of Lamb

1 (6-pound) lean leg of lamb
1 (6-ounce) can frozen apple juice
  concentrate, thawed and undiluted
½ cup cider vinegar
¼ cup honey
1 tablespoon low-sodium soy sauce
¼ teaspoon minced fresh rosemary
Vegetable cooking spray
2 carrots, scraped and cut into julienne
  strips (about 2 cups)
2 turnips, peeled and cut into julienne
  strips (about 2 cups)
Fresh spinach leaves (optional)
Fresh rosemary sprigs (optional)

Trim fat from lamb. Place lamb in a large shallow dish. Combine apple juice concentrate and next 4 ingredients; pour over lamb. Cover and marinate in refrigerator at least 8 hours, turning occasionally.

Remove lamb from marinade, reserving marinade. Place marinade in a small saucepan. Bring to a boil; reduce heat, and simmer 5 minutes.

Place lamb on a rack in a roasting pan coated with cooking spray. Brush lamb with reserved marinade. Insert meat thermometer into thickest part of lamb, making sure it does not touch bone.

Bake lamb, uncovered, at 350° for 2 hours, basting lamb frequently with reserved marinade. Shield with aluminum foil, and bake an additional 30 minutes or until meat thermometer registers 140° (rare) to 160° (medium). Remove lamb from oven; let stand 15 minutes before serving.

Arrange carrot strips in a vegetable steamer over boiling water; cover and steam 1 minute. Add turnips; cover and steam 2 minutes or until vegetables are crisp-tender. Drain well.

Place lamb on a spinach-lined serving platter, if desired. Arrange carrots and turnips around lamb, and garnish with fresh rosemary sprigs, if desired. Yield: 16 servings (206 calories and 30% fat per serving).

Protein 24.4 / Fat 6.8 (Saturated Fat 2.4) / Carbohydrate 10.8
Fiber 0.5 / Cholesterol 76 / Sodium 95

Asparagus Vinaigrette

3¾ pounds fresh asparagus spears
½ cup rice vinegar
¼ cup water
¼ cup lemon juice
1 (4-ounce) jar diced pimiento, drained
2 tablespoons olive oil
1 teaspoon dry mustard
1 teaspoon grated lemon rind
½ teaspoon ground white pepper

Snap off tough ends of asparagus. Remove scales from stalks with a knife or vegetable peeler, if desired. Cook asparagus, covered, in a small amount of boiling water 6 to 8 minutes or until crisp-tender; drain.

Place asparagus in a 13- x 9- x 2-inch baking dish. Combine vinegar and remaining ingredients in a small bowl; stir with a wire whisk until well blended. Pour over asparagus. Cover and chill thoroughly. Transfer asparagus to a large serving platter, using a slotted spoon. Yield: 16 servings (34 calories and 50% fat per serving).

Protein 2.3 / Fat 1.9 (Saturated Fat 0.3) / Carbohydrate 3.3
Fiber 1.5 / Cholesterol 0 / Sodium 3

Hot Cross Buns

4¼ cups all-purpose flour, divided
1 teaspoon ground cinnamon
½ teaspoon salt
¼ teaspoon ground nutmeg
¼ teaspoon ground cloves
1 package dry yeast
2 tablespoons sugar
¼ cup warm water (105° to 115°)
¾ cup skim milk
3 tablespoons margarine
2 eggs, beaten
⅓ cup currants
1 tablespoon grated lemon rind
3 tablespoons all-purpose flour
Vegetable cooking spray
¾ cup sifted powdered sugar
1 tablespoon skim milk

Combine 2 cups all-purpose flour and next 4 ingredients in a medium bowl; stir well, and set mixture aside.

Dissolve yeast and 2 tablespoons sugar in warm water in a large bowl, and let stand 5 minutes. Combine ¾ cup milk and margarine in a small saucepan; cook over medium heat until margarine melts, stirring constantly. Let milk mixture cool to 105° to 115°.

Add milk mixture, flour mixture, and eggs to yeast mixture; beat at medium speed of an electric mixer until well blended. Stir in currants, lemon rind, and enough of remaining 2¼ cups flour to make a soft dough.

Sprinkle 3 tablespoons flour evenly over work surface. Turn dough out onto floured surface, and knead until smooth and elastic (about 8 to 10 minutes). Place in a bowl coated with cooking spray, turning to coat top. Cover and let rise in a warm place (85°), free from drafts, 1 hour or until doubled in bulk.

Punch dough down, and divide into 24 equal portions; shape each portion into a ball. Place 2 inches apart on baking sheets coated with cooking spray. Cover and let rise in a warm place, free from drafts, 45 minutes or until doubled in bulk.

Bake at 375° for 10 to 12 minutes or until lightly browned. Remove from baking sheets, and cool completely on wire racks.

Combine powdered sugar and 1 tablespoon milk, stirring well. Drizzle ½ teaspoon glaze in the shape of a cross over top of each bun. Yield: 2 dozen (124 calories and 16% fat each).

Protein 3.2 / Fat 2.2 (Saturated Fat 0.4) / Carbohydrate 22.8
Fiber 0.7 / Cholesterol 18 / Sodium 76

Strawberries in Raspberry Sauce

2 (10-ounce) packages frozen raspberries
    in light syrup, thawed
2 tablespoons plus 2 teaspoons cornstarch
2 tablespoons lemon juice
2 tablespoons Cointreau or other orange-
    flavored liqueur
2 quarts fresh strawberries, hulled
¼ cup sugar
⅓ cup sliced almonds, toasted
Fresh mint sprigs (optional)

Press raspberries through a sieve, and discard seeds. Combine strained raspberries and cornstarch in a small saucepan; stir until smooth. Bring to a boil, stirring constantly, and cook 1 minute or until thickened. Remove sauce from heat; stir in lemon juice and liqueur.

Combine strawberries and sugar in a large bowl, tossing gently to coat. Pour raspberry sauce over strawberries; toss gently. Cover and chill 3 to 4 hours.

Toss gently, and spoon evenly into individual dessert dishes. Sprinkle evenly with toasted almonds. Garnish with fresh mint sprigs, if desired. Yield: 16 servings (94 calories and 14% fat per ½-cup serving).

Protein 1.1 / Fat 1.5 (Saturated Fat 0.1) / Carbohydrate 19.6
Fiber 4.5 / Cholesterol 0 / Sodium 1

Fourth of July Celebration

The all-American cookout doesn't always have to mean hamburgers and hot dogs. Try this healthy menu to set the tone for your outdoor celebration. Tuna steaks and onion slices are marinated in a sweet-and-sour mixture for Grilled Tuna and Onions. Serve each guest 1 cup of sparkling apple juice, a commercial carbonated beverage, to sip while the tuna is grilling. Herbed Potato Salad and Garlic-Basil Squash are the perfect side dishes for this summer meal.

Watermelon Ice is a treat that will delight both adults and kids. Serve ½ cup to each guest, and freeze the remainder to serve later.

Sparkling apple juice
Grilled Tuna and Onions
Herbed Potato Salad
Garlic-Basil Squash
Watermelon Ice
Serves 4
472 calories and 14% fat per serving

Grilled Tuna and Onions

4 (4-ounce) tuna steaks
1 small onion, thinly sliced and separated
  into rings
½ cup white wine vinegar
1 tablespoon plus 1 teaspoon sugar
2 teaspoons dried mint flakes
½ teaspoon salt
¼ teaspoon pepper
Vegetable cooking spray

Place tuna and onion in a large shallow baking dish. Combine vinegar and next 4 ingredients; pour vinegar mixture over tuna and onion. Cover and marinate in refrigerator at least 2 hours, turning tuna occasionally.

Remove tuna from marinade, reserving ¼ cup marinade and onion. Place reserved onion on a large square of heavy-duty aluminum foil; pour reserved marinade over onion. Fold foil over onion; seal tightly.

Coat grill rack with cooking spray; place on grill over medium-hot coals. Place foil packet on rack; cook 15 to 20 minutes or until onion is tender, turning packet frequently. Place tuna on rack; cook 6 to 8 minutes on each side or until fish flakes easily when tested with a fork.

To serve, place tuna on individual serving plates; spoon onion mixture evenly over tuna. Yield: 4 servings (190 calories and 27% fat per serving).

Protein 26.7 / Fat 5.8 (Saturated Fat 1.4) / Carbohydrate 5.5
Fiber 0.3 / Cholesterol 43 / Sodium 341

Herbed Potato Salad

¾ pound small round red potatoes
¼ pound fresh asparagus spears
½ cup chopped celery
1 tablespoon chopped fresh chives
1 tablespoon chopped fresh dillweed
2 tablespoons fat-free mayonnaise
1 tablespoon skim milk
⅛ teaspoon salt

Place potatoes in a large saucepan; add water to cover. Bring to a boil; cover, reduce heat, and simmer 15 minutes or until potatoes are tender. Drain; cover and chill.

Snap off tough ends of asparagus. Remove scales from stalks with a knife or vegetable peeler, if desired. Cut asparagus into 1-inch pieces. Arrange asparagus in a vegetable steamer over boiling water. Cover and steam 4 to 5 minutes or until crisp-tender; drain well, and set aside.

Cut potatoes into ¼-inch-thick slices. Combine potato slices, asparagus, celery, chives, and dillweed in a medium bowl; toss gently. Combine mayonnaise, milk, and salt in a small bowl; stir well. Add to vegetable mixture, tossing to coat. Cover and chill thoroughly. Yield: 4 servings (85 calories and 2% fat per 1-cup serving).

Protein 3.0 / Fat 0.2 (Saturated Fat 0.1) / Carbohydrate 18.8
Fiber 2.2 / Cholesterol 0 / Sodium 191

Grilled Tuna and Onions, Herbed Potato Salad, and Garlic-Basil Squash skimp on calories but not flavor.

Garlic-Basil Squash

1 tablespoon minced fresh basil
1½ teaspoons water
½ teaspoon lemon juice
½ teaspoon olive oil
⅛ teaspoon salt
1 clove garlic, crushed
4 small yellow squash, cut in half (about 1 pound)
Vegetable cooking spray

Combine first 6 ingredients in a small bowl. Brush cut surfaces of squash with half of basil mixture. Set aside.

Coat grill rack with cooking spray; place on grill over medium-hot coals. Place yellow squash halves, cut sides down, on rack and cook 3 minutes.

Turn squash; brush with remaining basil mixture, and cook an additional 5 minutes or until tender. Yield: 4 servings (32 calories and 31% fat per serving).

Protein 1.4 / Fat 1.1 (Saturated Fat 0.1) / Carbohydrate 5.3
Fiber 1.9 / Cholesterol 0 / Sodium 76

Watermelon Ice

½ cup water
¼ cup sugar
8 cups seeded, chopped watermelon
2 tablespoons lemon juice

Combine water and sugar in a small saucepan. Bring to a boil; reduce heat, and cook until sugar dissolves, stirring constantly. Remove from heat, and let cool completely.

Position knife blade in food processor bowl. Add 4 cups watermelon, and process until smooth; transfer to a bowl. Repeat procedure with enough of the remaining 4 cups watermelon to make 5 cups puree.

Combine sugar mixture, pureed melon, and lemon juice. Pour into a 13- x 9- x 2-inch pan; freeze until firm. Spoon mixture into processor bowl; process until smooth. Return to pan; freeze until firm. To serve, scoop ice into individual dessert bowls; serve immediately. Yield: 7 cups (48 calories and 8% fat per ½-cup serving).

Protein 0.7 / Fat 0.4 (Saturated Fat 0.2) / Carbohydrate 11.2
Fiber 0.6 / Cholesterol 0 / Sodium 2

TRADITIONAL HOLIDAY DINNER

Treat the ones you love to a heart-healthy holiday feast that is appropriate for either a Thanksgiving or Christmas dinner. Homemade cornbread stuffing, chockfull of good things like fresh mushrooms, herbs, currants, and chopped pecans, is rolled inside a lean and boneless turkey breast for a traditional entrée with a different look in Turkey Breast with Cornbread Stuffing.

Streusel-Topped Sweet Potato Casserole, a ¼-cup serving of Holiday Cranberry Relish, and

---

Turkey Breast with Cornbread Stuffing
Streusel-Topped Sweet Potato Casserole
Steamed green beans
Holiday Cranberry Relish
Ambrosia
Maple Pumpkin Pie
Serves 12
705 calories and 16% fat per serving

---

a ½-cup serving of green beans per person are colorful and attractive additions to the menu. Best of all, these recipes are healthier versions of the usual holiday favorites.

No celebration is complete without dessert. Just because you are eating healthier doesn't mean missing out on this meal's sweet ending. Offer each guest a serving of Ambrosia, a delicately sweet fruit dessert. There is also a slice of Maple Pumpkin Pie to round out this festive occasion.

Turkey Breast with Cornbread Stuffing

Basic Cornbread
1 (3-pound) boneless turkey breast, skinned
Vegetable cooking spray
2 teaspoons vegetable oil
1½ cups finely chopped fresh mushrooms
¾ cup finely chopped onion
1 clove garlic, minced
Dash of dried whole thyme
¼ cup minced fresh parsley
3 tablespoons currants
2 tablespoons chopped pecans
½ teaspoon salt
¼ teaspoon pepper
½ cup unsweetened apple juice
2 tablespoons honey
⅛ teaspoon dried whole thyme
1 small clove garlic, crushed
Fresh thyme sprigs (optional)

Cut Basic Cornbread into large chunks. Position knife blade in food processor bowl; add cornbread. Pulse 4 times or until cornbread is coarsely crumbled; set aside.

Trim fat from turkey; remove tendons. Place turkey breast, boned side up, on heavy-duty plastic wrap. From center, slice horizontally through thickest part of each side of breast almost to outer edge; flip each cut piece over to enlarge breast. Place heavy-duty plastic wrap over turkey; flatten to ½-inch thickness, using a meat mallet or rolling pin.

Coat a large nonstick skillet with cooking spray; add oil. Place over medium-high heat until hot. Add mushrooms, onion, minced garlic, and dash of thyme; sauté 5 minutes or until vegetables are tender. Stir in crumbled cornbread, parsley and next 4 ingredients.

Spoon cornbread mixture in center of turkey breast, leaving a 2-inch border at sides; roll up, jellyroll fashion, starting with short side. Tie turkey breast securely at 2-inch intervals with string. Place seam side down on a rack in a roasting pan coated with cooking spray. Insert meat thermometer.

Combine apple juice, honey, ⅛ teaspoon thyme, and crushed garlic in a small bowl; brush over turkey. Shield turkey with aluminum foil. Bake at 325° for 1 hour, basting frequently with apple juice mixture. Uncover and bake an additional 30 minutes or until meat thermometer registers 170°.

Remove string, and let stand 10 minutes. Slice turkey into 12 slices, and place on individual serving plates. Garnish with fresh thyme sprigs, if desired. Yield: 12 servings (193 calories and 16% fat per serving).

Basic Cornbread

¼ cup yellow cornmeal
¼ cup all-purpose flour
1 teaspoon baking powder
½ teaspoon sugar
¼ cup skim milk
1 tablespoon frozen egg substitute, thawed
1½ teaspoons vegetable oil
Vegetable cooking spray

Combine first 4 ingredients in a medium bowl; make a well in center of mixture. Combine milk, egg substitute, and oil; add to cornmeal mixture, stirring just until dry ingredients are moistened.

Pour batter into a 7½- x 3- x 2-inch loafpan coated with cooking spray. Bake at 400° for 10 to 12 minutes or until lightly browned. Let cool in pan on a wire rack. Yield: 1 (7½-inch) loaf.

Protein 26.7 / Fat 3.5 (Saturated Fat 1.1) / Carbohydrate 12.8
Fiber 0.8 / Cholesterol 70 / Sodium 174

Streusel-Topped Sweet Potato Casserole

3 pounds sweet potatoes
½ cup plus 1 tablespoon unsweetened orange juice, divided
3 tablespoons brandy
1 teaspoon grated orange rind
1 teaspoon butter flavoring
¼ teaspoon ground ginger
¼ teaspoon salt
⅛ teaspoon pepper
3 egg whites
½ cup firmly packed brown sugar, divided
Vegetable cooking spray
⅓ cup chopped pecans, toasted
3 tablespoons all-purpose flour
1 teaspoon ground cinnamon
1¼ cups finely chopped Rome apple

Cook sweet potatoes in boiling water to cover 35 to 40 minutes or until tender; drain and let cool. Peel and mash potatoes. Add ½ cup orange juice and next 6 ingredients; stir well, and set aside.

Beat egg whites at high speed of an electric mixer until soft peaks form. Gradually add ¼ cup brown sugar, 1 tablespoon at a time, beating until stiff peaks form. Gently stir one-fourth of egg white mixture into sweet potato mixture. Gently fold remaining egg white mixture into sweet potato mixture. Spoon mixture into an 11- x 7- x 2-inch baking dish coated with cooking spray; set aside.

Combine remaining ¼ cup brown sugar, pecans, flour, and cinnamon; stir well. Combine apple and remaining 1 tablespoon orange juice; add to pecan mixture, stirring well. Sprinkle evenly over sweet potato mixture. Bake at 350° for 30 to 35 minutes or until puffed. Let stand 10 minutes before serving. Yield: 12 servings (184 calories and 13% fat per ¾-cup serving).

Protein 3.0 / Fat 2.6 (Saturated Fat 0.3) Carbohydrate 38.1
Fiber 3.7 / Cholesterol 0 / Sodium 78

Holiday Cranberry Relish

1 orange
2 cups fresh cranberries
1 cup diced Red Delicious apple
1 (8-ounce) can unsweetened crushed pineapple, drained
⅓ cup sugar
Fresh spinach leaves (optional)

Cut orange into 4 pieces; remove seeds. Position knife blade in food processor bowl. Add orange, and process until finely chopped. Transfer to a nonaluminum bowl; set aside.

Place cranberries in food processor bowl; process until coarsely ground. Add cranberries and next 3 ingredients to chopped orange; stir well. Cover and refrigerate at least 8 hours.

Place spinach leaves on individual serving plates, if desired. Spoon ¼ cup relish over spinach leaves on each plate. Yield: 3 cups (52 calories and 2% fat per ¼-cup serving).

Protein 0.3 / Fat 0.1 (Saturated Fat 0) / Carbohydrate 13.5
Fiber 1.4 / Cholesterol 0 / Sodium 0

Ambrosia

3 medium-size pink grapefruit, peeled and
   sectioned
3 large oranges, peeled and sectioned
1 medium-size Red Delicious apple, cored
   and sliced
½ cup unsweetened orange juice
¼ teaspoon coconut extract
Fresh mint sprigs (optional)

Combine first 5 ingredients in a medium bowl; stir gently. Cover and chill at least 1 hour. To serve, spoon fruit evenly into individual dessert bowls. Garnish with fresh mint sprigs, if desired. Yield: 12 servings (50 calories and 4% fat per ½-cup serving).

Protein 0.8 / Fat 0.2 (Saturated Fat 0) / Carbohydrate 12.6
Fiber 2.7 / Cholesterol 0 / Sodium 0

Maple Pumpkin Pie

2 cups sifted cake flour
2 tablespoons sugar
½ teaspoon ground cinnamon
¼ teaspoon ground nutmeg
½ cup cold margarine
¼ cup cold water
Vegetable cooking spray
3 cups cooked, mashed pumpkin
1½ cups evaporated skimmed milk
1 cup frozen egg substitute, thawed
½ cup sugar
½ cup maple syrup
1½ teaspoons ground cinnamon
½ teaspoon salt
½ teaspoon ground allspice
½ teaspoon ground cloves
1 (16-ounce) carton vanilla low-fat yogurt

Combine flour, 2 tablespoons sugar, ½ teaspoon cinnamon, and nutmeg; stir well. Cut in margarine with a pastry blender until mixture resembles coarse meal. Sprinkle cold water, 1 tablespoon at a time, evenly over surface; stir with a fork until dry ingredients are moistened. Divide dough in half, and shape each half into a ball.

Place 1 ball of dough between 2 sheets of heavy-duty plastic wrap, and gently press to a 4-inch circle. Chill 15 minutes. Roll dough to a 13-inch circle. Place in freezer 10 minutes or until plastic wrap can be removed easily.

Remove top sheet of plastic wrap. Invert and fit pastry into a 9-inch pieplate coated with cooking spray. Remove remaining sheet of plastic wrap. Trim excess dough, and set aside. Fold edges of pastry under and flute; seal to edge of pieplate. Repeat procedure with remaining ball of dough.

Shape excess dough into a ball; place between 2 sheets of heavy-duty plastic wrap. Roll dough to ⅛-inch thickness. Freeze 10 minutes or until plastic wrap can be removed easily. Remove top sheet of plastic wrap; cut 4 leaf shapes in pastry, making vein markings with the back of a knife. Cover and freeze 15 minutes.

Combine pumpkin and next 8 ingredients in a large bowl. Pour mixture evenly into pastry shells. Arrange 2 pastry leaves on top of each pie. Bake at 350° for 1 hour or until a knife inserted in center comes out clean. Cool completely on a wire rack.

Spoon yogurt onto several layers of heavy-duty paper towels; spread to ½-inch thickness. Cover with additional paper towels; let stand 5 minutes. Scrape yogurt into a bowl, using a rubber spatula; cover and chill thoroughly. Serve chilled yogurt with pie. Yield: 16 servings (211 calories and 27% fat per slice and 1 tablespoon yogurt).

Protein 6.1 / Fat 6.4 (Saturated Fat 0.8) / Carbohydrate 33.1
Fiber 0.5 / Cholesterol 2 / Sodium 211

Enjoy these lighter versions of traditional holiday favorites when you serve Turkey Breast with Cornbread Stuffing (page 80), green beans, Streusel-Topped Sweet Potato Casserole (page 81), and Holiday Cranberry Relish (page 81).

HEALTHY HEART Recipes

From upscale fare to down-home favorites, the following recipes are sure to find their way into your daily meals. Each recipe has been analyzed per serving for calories and the percent of calories from fat to help you meet the American Heart Association (AHA) goal of no more than 30 percent of total calories from fat for a healthy heart. Other nutrients included in the nutritional analysis are protein, fat and saturated fat, carbohydrate, fiber, cholesterol, and sodium.

As you will see, a few of the recipes exceed 30 percent of calories from fat per serving due to the nature of the recipe or ingredients used. Rest assured that fat has been trimmed as much as possible from these recipes. And keep in mind that the AHA guideline to keep the total fat consumption under 30 percent refers to the average of all food eaten. By combining a recipe that exceeds 30 percent fat with a low-fat recipe such as a vegetable or bread, you will keep the total fat intake under 30 percent.

You'll find a wide variety of recipes for breads, grains, legumes, pastas, and meatless main dishes. This is to encourage the use of nutritious grains and vegetables that are low in fat and cholesterol, boosting the amount of complex carbohydrate and fiber in the diet as recommended by the AHA.

The amount of calories, fat, saturated fat, and cholesterol in these recipes is significantly lower than the amounts found in traditional recipes because the amount or type of fat used has been modified. Small amounts of vegetable oil or reduced-calorie margarine that are high in monounsaturated fats are called for when added fat is necessary. Regular margarine is used occasionally when a desirable outcome of the recipe would be sacrificed by using a lower fat substitute.

Products high in fat such as mayonnaise, sour cream, Cheddar cheese, and cream cheese have been replaced with their fat-free or lower fat counterparts. And cooking techniques are used that help keep fat to a minimum.

Most recipes in this book use a small amount of salt for flavor; however, sodium is significantly lower in these recipes than in similar traditional recipes. Low-sodium versions of soy sauce, Worcestershire sauce, canned vegetables, and other products are used instead of their higher sodium counterparts. Herbs and spices frequently enhance flavor and decrease the need for salt. With these recipes you'll realize that heart-healthy eating can be delicious and satisfying.

Traditional Tex-Mex favorites take a break from fat and sodium with healthy alternatives such as Garbanzo Guacamole (page 88) and Mock Margaritas (page 94).

Appetizers & Beverages

Lemon-Marinated Mushrooms

60 small fresh mushrooms (about 1 pound)
½ cup fresh lemon juice
¼ cup water
2 tablespoons minced fresh parsley
2 tablespoons Dijon mustard
1 tablespoon low-sodium Worcestershire sauce
1 teaspoon dried whole oregano
1 teaspoon olive oil
¼ teaspoon garlic powder
⅛ teaspoon ground red pepper

Clean mushrooms with damp paper towels. Place in a 13- x 9- x 2-inch baking dish.

Combine lemon juice and remaining ingredients in a small bowl; stir well. Pour over mushrooms, stirring to coat. Cover and marinate in refrigerator at least 8 hours, stirring occasionally. Drain well before serving. Yield: 5 dozen appetizers (4 calories and 23% fat each).

Protein 0.2 / Fat 0.2 (Saturated Fat 0) / Carbohydrate 0.6
Fiber 0.1 / Cholesterol 0 / Sodium 9

Stuffed Cherry Tomatoes

24 small cherry tomatoes
½ cup fat-free mayonnaise
3 tablespoons light process cream cheese product, softened
1½ teaspoons minced fresh parsley
1½ teaspoons grated onion
1 teaspoon capers
½ teaspoon fines herbes
¼ teaspoon low-sodium Worcestershire sauce
Fresh parsley sprigs (optional)

Cut top off each cherry tomato. Scoop out and discard pulp, leaving shells intact. Invert tomato shells on paper towels to drain.

Combine mayonnaise and next 6 ingredients; stir well. Spoon 1½ teaspoons mixture into each tomato. Cover and chill thoroughly.

Garnish with fresh parsley sprigs, if desired. Yield: 2 dozen appetizers (10 calories and 27% fat each).

Protein 0.3 / Fat 0.3 (Saturated Fat 0.2) / Carbohydrate 1.6
Fiber 0.1 / Cholesterol 1 / Sodium 84

Grilled Quesadillas With Yogurt Salsa

½ cup (2 ounces) shredded reduced-fat Monterey Jack cheese
⅓ cup (1.3 ounces) shredded reduced-fat Colby cheese
4 (8-inch) flour tortillas
1½ tablespoons canned chopped green chiles
Vegetable cooking spray
Yogurt Salsa

Divide cheeses evenly among tortillas, arranging just off center of each. Top each evenly with green chiles.

Coat grill rack with cooking spray; place on grill over medium-hot coals. Place tortillas on rack, and cook 30 seconds or until bottoms of tortillas are golden. Fold each tortilla in half; cook 30 seconds or until cheese melts.

Cut each tortilla into 4 wedges; serve immediately with Yogurt Salsa. Yield: 16 appetizer servings (42 calories and 30% fat per wedge and 1½ teaspoons salsa).

Yogurt Salsa

¼ cup plain nonfat yogurt
2 tablespoons chopped tomato
1 tablespoon chopped onion
2 teaspoons minced fresh cilantro
½ teaspoon lemon juice

Combine all ingredients in a small bowl; stir well. Cover and chill salsa at least 2 hours. Yield: ½ cup.

Protein 2.0 / Fat 1.4 (Saturated Fat 0.6) / Carbohydrate 5.8
Fiber 0.3 / Cholesterol 3 / Sodium 44

Add south-of-the-border flavor to your next cookout with Grilled Quesadillas with Yogurt Salsa. The salsa is a flavorful nonfat accompaniment.

Cheese Tortellini with Basil Sauce

½ (9-ounce) package fresh cheese tortellini, uncooked
1 (8-ounce) can no-salt-added tomato sauce
1 clove garlic, crushed
½ teaspoon dried whole basil
¼ teaspoon dried whole oregano
1 tablespoon grated Parmesan cheese

Cook tortellini according to package directions; omit salt and fat. Drain; keep warm.

Combine tomato sauce, crushed garlic, basil, and oregano in a small saucepan; bring to a boil. Cover, reduce heat, and simmer 5 minutes; stir in Parmesan cheese.

Transfer sauce to a serving bowl. Serve tortellini with warm sauce. Yield: 14 appetizer servings (36 calories and 23% fat per 3 tortellini and 1 tablespoon sauce).

Protein 1.8 / Fat 0.9 (Saturated Fat 0.3) / Carbohydrate 7.2
Fiber 0 / Cholesterol 6 / Sodium 45

Parmesan Chicken Strips

8 (4-ounce) skinned, boned chicken breast halves
¼ cup skim milk
¼ cup frozen egg substitute, thawed
⅔ cup fine, dry breadcrumbs
⅔ cup grated Parmesan cheese
1¼ teaspoons dried whole basil
¾ teaspoon dried whole thyme
¼ teaspoon onion powder
¼ teaspoon freshly ground pepper
Vegetable cooking spray

Cut chicken into 4- x 1-inch strips. Combine milk and egg substitute in a small bowl; stir well. Combine breadcrumbs and next 5 ingredients; stir well. Dip chicken strips in milk mixture; dredge in breadcrumb mixture.

Place chicken strips on baking sheets coated with cooking spray. Bake at 400° for 18 minutes or until lightly browned. Yield: 3½ dozen appetizers (36 calories and 18% fat each).

Protein 5.6 / Fat 0.7 (Saturated Fat 0.3) / Carbohydrate 1.4
Fiber 0.1 / Cholesterol 13 / Sodium 52

Meatballs with Piquant Cranberry Dip

Vegetable cooking spray
¼ cup minced onion
1 pound freshly ground raw turkey
⅓ cup fine, dry breadcrumbs
¼ cup minced fresh parsley
¼ teaspoon salt
⅛ teaspoon ground nutmeg
¼ cup skim milk
1 egg white, lightly beaten
Piquant Cranberry Dip

Coat a small nonstick skillet with cooking spray; place over medium-high heat until hot. Add onion; sauté 4 to 5 minutes or until tender.

Combine onion, turkey, and next 6 ingredients in a medium bowl; stir well. Shape mixture into 36 (1-inch) meatballs; place on a rack in a roasting pan coated with cooking spray. Bake at 375° for 20 to 24 minutes or until done. Drain and pat dry with paper towels.

Transfer meatballs to a serving dish, and serve warm with Piquant Cranberry Dip. Yield: 1½ dozen appetizer servings (48 calories and 15% fat per 2 meatballs and 2 teaspoons dip).

Piquant Cranberry Dip

½ cup fresh cranberries, finely chopped
½ cup low-sugar grape spread
1 to 2 teaspoons dry mustard
⅛ teaspoon ground red pepper

Combine chopped cranberries, grape spread, dry mustard, and ground red pepper in a small saucepan, stirring well. Cook over medium heat until thoroughly heated, stirring occasionally. Serve warm. Yield: ¾ cup.

Protein 4.8 / Fat 0.8 (Saturated Fat 0.2) / Carbohydrate 5.4
Fiber 0.2 / Cholesterol 12 / Sodium 72

Ham-Stuffed Potatoes

21 small round red potatoes (about 1½
   pounds)
1 cup diced cooked lean low-salt ham
⅓ cup plus 1 tablespoon lite ricotta cheese
¼ cup light process cream cheese product
1 tablespoon minced onion
1 tablespoon Dijon mustard
Fresh parsley sprigs (optional)

Arrange potatoes in a vegetable steamer over boiling water. Cover and steam 15 to 20 minutes or until potatoes are tender. Remove potatoes from steamer, and let cool. Scoop out centers of potatoes with a melon ball scoop; reserve pulp for other uses.

Combine ham and next 4 ingredients; stir well. Fill center of each potato with 2 teaspoons ham mixture. Garnish with fresh parsley sprigs, if desired. Yield: 21 appetizers (37 calories and 29% fat each).

Protein 2.8 / Fat 1.2 (Saturated Fat 0.5) / Carbohydrate 3.9
Fiber 0.4 / Cholesterol 6 / Sodium 96

Few guests will be able to resist Ham-Stuffed Potatoes, a flavorful appetizer that will have everyone reaching for seconds.

Pickled Shrimp and Onions

1½ quarts water
36 medium-size fresh unpeeled shrimp
  (about 1½ pounds)
1 medium onion, thinly sliced and separated
  into rings
1⅓ cups water
1⅓ cups white wine vinegar
1 tablespoon sugar
1 tablespoon minced fresh parsley
2 teaspoons coriander seeds
½ teaspoon crushed red pepper
3 bay leaves

Bring 1½ quarts water to a boil in a Dutch oven; add shrimp, and cook 3 to 5 minutes.

Drain well; rinse with cold water. Chill. Peel and devein shrimp. Combine shrimp and onion in a 1½-quart casserole; toss gently.

Combine 1⅓ cups water and remaining ingredients in a medium saucepan; bring to a boil. Cover, reduce heat, and simmer 10 minutes. Pour over shrimp mixture; toss gently. Cover and marinate in refrigerator 24 hours, stirring occasionally.

Remove and discard bay leaves. To serve, spoon onto a serving platter, using a slotted spoon. Yield: 1½ dozen appetizer servings (30 calories and 6% fat per 2 shrimp and 4 onion rings).

Protein 4.0 / Fat 0.2 (Saturated Fat 0) / Carbohydrate 2.2
Fiber 0.4 / Cholesterol 36 / Sodium 44

Turkey and Melon Roll-Ups

1 tablespoon coarse-grained mustard
½ teaspoon honey
Dash of ground white pepper
3 (1-ounce) slices deli-style turkey breast
6 (4- x 1-inch) slices peeled, seeded
  cantaloupe

Combine mustard, honey, and pepper; stir well. Spread 1 teaspoon mustard mixture on

each turkey slice. Cut turkey slices in half lengthwise. Wrap 1 turkey slice spirally around each cantaloupe slice. Repeat procedure with remaining mustard mixture, turkey, and cantaloupe. Yield: 6 appetizers (41 calories and 13% fat each).

Protein 3.4 / Fat 0.6 (Saturated Fat 0.1) / Carbohydrate 5.5
Fiber 0.7 / Cholesterol 0 / Sodium 155

Mock Margaritas

1 (6-ounce) can frozen lemonade
  concentrate, thawed and undiluted
1 (6-ounce) can frozen limeade
  concentrate, thawed and undiluted
½ cup sifted powdered sugar
3¼ cups crushed ice
1½ cups club soda, chilled
Lime slices (optional)

Combine lemonade and limeade concentrates, powdered sugar, and crushed ice in a

large plastic container, and stir mixture well. Freeze mixture. Remove mixture from freezer 30 minutes before serving.

Spoon mixture into container of an electric blender; add club soda. Top with cover, and process until smooth. Pour into glasses; garnish with lime, if desired. Yield: 6 cups (143 calories and 1% fat per 1-cup serving).

Protein 0.1 / Fat 0.1 (Saturated Fat 0) / Carbohydrate 37.3
Fiber 0.1 / Cholesterol 0 / Sodium 13

Serve refreshing Tutti-Frutti Punch anytime you want a thirst-quenching treat that's low in fat and calories.

Tutti-Frutti Punch

1 (16-ounce) package frozen unsweetened
   strawberries, thawed
1 (6-ounce) can frozen pineapple juice
   concentrate, thawed and undiluted
½ (6-ounce) can frozen apple juice
   concentrate, thawed and undiluted
½ (6-ounce) can frozen orange juice
   concentrate, thawed and undiluted
1½ cups water
1 (33.8-ounce) bottle salt-free seltzer
   water, chilled

Combine first 4 ingredients in container of
an electric blender; top with cover, and process
until smooth. Combine strawberry mixture and
1½ cups water in a large pitcher; cover and chill
at least 3 hours.

To serve, add chilled seltzer water to juice
mixture, and stir gently. Serve punch
immediately. Yield: 2½ quarts (37 calories and
2% fat per ½-cup serving).

Protein 0.3 / Fat 0.1 (Saturated Fat 0) / Carbohydrate 9.2
Fiber 0.2 / Cholesterol 0 / Sodium 12

Fruit Juice Spritzer

1 (6-ounce) can frozen orange juice
concentrate, thawed and undiluted
1 (6-ounce) can frozen apple juice
concentrate, thawed and undiluted
4½ cups club soda, chilled
Orange slices (optional)

Combine first 3 ingredients in a pitcher; stir well. Serve over ice. Garnish with orange slices, if desired. Yield: 6 cups (92 calories and 2% fat per 1-cup serving).

Protein 0.8 / Fat 0.2 (Saturated Fat 0) / Carbohydrate 22.4
Fiber 0.2 / Cholesterol 0 / Sodium 44

Chocolate-Banana Shake

½ cup sliced ripe banana
(about 1 small)
½ cup ice water
¼ cup instant nonfat dry milk powder
1 tablespoon sugar
1 tablespoon chocolate-flavored
syrup
½ teaspoon vanilla extract
Ice cubes

Combine first 6 ingredients in container of an electric blender; top with cover, and process chocolate mixture 30 seconds or until well blended. With blender running, add enough ice cubes, one at a time, to make 2 cups chocolate mixture; process until smooth. Yield: 2 cups (152 calories and 3% fat per 1-cup serving).

Protein 6.2 / Fat 0.5 (Saturated Fat 0.2) / Carbohydrate 31.5
Fiber 1.5 / Cholesterol 3 / Sodium 87

Mulled Cranberry Juice

4½ cups cranberry juice cocktail
4 dried apricot halves
2 tablespoons cranberries
2 tablespoons raisins
4 whole cloves
1 (3-inch) stick cinnamon
⅛ teaspoon ground nutmeg
4 (3-inch) sticks cinnamon (optional)

Place cranberry juice in a large non-aluminum saucepan. Add apricot halves and next 5 ingredients; bring juice mixture to a boil, stirring frequently. Cover, reduce heat, and simmer 10 minutes, stirring occasionally. Strain juice mixture, and discard fruits, cloves, and cinnamon stick.

Pour mixture into individual mugs, and garnish each serving with a cinnamon stick, if desired. Serve warm. Yield: 4 cups (169 calories and 1% fat per 1-cup serving).

Protein 0.1 / Fat 0.2 (Saturated Fat 0) / Carbohydrate 43.3
Fiber 0 / Cholesterol 0 / Sodium 12

These yeast breads offer a variety of flavor options: (clockwise from top) Onion and Poppy Seed Breadsticks (page 106), Cinnamon-Oatmeal Rolls (page 106), Peppered Parmesan Twist (page 110), and Honey-Wheat Crescents (page 104).

Sprinkle powdered sugar over crisp Belgian Waffles to add a touch of sweetness to this healthy breakfast treat.

Raisin-Applesauce Bran Muffins

1½ cups shreds of wheat
  bran cereal
¾ cup unsweetened applesauce
½ cup nonfat buttermilk
¼ cup firmly packed brown sugar
¼ cup frozen egg substitute, thawed
2 tablespoons vegetable oil
1¼ cups all-purpose flour
2 teaspoons baking powder
¼ teaspoon salt
½ teaspoon ground cinnamon
¾ cup raisins
Vegetable cooking spray

Combine first 3 ingredients; let stand 5 minutes. Add brown sugar, egg substitute, and oil; stir well.

Combine flour, baking powder, salt, and cinnamon; make a well in center of mixture. Add cereal mixture, stirring just until dry ingredients are moistened. Fold in raisins.

Spoon batter into muffin pans coated with cooking spray, filling three-fourths full. Bake at 400° for 20 minutes or until lightly browned. Yield: 1 dozen (150 calories and 19% fat each).

Protein 3.9 / Fat 3.1 (Saturated Fat 0.7) / Carbohydrate 31.5
Fiber 4.8 / Cholesterol 0 / Sodium 217

Buttermilk-Buckwheat Pancakes

½ cup buckwheat flour
¼ cup all-purpose flour
2 teaspoons baking powder
1 tablespoon sugar
½ cup nonfat buttermilk
¼ cup frozen egg substitute, thawed
¼ cup water
2 teaspoons reduced-calorie margarine, melted
Vegetable cooking spray

Combine first 4 ingredients in a medium bowl; make a well in center of mixture.

Combine buttermilk, egg substitute, water, and margarine in a small bowl, stirring well; add to flour mixture, stirring just until dry ingredients are moistened.

For each pancake, spoon 2 tablespoons batter onto a hot griddle coated with cooking spray, spreading batter to a 4-inch circle. Turn pancakes when tops are covered with bubbles and edges look cooked. Yield: 12 (4-inch) pancakes (46 calories and 15% fat each).

Protein 1.9 / Fat 0.8 (Saturated Fat 0.1) / Carbohydrate 8.1
Fiber 0.1 / Cholesterol 0 / Sodium 75

Belgian Waffles

2 cups all-purpose flour
1 tablespoon plus 1 teaspoon baking powder
¼ teaspoon salt
1 tablespoon sugar
1½ cups skim milk
½ cup frozen egg substitute, thawed
¼ cup reduced-calorie margarine, melted
½ teaspoon vanilla extract
Vegetable cooking spray
2 tablespoons powdered sugar
Sliced strawberries (optional)
Fresh mint sprigs (optional)

Combine first 4 ingredients in a medium bowl, and stir well. Combine milk, egg substitute, margarine, and vanilla in a medium bowl, stirring well; add to flour mixture. Beat at medium speed of an electric mixer until blended.

Coat a Belgian waffle iron with vegetable cooking spray; allow waffle iron to preheat. For each waffle, spoon ¼ cup batter onto hot waffle iron, spreading batter to edges. Bake 4 to 5 minutes or until steaming stops.

Sprinkle powdered sugar evenly over waffles. If desired, garnish waffles with sliced strawberries and fresh mint sprigs. Yield: 12 (4-inch) waffles (118 calories and 22% fat each).

Protein 4.0 / Fat 2.9 (Saturated Fat 0.4) / Carbohydrate 18.9
Fiber 0.5 / Cholesterol 1 / Sodium 217

Buttermilk Corn Muffins and Mexican Corn Sticks are delicious evidence that you don't have to pass up old-fashioned cornbread when you're eating healthy.

Buttermilk Corn Muffins

1 cup yellow cornmeal
1 cup all-purpose flour
2 teaspoons baking powder
¼ teaspoon baking soda
¼ teaspoon salt
1½ cups nonfat buttermilk
¼ cup frozen egg substitute, thawed
1 tablespoon vegetable oil
Vegetable cooking spray

Combine first 5 ingredients in a large bowl; make a well in center of mixture. Combine buttermilk, egg substitute, and vegetable oil in a small bowl, stirring well; add to cornmeal mixture, stirring just until dry ingredients are moistened.

Spoon batter evenly into muffin pans coated with cooking spray, filling three-fourths full. Bake at 425° for 20 minutes or until golden. Remove corn muffins from pans immediately. Let cool on wire racks. Yield: 1 dozen (103 calories and 16% fat each).

Protein 4.3 / Fat 1.8 (Saturated Fat 0.3) / Carbohydrate 17.9
Fiber 0.9 / Cholesterol 0 / Sodium 154

Mexican Corn Sticks

¾ cup yellow cornmeal
¾ cup all-purpose flour
¾ teaspoon baking powder
½ teaspoon baking soda
¼ teaspoon salt
1 teaspoon ground cumin
½ teaspoon chili powder
1 (8¾-ounce) can no-salt-added whole
  kernel corn, drained
½ cup nonfat buttermilk
¼ cup frozen egg substitute, thawed
¼ cup canned chopped green chiles, drained
2 tablespoons margarine, melted
Vegetable cooking spray

Combine first 7 ingredients in a large bowl; make a well in center of mixture. Combine corn, buttermilk, egg substitute, chiles, and margarine; add to cornmeal mixture, stirring just until dry ingredients are moistened.

Heavily coat a cast-iron corn stick pan with cooking spray; place in a 425° oven for 5 minutes. Spoon batter into hot pan, filling two-thirds full. Bake at 425° for 12 minutes or until golden. Remove corn sticks from pan immediately. Yield: 15 corn sticks (80 calories and 24% fat each).

Protein 2.2 / Fat 2.1 (Saturated Fat 0.1) / Carbohydrate 12.8
Fiber 0.7 / Cholesterol 0 / Sodium 194

Apple-Yogurt Bread

1 cup whole wheat flour
¾ cup all-purpose flour
1½ teaspoons baking powder
1 teaspoon baking soda
¼ teaspoon salt
⅓ cup firmly packed brown sugar
½ teaspoon ground cinnamon
1 (8-ounce) carton Dutch apple low-fat
  yogurt with fruit on the bottom
½ cup frozen egg substitute, thawed
¼ cup vegetable oil
2 tablespoons skim milk
Vegetable cooking spray

Combine first 7 ingredients in a large bowl; stir well. Combine yogurt, egg substitute, oil, and milk; add to flour mixture, stirring just until dry ingredients are moistened.

Spoon batter into an 8½- x 4½- x 3-inch loafpan coated with cooking spray. Bake at 350° for 40 minutes or until a wooden pick inserted in center comes out clean. Cool in pan 10 minutes; remove from pan, and let cool completely on a wire rack. Yield: 16 servings (112 calories and 30% fat per ½-inch slice).

Protein 3.0 / Fat 3.8 (Saturated Fat 0.8) / Carbohydrate 17.0
Fiber 1.1 / Cholesterol 1 / Sodium 138

Facts About Fiber

The National Cancer Institute recommends 25 to 35 grams of dietary fiber daily. To get this much fiber in your diet each day, eat at least 6 servings of whole grains and/or legumes and 5 servings of fruits and vegetables. The following foods are good sources of dietary fiber and contain less than 100 calories per serving:

1 to 4 grams dietary fiber
1 slice whole wheat bread
1 slice cracked wheat bread
1 slice seven-grain bread
1 cup fresh cauliflower flowerets
½ cup seedless grapes
1 cup raw spinach

5 to 10 grams dietary fiber
½ cup 100% bran cereal
¾ cup 40% bran flakes cereal
1 cup cooked broccoli
3 medium carrots
1 medium apple, unpeeled
1 medium pear, unpeeled

Whole Wheat Yeast Biscuits

1 package dry yeast
⅓ cup warm water (105° to 115°)
2½ cups whole wheat flour
½ cup all-purpose flour
2 teaspoons baking powder
½ teaspoon baking soda
½ teaspoon salt
1 tablespoon sugar
½ teaspoon dried whole oregano
½ teaspoon dried whole basil
3 tablespoons margarine
1 cup nonfat buttermilk
2 tablespoons all-purpose flour
Vegetable cooking spray

Dissolve yeast in warm water in a small bowl; let stand 5 minutes.

Combine whole wheat flour and next 7 ingredients in a large bowl; cut in margarine with a pastry blender until flour mixture resembles coarse meal. Add yeast mixture and buttermilk to flour mixture, stirring just until dry ingredients are moistened.

Sprinkle 2 tablespoons flour evenly over work surface. Turn dough out onto floured surface, and knead 3 or 4 times. Roll dough to ½-inch thickness; cut with a 2-inch biscuit cutter. Place rounds on baking sheets coated with vegetable cooking spray. Bake at 400° for 10 to 12 minutes or until biscuits are lightly browned. Yield: 2 dozen (73 calories and 22% fat each).

Protein 2.5 / Fat 1.8 (Saturated Fat 0.3) / Carbohydrate 12.6
Fiber 1.8 / Cholesterol 0 / Sodium 119

Honey-Wheat Crescents

1 package dry yeast
½ cup warm water (105° to 115°)
2 tablespoons honey, divided
½ cup skim milk
3 tablespoons margarine
½ teaspoon salt
¼ cup frozen egg substitute, thawed
2 cups whole wheat flour
1¼ cups all-purpose flour
2 tablespoons all-purpose flour, divided
Vegetable cooking spray

Dissolve yeast in warm water in a large bowl. Stir in 1 teaspoon honey; let stand 5 minutes.

Combine remaining 1 tablespoon plus 2 teaspoons honey, milk, margarine, and salt in a small saucepan. Cook over medium heat, stirring occasionally, until margarine melts. Cool to 105° to 115°.

Add milk mixture, egg substitute, and whole wheat flour to yeast mixture; beat at medium speed of an electric mixer until well blended.

Gradually stir in enough of the 1¼ cups all-purpose flour to make a soft dough.

Place dough in a large bowl coated with cooking spray, turning to coat top. Cover and let rise in a warm place (85°), free from drafts, 1 hour or until doubled in bulk.

Sprinkle 1 tablespoon all-purpose flour evenly over work surface. Punch dough down; cover and let rest 10 minutes. Divide dough in half. Turn 1 portion out onto floured surface, and roll to a 12-inch circle; cut into 12 wedges. Roll up wedges, beginning at wide end; seal points. Place rolls, point side down, on a baking sheet coated with cooking spray; curve into crescents. Repeat procedure with remaining 1 tablespoon flour and dough.

Cover and let rise in a warm place, free from drafts, 45 minutes or until doubled in bulk. Bake at 400° for 10 minutes or until lightly browned. Yield: 2 dozen (81 calories and 20% fat each).

Protein 2.6 / Fat 1.8 (Saturated Fat 0.3) / Carbohydrate 14.2
Fiber 1.5 / Cholesterol 0 / Sodium 73

Dried herbs, garlic powder, and Parmesan cheese give Herbed Dinner Rolls an authentic Italian flavor.

Herbed Dinner Rolls

2 packages dry yeast
½ cup warm water (105° to 115°)
1 cup skim milk
2 tablespoons margarine
1 tablespoon sugar
1 teaspoon dried Italian seasoning
½ teaspoon salt
¼ teaspoon garlic powder
¼ cup frozen egg substitute, thawed
2 cups whole wheat flour
¼ cup grated Parmesan cheese
2½ cups all-purpose flour
2 tablespoons all-purpose flour, divided
Vegetable cooking spray

Dissolve yeast in warm water in a large bowl; let stand 5 minutes.

Combine milk and next 5 ingredients in a small saucepan. Cook over medium heat, stirring occasionally, until margarine melts. Let cool to 105° to 115°.

Add milk mixture, egg substitute, and whole wheat flour to yeast mixture. Beat at low speed of an electric mixer just until blended; beat at high speed for an additional 3 minutes.

Gradually stir in grated Parmesan cheese and enough of the 2½ cups all-purpose flour to make a stiff dough.

Sprinkle 1 tablespoon all-purpose flour evenly over work surface. Turn dough out onto floured surface, and knead until dough is smooth and elastic (about 5 to 7 minutes). Place dough in a large bowl coated with cooking spray, turning to coat top. Cover and let rise in a warm place (85°), free from drafts, 45 minutes or until dough is doubled in bulk.

Sprinkle remaining 1 tablespoon all-purpose flour evenly over work surface. Punch dough down; turn out onto floured surface. Cover and let rest 10 minutes.

Divide dough into 30 equal portions; shape each portion into a ball. Place 15 balls in each of two 9-inch round cakepans coated with cooking spray. Cover and let rise in a warm place, free from drafts, 35 minutes or until doubled in bulk. Bake at 375° for 25 minutes or until golden. Remove from pans; serve warm. Yield: 2½ dozen (81 calories and 14% fat each).

Protein 3.1 / Fat 1.3 (Saturated Fat 0.3) / Carbohydrate 14.6
Fiber 1.4 / Cholesterol 1 / Sodium 69

Cinnamon-Oatmeal Rolls

1¾ cups all-purpose flour, divided
½ cup regular oats, uncooked
1 package dry yeast
1 tablespoon sugar
¼ teaspoon salt
¼ cup water
¼ cup skim milk
2 tablespoons margarine
¼ cup frozen egg substitute, thawed
3 tablespoons all-purpose flour, divided
Vegetable cooking spray
¼ cup firmly packed brown sugar
1 teaspoon ground cinnamon
1 tablespoon margarine, melted
¾ cup sifted powdered sugar
2¼ teaspoons skim milk

Combine ½ cup flour and next 4 ingredients in a large bowl; stir well.

Combine water, ¼ cup milk, and 2 tablespoons margarine in a small saucepan. Cook over medium heat, stirring occasionally, until margarine melts. Let cool to 120° to 130°.

Add milk mixture to flour mixture. Beat at low speed of an electric mixer just until blended; beat at high speed 2 minutes. Gradually add ½ cup flour and egg substitute, beating 2 minutes at medium speed. Stir in enough of the remaining ¾ cup flour to make a soft dough.

Sprinkle 2 tablespoons flour over work surface. Turn dough out onto floured surface; knead until smooth and elastic (about 8 to 10 minutes). Place dough in a large bowl coated with cooking spray, turning to coat top. Cover and let rise in a warm place (85°), free from drafts, 1 hour or until doubled in bulk.

Sprinkle remaining 1 tablespoon flour over work surface. Punch dough down, and turn out onto floured surface. Cover and let rest 10 minutes.

Combine brown sugar and cinnamon in a small bowl; set aside.

Roll dough to a 12- x 9-inch rectangle. Brush with melted margarine; sprinkle with brown sugar mixture. Roll up, jellyroll fashion, starting with long side; pinch seam to seal (do not seal ends). Cut roll into 1-inch slices. Place slices, cut side down, in a 9-inch square baking pan coated with cooking spray. Cover and let rise in a warm place, free from drafts, 45 minutes or until doubled in bulk.

Bake at 400° for 15 minutes or until golden. Cool in pan 5 minutes; remove from pan. Combine powdered sugar and 2¼ teaspoons milk; drizzle over warm rolls. Serve warm. Yield: 1 dozen (166 calories and 18% fat each).

Protein 3.5 / Fat 3.4 (Saturated Fat 0.6) / Carbohydrate 30.6
Fiber 1.1 / Cholesterol 0 / Sodium 95

Onion and Poppy Seed Breadsticks

1 (16-ounce) package hot roll mix
2 tablespoons instant minced onion, toasted
2 tablespoons grated Parmesan cheese
1 cup warm water (105° to 115°)
¼ cup frozen egg substitute, thawed
2 tablespoons all-purpose flour
Vegetable cooking spray
1 egg white, lightly beaten
1 tablespoon water
2 teaspoons poppy seeds

Combine hot roll mix, yeast from foil packet, onion, and cheese. Add warm water and egg substitute; stir until dry ingredients are moistened. Shape dough into a ball.

Sprinkle 2 tablespoons flour over work surface. Turn dough out onto floured surface; knead until smooth and elastic (about 5 minutes). Cover and let rest 5 minutes.

Divide dough into 32 equal portions; shape each portion into a 10-inch rope. (Keep unrolled dough covered.) Place ropes 1 inch apart on baking sheets coated with cooking spray. Cover and let rise in a warm place (85°), free from drafts, 15 minutes.

Combine egg white and 1 tablespoon water in a small bowl, stirring well. Brush breadsticks with egg white mixture, and sprinkle with poppy seeds. Bake at 375° for 14 minutes or until golden. Remove from baking sheets; let cool on wire racks. Yield: 32 breadsticks (57 calories and 3% fat each).

Protein 3.6 / Fat 0.2 (Saturated Fat 0.1) / Carbohydrate 11.2
Fiber 0.1 / Cholesterol 0 / Sodium 111

Sesame Seed Bagels

1 package dry yeast
2 tablespoons sugar, divided
1½ cups warm water (105° to 115°)
4½ cups all-purpose flour, divided
1 teaspoon salt
2 tablespoons all-purpose flour, divided
Vegetable cooking spray
1 gallon water
1 egg white, lightly beaten
1 tablespoon water
3 tablespoons sesame seeds

Dissolve yeast and 1 tablespoon sugar in warm water in a large bowl; let stand 5 minutes. Add 2½ cups flour and salt; beat at medium speed of an electric mixer until well blended. Gradually stir in enough of the remaining 2 cups flour to make a soft dough.

Sprinkle 1 tablespoon flour over work surface. Turn dough out onto floured surface; knead until smooth and elastic (about 8 to 10 minutes). Place in a bowl coated with cooking spray, turning to coat top. Cover and let rise in a warm place (85°), free from drafts, 15 minutes.

Sprinkle remaining 1 tablespoon flour over work surface. Punch dough down; turn dough out onto floured surface, and knead lightly 4 or 5 times.

Divide dough into 18 equal portions; shape each portion into a ball. Punch a hole in the center of each ball with a floured finger. Gently pull dough away from center to make a 1- to 1½-inch hole. Return bagels to floured surface; cover and let rest 20 minutes.

Bring 1 gallon water and remaining 1 tablespoon sugar to a boil in a large Dutch oven. Reduce heat to medium, and drop bagels, 6 at a time, into gently boiling water. Simmer, uncovered, 2½ minutes on each side. Drain bagels on paper towels.

Place bagels on ungreased baking sheets. Bake at 375° for 10 minutes; remove from oven. Combine egg white and 1 tablespoon water, stirring well. Brush bagels with egg white mixture; sprinkle with sesame seeds. Bake an additional 20 minutes or until golden. Remove from baking sheets, and let cool on wire racks. Yield: 1½ dozen (124 calories and 8% fat each).

Protein 3.7 / Fat 1.1 (Saturated Fat 0.2) / Carbohydrate 24.5
Fiber 1.0 / Cholesterol 0 / Sodium 134

Savory Sandwich Buns

2 packages dry yeast
2 tablespoons sugar
2 cups warm water (105° to 115°)
5 cups bread flour, divided
½ cup grated Parmesan cheese
1 teaspoon dried Italian seasoning
¾ teaspoon salt
Vegetable cooking spray
1 teaspoon cornmeal
1 cup boiling water

Dissolve yeast and sugar in 2 cups warm water in a large bowl; let stand 5 minutes. Add 2 cups flour and next 3 ingredients; beat at low speed of an electric mixer until blended. Gradually stir in 2½ cups flour; cover and let rest 15 minutes.

Sprinkle 1 tablespoon flour evenly over work surface. Turn dough out onto floured surface, and knead until dough is smooth and elastic (about 8 to 10 minutes). Work in enough of the remaining flour, 1 tablespoon at a time, to prevent dough from sticking to hands. Place dough in a large bowl coated with cooking spray, turning to coat top. Cover and let rise in a warm place (85°), free from drafts, 45 minutes or until doubled in bulk.

Punch dough down, and divide into 16 equal portions; shape each portion into a ball. Place on a large ungreased baking sheet sprinkled with cornmeal. Cover and let rise in a warm place, free from drafts, 35 minutes or until doubled in bulk.

Place a 15- x 10- x 1-inch jellyroll pan on bottom rack of oven; add 1 cup boiling water. Uncover rolls, and place baking sheet on middle rack of oven above jellyroll pan. Bake at 450° for 10 minutes or until golden. Remove from baking sheet, and let cool on wire racks. Yield: 16 buns (154 calories and 9% fat each).

Protein 5.9 / Fat 1.6 (Saturated Fat 0.7) / Carbohydrate 28.3
Fiber 0.3 / Cholesterol 2 / Sodium 168

Whole Wheat Pita Bread

1 package dry yeast
1 tablespoon sugar, divided
2½ cups warm water (105° to 115°)
2 tablespoons vegetable oil
1 teaspoon salt
5¼ cups all-purpose flour, divided
3 cups whole wheat flour
Vegetable cooking spray

Dissolve yeast and 1 teaspoon sugar in warm water in a large bowl; let stand 5 minutes. Add remaining 2 teaspoons sugar, oil, salt, 2 cups all-purpose flour, and whole wheat flour; beat at medium speed of an electric mixer until well blended. Gradually stir in 3 cups all-purpose flour to make a soft dough.

Sprinkle 3 tablespoons all-purpose flour evenly over work surface. Turn dough out onto floured surface, and knead until smooth and elastic (about 8 to 10 minutes). Place dough in a large bowl coated with cooking spray, turning to coat top. Cover dough with heavy-duty plastic wrap and a towel. Let dough rest 20 minutes.

Punch dough down. Divide into 24 equal portions; shape each portion into a ball. Place balls on 4 large baking sheets coated with cooking spray. Cover and let rise in a warm place (85°), free from drafts, 30 minutes or until doubled in bulk.

Sprinkle remaining 1 tablespoon all-purpose flour evenly over work surface. Roll each ball into a 5-inch circle on floured surface. Place 6 circles on a large mesh wire rack. Place wire rack directly on middle oven rack. Bake at 500° for 4 to 5 minutes or until bread rounds are puffed and brown.

Remove bread and wire rack from oven; let bread cool completely on wire racks. Repeat procedure with remaining circles. Cut pita bread in half, if desired. Yield: 2 dozen rounds (156 calories and 10% fat each).

Protein 4.8 / Fat 1.8 (Saturated Fat 0.3) / Carbohydrate 30.7
Fiber 2.7 / Cholesterol 0 / Sodium 99

Whole Wheat French Bread

1 package dry yeast
2 teaspoons sugar
1½ cups warm water (105° to 115°)
1½ cups whole wheat flour, divided
2½ cups all-purpose flour
¾ teaspoon salt
Vegetable cooking spray
2 tablespoons cornmeal
1 tablespoon all-purpose flour
1 tablespoon water
2 teaspoons sesame seeds

Dissolve yeast and sugar in warm water in a large bowl; let stand 5 minutes. Add 1 cup whole wheat flour, stirring well. Let stand in a warm place (85°), free from drafts, 10 minutes. (Bubbles will appear on surface.)

Add remaining ½ cup whole wheat flour, 2½ cups all-purpose flour, and salt to yeast mixture; stir well. Shape dough into a ball, and place in a large bowl coated with cooking spray, turning to coat top. Cover and let rise in a warm place (85°), free from drafts, 1 hour or until doubled in bulk.

Coat 2 French bread loafpans with cooking spray; sprinkle evenly with cornmeal. Set aside.

Sprinkle 1 tablespoon all-purpose flour evenly over work surface. Turn dough out onto floured surface, and knead until smooth and elastic (about 5 to 7 minutes). Divide dough in half; shape each portion into a 15-inch rope. Place ropes in prepared pans; brush with 1 tablespoon water, and sprinkle with sesame seeds. Cover and let rise in a warm place, free from drafts, 40 minutes or until doubled in bulk.

Gently make 3 or 4 slits, about ½-inch deep, diagonally across each loaf, using a sharp knife. Spray loaves with water.

Bake at 450° for 15 minutes, spraying with water every 3 minutes without removing loaves from oven. Continue to bake, without spraying, an additional 5 minutes or until loaves are golden and sound hollow when tapped. Remove from pans, and let loaves cool on wire racks. Yield: 36 servings (51 calories and 6% fat per ½-inch slice).

Protein 1.7 / Fat 0.3 (Saturated Fat 0.1) / Carbohydrate 10.6
Fiber 0.9 / Cholesterol 0 / Sodium 49

Honey-Grain Bread

2 packages dry yeast
½ cup warm water (105° to 115°)
⅓ cup honey, divided
1 cup skim milk
¼ cup margarine
¼ cup frozen egg substitute, thawed
½ cup bulgur wheat, uncooked
½ cup wheat germ
1 teaspoon salt
½ teaspoon ground nutmeg
1½ cups whole wheat flour
4¼ cups all-purpose flour, divided
Vegetable cooking spray

Dissolve yeast in ½ cup warm water in a large bowl; stir in 2 tablespoons honey, and let stand 5 minutes.

Combine remaining 3 tablespoons plus 1 teaspoon honey, milk, and margarine in a small saucepan. Cook over medium heat, stirring occasionally, until margarine melts. Let cool to 105° to 115°.

Add milk mixture, egg substitute, bulgur, wheat germ, salt, nutmeg, whole wheat flour, and 3 cups all-purpose flour to yeast mixture. Gradually stir in 1 cup all-purpose flour to make a stiff dough.

Sprinkle 2 tablespoons all-purpose flour over work surface. Turn dough out onto floured surface; knead until smooth and elastic (about 8 to 10 minutes). Place dough in a bowl coated with vegetable cooking spray, turning to coat top. Cover and let rise in a warm place (85°), free from drafts, 1 hour or until doubled in bulk.

Punch dough down, and divide in half. Sprinkle 1 tablespoon all-purpose flour over work surface. Roll 1 portion of dough to a 10- x 6-inch rectangle. Roll up dough, jellyroll fashion, starting at short side, pressing firmly to

Enjoy one loaf of Honey-Grain Bread fresh from the oven and freeze the second loaf to serve later.

eliminate air pockets. Pinch ends to seal. Shape into a loaf. Place dough, seam side down, in an 8½- x 4½- x 3-inch loafpan coated with vegetable cooking spray. Repeat procedure with remaining dough and remaining 1 tablespoon all-purpose flour.

Cover and let rise in a warm place, free from drafts, 30 minutes or until doubled in bulk. Bake at 350° for 25 minutes or until loaves sound hollow when tapped. Remove from pans; let cool on wire racks. Yield: 34 servings (111 calories and 15% fat per ½-inch slice).

Protein 3.4 / Fat 1.8 (Saturated Fat 0.1) / Carbohydrate 20.5
Fiber 1.5 / Cholesterol 0 / Sodium 92

Peppered Parmesan Twist

2¼ cups bread flour, divided
2 tablespoons sugar
1 package dry yeast
1 cup warm water (105° to 115°), divided
¾ cup all-purpose flour, divided
½ cup freshly grated Parmesan cheese
1 teaspoon coarsely ground pepper
½ teaspoon salt
1 tablespoon olive oil
Vegetable cooking spray

Combine ½ cup bread flour, sugar, and yeast in a medium bowl, stirring well. Add ½ cup warm water, and stir well. Cover mixture, and let stand 10 minutes.

Combine remaining 1¾ cups bread flour, ½ cup plus 2 tablespoons all-purpose flour, cheese, pepper, and salt in a large bowl; stir well. Stir in yeast mixture, oil, and enough of the remaining ½ cup warm water to make a soft dough.

Sprinkle 1 tablespoon all-purpose flour evenly over work surface. Turn dough out onto floured surface, and knead until smooth and elastic (about 8 to 10 minutes). Place dough in a large bowl coated with cooking spray, turning to coat top. Cover dough, and let rise in a warm place (85°), free from drafts, 1 hour or until doubled in bulk.

Sprinkle remaining 1 tablespoon all-purpose flour evenly over work surface. Punch dough down, and turn out onto floured surface; knead lightly 4 or 5 times. Divide dough into thirds. Shape each third into a 20-inch rope. Place ropes on a baking sheet coated with cooking spray (do not stretch). Braid ropes together; pinch ends to seal. Cover and let rise in a warm place, free from drafts, 30 minutes or until doubled in bulk.

Spray loaf with water. Bake at 400° for 10 minutes. Remove from oven; spray loaf with water. Reduce oven temperature to 375°; rotate baking sheet, and bake 15 minutes or until loaf sounds hollow when tapped. (Cover loaf with aluminum foil the last 5 to 10 minutes of baking to prevent excess browning, if necessary.) Remove from baking sheet; let cool on a wire rack. Yield: 32 servings (54 calories and 18% fat per ½-inch slice).

Protein 2.0 / Fat 1.1 (Saturated Fat 0.4) / Carbohydrate 8.9
Fiber 0.2 / Cholesterol 1 / Sodium 65

A scoop of tangy Apple-Cranberry Ice (page 114) or sweet Peach Sherbet (page 115) will be a refreshing ending to a casual lunch or dinner.

Festive Fruit Trifle

1 (10½-ounce) loaf commercial angel
   food cake
1½ cups skim milk
½ cup 1% low-fat cottage cheese
¼ cup sugar
3 tablespoons cornstarch
2 tablespoons instant nonfat dry milk
   powder
1 tablespoon grated orange rind
2 teaspoons vanilla extract
½ cup reduced-calorie strawberry spread
2 tablespoons Cointreau or other
   orange-flavored liqueur
5 cups fresh strawberries, hulled and halved
5 kiwifruit, peeled and thinly sliced
4 medium oranges, peeled and sectioned
Fresh whole strawberries (optional)

Cut angel food cake into 1-inch cubes; set aside. Combine milk and next 4 ingredients in container of an electric blender or food processor; top with cover, and process until mixture is smooth.

Pour mixture into top of a double boiler; bring water to a boil. Reduce heat to medium-low; cook, stirring constantly, 10 to 12 minutes or until mixture is thickened. Remove from heat; add orange rind and vanilla, stirring well. Transfer mixture to a bowl; cover and chill.

Combine strawberry spread and liqueur in a small saucepan; bring to a boil, stirring constantly. Remove from heat.

Arrange half of cake cubes in bottom of a 3-quart trifle bowl. Brush cubes with half of strawberry spread mixture. Arrange enough strawberry halves, cut side out, to line lower edge of bowl. Place half of remaining strawberries over cake cubes. Arrange half of kiwifruit and half of orange sections over strawberries. Spoon half of chilled custard over fruit layer. Repeat layering procedure with remaining fruit and chilled custard. Cover and refrigerate 8 hours. Garnish with strawberries, if desired. Yield: 12 servings (171 calories and 4% fat per serving).

Protein 5.2 / Fat 0.7 (Saturated Fat 0.2) / Carbohydrate 38.2
Fiber 4.0 / Cholesterol 1 / Sodium 99

Honeyed Banana Sauté

3 medium bananas, peeled and cut into
   ½-inch pieces
1 tablespoon lemon juice
2 teaspoons reduced-calorie margarine
1½ tablespoons honey
⅛ teaspoon grated lemon rind
Dash of ground nutmeg
3 cups vanilla ice milk

Combine bananas and lemon juice in a small bowl, tossing gently; set aside. Melt margarine in a large nonstick skillet over

medium heat; add honey, lemon rind, and nutmeg, stirring well to combine. Add banana mixture to honey mixture in skillet. Cook 2 minutes or until banana is slightly soft, basting frequently with honey mixture.

To serve, spoon ½ cup ice milk into each of 6 individual dessert bowls. Spoon warm banana mixture evenly over each serving. Serve immediately. Yield: 6 servings (158 calories and 22% fat per serving).

Protein 3.1 / Fat 3.8 (Saturated Fat 2.0) / Carbohydrate 29.9
Fiber 1.4 / Cholesterol 9 / Sodium 65

The perfect make-ahead dessert, Festive Fruit Trifle looks similar to its traditionally rich counterpart, but angel food cake and a low-fat custard keep this version healthy.

Oatmeal-Molasses Cookies

¼ cup margarine, softened
¾ cup sugar
¼ cup molasses
1 egg
1 teaspoon vanilla extract
1¾ cups all-purpose flour
½ teaspoon baking soda
½ teaspoon salt
1 cup regular oats, uncooked
1 teaspoon ground cinnamon
½ teaspoon ground ginger
Vegetable cooking spray

Cream margarine; gradually add sugar, beating at medium speed of an electric mixer until well blended. Add molasses, egg, and vanilla; beat well.

Combine flour and next 5 ingredients in a medium bowl, stirring mixture well. Gradually add flour mixture to creamed mixture, mixing well to combine.

Drop dough by level tablespoonfuls, 2 inches apart, onto cookie sheets coated with cooking spray. Bake at 350° for 10 minutes or until very lightly browned. Cool slightly on cookie sheets. Remove from cookie sheets, and cool completely on wire racks. Yield: 32 cookies (73 calories and 22% fat each).

Protein 1.3 / Fat 1.8 (Saturated Fat 0.3) / Carbohydrate 12.8
Fiber 0.4 / Cholesterol 7 / Sodium 69

Peppermint Brownies

¼ cup margarine, softened
¾ cup sugar
¼ cup frozen egg substitute, thawed
2 tablespoons water
2 teaspoons vanilla extract
¾ cup all-purpose flour
¼ teaspoon baking powder
⅛ teaspoon salt
⅓ cup unsweetened cocoa
¼ cup finely crushed peppermint candy
1 egg white
Vegetable cooking spray

Cream margarine; gradually add sugar, beating well at medium speed of an electric mixer until crumbly. Add egg substitute, water, and vanilla; beat at low speed until well blended.

Combine flour and next 4 ingredients; add to sugar mixture, stirring just until dry ingredients are moistened. Set aside.

Beat egg white at high speed of an electric mixer until stiff peaks form; gently fold into flour mixture. Spoon batter into an 8-inch square baking pan coated with cooking spray. Bake at 350° for 20 to 25 minutes or until a wooden pick inserted in center comes out clean. Cool in pan on a wire rack. Cut into squares. Yield: 1 dozen (139 calories and 28% fat each).

Protein 2.3 / Fat 4.3 (Saturated Fat 0.8) / Carbohydrate 23.0
Fiber 0.2 / Cholesterol 0 / Sodium 90

A simple side dish of sliced potatoes is the perfect accompaniment to Catfish Fillets with Crabmeat Topping (page 126), a colorful and filling entrée.

Catfish Fillets with Crabmeat Topping

3 tablespoons fresh lemon juice
1 tablespoon reduced-calorie margarine, melted
2 teaspoons low-sodium Worcestershire sauce
6 (4-ounce) farm-raised catfish fillets
½ teaspoon garlic powder
½ teaspoon creole seasoning
¼ teaspoon ground red pepper
Vegetable cooking spray
1 cup chopped onion
½ cup chopped green onions
½ medium-size green pepper, chopped
½ medium-size sweet red pepper, chopped
6 ounces fresh lump crabmeat, drained

Combine first 3 ingredients in a small bowl; brush mixture on both sides of fillets. Combine garlic powder, creole seasoning, and ground red pepper; sprinkle evenly over both sides of fillets. Place fillets in a 13- x 9- x 2-inch baking dish. Bake, uncovered, at 350° for 25 minutes.

Coat a large nonstick skillet with cooking spray; place over medium-high heat until hot. Add chopped onion, green onions, green pepper, and sweet red pepper; sauté 5 minutes or until vegetables are tender. Add crabmeat, and cook 30 seconds or until thoroughly heated, stirring constantly.

Spoon crabmeat mixture evenly over baked fillets. Bake an additional 5 minutes or until fish flakes easily when tested with a fork. Yield: 6 servings (194 calories and 27% fat per serving).

Protein 29.7 / Fat 5.8 (Saturated Fat 1.0) / Carbohydrate 4.8
Fiber 1.0 / Cholesterol 93 / Sodium 332

Orange Flounder en Papillote

½ cup unsweetened orange juice
1 teaspoon peeled, grated gingerroot
1 teaspoon honey
¾ teaspoon cornstarch
¼ teaspoon salt
1 large orange, peeled and sectioned
4 (4-ounce) flounder fillets
2 cups fresh broccoli flowerets

Combine orange juice, gingerroot, honey, cornstarch, and salt in a saucepan. Cook over medium heat, stirring constantly, until thickened and bubbly. Remove from heat; gently stir in orange sections, and set aside.

Cut 4 (15-inch) squares of parchment paper; fold each square in half, and trim each into a large heart shape. Place hearts on 2 large baking sheets, and open out flat. Place a fillet on one half of each heart near the crease.

Spoon orange mixture evenly over fillets; top each with ½ cup broccoli flowerets.

Fold edges over to seal securely. Starting with rounded edge of heart, pleat and crimp edges of parchment paper to make an airtight seal. Bake at 400° for 10 to 12 minutes or until packets are puffed and browned.

Place packets on individual serving plates; cut an opening in the top of each packet, and fold paper back. Yield: 4 servings (150 calories and 9% fat per serving).

Protein 22.9 / Fat 1.5 (Saturated Fat 0.4) / Carbohydrate 11.1
Fiber 2.5 / Cholesterol 54 / Sodium 248

Broiled Dijon Grouper

3 tablespoons Dijon mustard
1 tablespoon sliced green onions
¼ teaspoon coarsely ground pepper
6 (4-ounce) grouper fillets
Vegetable cooking spray
1 tablespoon reduced-calorie margarine,
  melted

Combine first 3 ingredients in a small bowl.
Place fillets on rack of a broiler pan coated with cooking spray; brush with margarine. Broil 5½ inches from heat 8 minutes. Turn fish; spread mustard mixture evenly over fillets. Broil an additional 3 minutes or until fish flakes easily when tested with a fork. Yield: 6 servings (127 calories and 21% fat per serving).

Protein 22.4 / Fat 3.0 (Saturated Fat 0.4) / Carbohydrate 0.7
Fiber 0.1 / Cholesterol 42 / Sodium 289

Grouper and Sautéed Vegetables

4 (4-ounce) grouper fillets
¼ cup lemon juice
½ teaspoon garlic powder
¼ teaspoon dried whole thyme
¼ teaspoon hot sauce
Vegetable cooking spray
1 teaspoon olive oil
½ cup chopped onion
½ cup chopped green pepper
1 clove garlic, minced
¾ cup peeled, seeded, and chopped tomato
½ teaspoon dried whole thyme
¼ teaspoon salt
½ cup (2 ounces) shredded part-skim
  mozzarella cheese

Place fillets in an 8-inch square baking dish. Combine lemon juice and next 3 ingredients; pour over fish. Cover and marinate in refrigerator 2 hours.
Bake fillets in marinade, uncovered, at 350° for 25 minutes or until fish flakes easily when tested with a fork. Drain excess liquid. Keep warm.
Coat a large nonstick skillet with cooking spray; add oil. Place over medium-high heat until hot. Add onion, green pepper, and garlic; sauté 3 minutes or until vegetables are tender. Add tomato, ½ teaspoon thyme, and salt; cook 1 minute, stirring frequently.
Top fillets with vegetable mixture; sprinkle evenly with cheese. Bake an additional 3 minutes or until cheese melts. Yield: 4 servings (174 calories and 25% fat per serving).

Protein 26.2 / Fat 4.9 (Saturated Fat 1.9) / Carbohydrate 5.8
Fiber 1.0 / Cholesterol 50 / Sodium 266

Halibut Steaks with Tangy Mustard Sauce

6 (4-ounce) halibut steaks (¾ inch thick)
⅓ cup unsweetened orange juice
¼ cup lemon juice
1 teaspoon dried whole basil
1 teaspoon dried whole tarragon
1 teaspoon curry powder
⅛ teaspoon ground red pepper
Vegetable cooking spray
1 tablespoon olive oil, divided
3 tablespoons Dijon mustard
2 tablespoons minced purple onion
1½ tablespoons capers, drained
1 tablespoon minced fresh parsley

Arrange halibut steaks in a large, shallow baking dish. Combine orange juice and next 5 ingredients in a small bowl, stirring well; pour over steaks. Cover and marinate in refrigerator 1 hour, turning once.
Remove steaks from marinade, reserving marinade. Place steaks on rack of a broiler pan coated with cooking spray; brush with ¼ teaspoon olive oil. Broil 3½ inches from heat 5 minutes. Turn steaks, and brush with ¼ teaspoon oil. Broil an additional 3 minutes or until fish flakes easily when tested with a fork. Arrange on a serving platter, and keep warm.
Combine reserved marinade, remaining 2½ teaspoons olive oil, and mustard in a small saucepan; bring to a boil. Add onion, capers, and parsley; reduce heat, and simmer 5 minutes, stirring occasionally. Spoon sauce evenly over fish. Yield: 6 servings (167 calories and 30% fat per serving).

Protein 24.0 / Fat 5.6 (Saturated Fat 0.7) / Carbohydrate 3.7
Fiber 0.3 / Cholesterol 36 / Sodium 452

Monkfish en Brochette

¼ cup plus 2 tablespoons lemon
  juice
1 tablespoon olive oil
¾ teaspoon paprika
¾ teaspoon pepper
½ teaspoon dried whole marjoram
1 (1-pound) monkfish fillet, cut into
  1-inch pieces
1 (14-ounce) can artichoke hearts,
  drained and quartered
Vegetable cooking spray

  Combine first 5 ingredients in a large,
shallow dish. Add fish and artichoke quarters,
tossing gently to coat. Cover and marinate in
refrigerator 30 minutes.

  Remove fish and artichoke quarters from
marinade, reserving marinade. Place marinade
in a small saucepan. Bring marinade to a boil;
reduce heat, and simmer 5 minutes. Set
marinade aside.

  Thread fish and artichoke quarters alternately on 4 (12-inch) skewers.

  Coat grill rack with cooking spray; place on
grill over medium-hot coals. Place kabobs on
rack; cook 8 minutes or until fish flakes easily
when tested with a fork, turning once and
basting frequently with reserved marinade.
Yield: 4 servings (171 calories and 26% fat per
serving).

Protein 23.6 / Fat 4.9 (Saturated Fat 0.7) / Carbohydrate 8.7
Fiber 0.8 / Cholesterol 102 / Sodium 257

Peppered Perch

4 (6-ounce) pan-dressed freshwater
  perch
½ cup Chablis or other dry white
  wine
¼ cup lemon juice
2 tablespoons low-sodium soy sauce
1 tablespoon low-sodium Worcestershire
  sauce
2 cloves garlic, minced
Vegetable cooking spray
¼ teaspoon cracked pepper, divided
Lemon wedges (optional)

  Place fish in an 11- x 7- x 2-inch baking
dish. Combine wine and next 4 ingredients; stir
well, and pour over fish. Cover and marinate in
refrigerator 4 hours, turning twice.

  Remove fish from marinade, reserving
marinade. Place marinade in a small saucepan.
Bring to a boil; reduce heat, and simmer 5
minutes. Remove from heat.

  Place fish on rack of a broiler pan coated with
cooking spray. Broil 5½ inches from heat 5 minutes,
basting occasionally with reserved marinade.

  Turn fish, and sprinkle with ⅛ teaspoon
cracked pepper. Broil an additional 8 minutes or
until fish flakes easily when tested with a fork,
basting occasionally with reserved marinade.

  Transfer fish to a serving platter; sprinkle
with remaining ⅛ teaspoon cracked pepper.
Garnish with lemon wedges, if desired. Yield: 4
servings (115 calories and 9% fat per serving).

Protein 21.4 / Fat 1.2 (Saturated Fat 0.2) / Carbohydrate 3.0
Fiber 0.1 / Cholesterol 98 / Sodium 279

*Healthy cooking is easy when you serve
Lemon-Broiled Orange Roughy as the
main course.*

Lemon-Broiled Orange Roughy

4 (4-ounce) orange roughy fillets
Vegetable cooking spray
3 tablespoons lemon juice
1 tablespoon Dijon mustard
1 tablespoon reduced-calorie margarine,
  melted
¼ teaspoon coarsely ground pepper
Coarsely ground pepper (optional)
Lemon slices (optional)

Place fillets on rack of a broiler pan coated with cooking spray. Combine lemon juice and next 3 ingredients; stir well. Brush half of lemon juice mixture over fillets.

Broil fillets 5½ inches from heat 8 to 10 minutes or until fish flakes easily when tested with a fork.

Drizzle remaining lemon juice mixture over fillets; transfer to a serving platter. If desired, sprinkle with ground pepper, and garnish with lemon slices. Yield: 4 servings (204 calories and 56% fat per serving).

Protein 20.2 / Fat 12.6 (Saturated Fat 4.1) / Carbohydrate 1.3
Fiber 0 / Cholesterol 54 / Sodium 204

Garnished with lemon and fresh thyme, Grilled Herbed Salmon offers a distinctive flavor and elegant appearance.

Grilled Herbed Salmon

2 teaspoons cracked pepper
4 (4-ounce) salmon steaks (¾ inch thick)
1 medium onion, thinly sliced
1 lemon, thinly sliced
Vegetable cooking spray
1 bunch fresh thyme (about ½ ounce)
Lemon slices (optional)
Fresh thyme sprigs (optional)

Press pepper onto both sides of salmon. Top with onion and lemon slices; set aside.

Coat grill rack with cooking spray; place on grill over medium-hot coals. Arrange fresh thyme on grill rack; place salmon on fresh thyme. Cover and cook 10 to 12 minutes or until fish flakes easily when tested with a fork.

Transfer to a serving platter, discarding thyme and lemon slices. If desired, garnish with lemon slices and fresh thyme sprigs. Yield: 4 servings (215 calories and 43% fat per serving).

Protein 24.8 / Fat 10.2 (Saturated Fat 1.7) / Carbohydrate 4.7
Fiber 1.1 / Cholesterol 77 / Sodium 60

Orange Snapper

6 (4-ounce) red snapper fillets (½ inch thick)
Vegetable cooking spray
3 tablespoons water
2 tablespoons frozen orange juice
    concentrate, thawed and undiluted
2 teaspoons olive oil
½ teaspoon grated orange rind
⅛ teaspoon ground nutmeg
Dash of freshly ground pepper
Orange wedges (optional)

Arrange fillets in a 13- x 9- x 2-inch baking dish coated with cooking spray. Combine water and next 5 ingredients; pour over fillets.

Bake, uncovered, at 350° for 20 minutes or until fish flakes easily when tested with a fork. Transfer fillets to a serving platter, using a slotted spoon. Garnish with orange wedges, if desired. Yield: 6 servings (133 calories and 21% fat per serving).

Protein 22.5 / Fat 3.1 (Saturated Fat 0.5) / Carbohydrate 2.3
Fiber 0.1 / Cholesterol 40 / Sodium 49

Red Snapper Veracruz

6 (4-ounce) red snapper fillets (½ inch
　thick)
½ cup lime juice
½ teaspoon salt
Vegetable cooking spray
1 teaspoon vegetable oil
1 cup sliced onion
2 cups chopped tomato
1 (4-ounce) jar diced pimiento,
　drained
1 teaspoon canned chopped green chiles
½ teaspoon capers
1 fresh parsley sprig
Lime slices (optional)
Fresh parsley sprigs (optional)

Arrange fillets in a shallow baking dish; pour lime juice over fillets, and sprinkle with salt. Cover and marinate in refrigerator 2 hours.

Coat a large nonstick skillet with cooking spray; add oil. Place over medium-high heat until hot. Add onion; sauté until tender. Add tomato and next 4 ingredients; cover and cook 7 minutes, stirring occasionally.

Remove fillets from marinade; discard marinade. Arrange fillets over mixture in skillet. Cover and cook 6 minutes on each side or until fish flakes easily when tested with a fork.

Transfer fillets to a serving platter; keep warm. Continue cooking tomato mixture, uncovered, until liquid is absorbed (about 10 minutes). Remove and discard parsley sprig. Spoon vegetable mixture evenly over fillets. If desired, garnish with lime slices and fresh parsley sprigs. Yield: 6 servings (142 calories and 17% fat per serving).

Protein 24.0 / Fat 2.6 (Saturated Fat 0.5) / Carbohydrate 4.8
Fiber 1.0 / Cholesterol 42 / Sodium 195

Baked Sole with Mushroom Sauce

Vegetable cooking spray
2 teaspoons reduced-calorie margarine
¾ cup minced onion
1 tablespoon all-purpose flour
1 pound sliced fresh mushrooms
2 tablespoons water
3 tablespoons Chablis or other dry white
　wine, divided
¼ cup thinly sliced green onions
6 (4-ounce) sole fillets
⅛ teaspoon pepper

Coat a large nonstick skillet with cooking spray; add margarine. Place over medium-high heat until margarine melts. Add onion; sauté until tender. Add flour; cook 1 minute, stirring constantly.

Add mushrooms, water, and 1 tablespoon wine. Cook over medium heat 5 to 7 minutes or until mushrooms are tender, stirring constantly, and adding 1 tablespoon water, if necessary, to prevent sticking. Stir in green onions. Remove from heat; cover and set aside.

Arrange fillets in a 13- x 9- x 2-inch baking dish coated with cooking spray. Drizzle with remaining 2 tablespoons wine, and sprinkle with pepper. Cover and bake at 400° for 10 to 12 minutes or until fish flakes easily when tested with a fork.

Transfer fillets to a serving platter, using a slotted spoon; set aside, and keep warm. Combine pan drippings with mushroom mixture in skillet. Bring to a boil over medium-high heat, stirring constantly. Spoon sauce over fillets. Yield: 6 servings (138 calories and 18% fat per serving).

Protein 23.2 / Fat 2.7 (Saturated Fat 0.5) / Carbohydrate 5.1
Fiber 1.2 / Cholesterol 54 / Sodium 109

Honey-Mustard Swordfish

2 (8-ounce) swordfish steaks (1 inch thick)
¼ cup Chablis or other dry white wine
2 tablespoons Dijon mustard
2 tablespoons low-sodium soy sauce
1 tablespoon honey
½ teaspoon curry powder
Vegetable cooking spray

Arrange steaks in a baking dish. Combine wine and next 4 ingredients; pour over steaks. Cover and marinate in refrigerator 1 hour.

Remove steaks from marinade, reserving ¼ cup marinade. Place reserved marinade in a small saucepan; bring to a boil. Reduce heat, and simmer 5 minutes.

Coat grill rack with cooking spray; place on grill over medium-hot coals. Place steaks on rack; cook 15 minutes or until fish flakes easily when tested with a fork, turning once, and basting frequently with marinade. Yield: 4 servings (189 calories and 30% fat per serving).

Protein 28.2 / Fat 6.2 (Saturated Fat 1.6) / Carbohydrate 2.6
Fiber 0 / Cholesterol 55 / Sodium 337

Pesto Swordfish Kabobs

1 cup tightly packed fresh basil leaves
1 clove garlic
2 tablespoons commercial oil-free Italian dressing
1 pound swordfish steaks (¾ inch thick)
⅛ teaspoon pepper
Vegetable cooking spray

Position knife blade in food processor bowl; add basil and garlic. Process until finely chopped; transfer to a small bowl. Stir in Italian dressing, and set aside.

Cut swordfish steaks into 1-inch pieces; sprinkle with pepper. Thread steak pieces on 4 (10-inch) skewers.

Coat grill rack with cooking spray; place on grill over medium-hot coals. Place kabobs on rack; cook 8 minutes or until fish flakes easily when tested with a fork, turning once, and basting frequently with basil mixture. Yield: 4 servings (147 calories and 29% fat per serving).

Protein 22.9 / Fat 4.8 (Saturated Fat 1.3) / Carbohydrate 1.7
Fiber 0 / Cholesterol 44 / Sodium 118

Omega-3—A Fat that's Good for You

Two polyunsaturated fatty acids found in fish, docosahexaenoic acid and eicosapentaenoic acid, appear to decrease heart disease risk. Known as omega-3 fatty acids, these healthful fats are found in fish with darker, moist flesh that tend to come from deep, cold waters where the oil in the flesh provides insulation. Even though lighter, firm-fleshed fish have less omega-3 fatty acids, don't hesitate to include them in your menu.

High in Omega-3s	Moderately High in Omega-3s
anchovy	bass
mackerel	bluefish
pompano	catfish
sablefish	halibut
salmon	ocean perch
sardine	pollock
lake trout	rainbow and sea trout
canned albacore tuna	swordfish
fresh tuna	whiting

Zesty Crab Cakes

1 pound fresh crabmeat, drained and flaked
¾ cup shredded carrot
½ cup fine, dry breadcrumbs
½ cup frozen egg substitute, thawed
2 teaspoons chopped fresh parsley
½ teaspoon dried Italian seasoning
½ teaspoon dry mustard
¼ teaspoon pepper
⅛ teaspoon garlic powder
2 teaspoons fat-free mayonnaise
1½ teaspoons low-sodium Worcestershire
  sauce
Vegetable cooking spray
Creamy Seafood Sauce

   Combine first 11 ingredients in a medium
bowl; stir well. Shape mixture into 6 patties.
Cover and chill 1 hour.
   Coat a large nonstick skillet with cooking
spray; place over medium heat until hot. Add
patties; cook 4 to 5 minutes on each side or
until golden. Serve with Creamy Seafood
Sauce. Yield: 6 servings (150 calories and 14%
fat per crab cake and 2 tablespoons sauce).

Creamy Seafood Sauce

¼ cup fat-free mayonnaise
¼ cup nonfat sour cream
¼ cup reduced-calorie catsup
1½ tablespoons finely chopped green onions
2 tablespoons prepared horseradish
1 teaspoon chopped fresh parsley
1½ teaspoons lemon juice

   Combine all ingredients in a small bowl,
stirring well. Cover and chill at least 3 hours.
Yield: ¾ cup.

Protein 19.3 / Fat 2.0 (Saturated Fat 0.3) / Carbohydrate 12.1
Fiber 0.9 / Cholesterol 76 / Sodium 449

Lobster in Orange Sauce

4 (8-ounce) fresh or frozen lobster tails,
  thawed
Vegetable cooking spray
1½ tablespoons reduced-calorie margarine
1 tablespoon peeled, grated gingerroot
1 clove garlic, minced
1½ cups unsweetened orange juice
1½ tablespoons cornstarch
1½ tablespoons honey
1½ teaspoons grated orange rind
¼ teaspoon curry powder
3 cups cooked long-grain rice (cooked
  without salt or fat)
¼ cup chopped green onions

   Cook lobster tails in boiling water 6 to 8
minutes or until done; drain. Rinse with cold
water. Split and clean tails. Cut lobster meat
into bite-size pieces; set aside.
   Coat a large nonstick skillet with cooking
spray; add margarine. Place over medium heat
until margarine melts. Add gingerroot and
garlic; sauté 1 minute.
   Combine orange juice, cornstarch, honey,
grated orange rind, and curry powder, stirring
well. Add orange juice mixture to skillet,
stirring constantly until thickened and bubbly.
   Stir in lobster, and cook until thoroughly
heated. Spoon lobster mixture over cooked rice
on a serving platter, and sprinkle with green
onions. Yield: 6 servings (310 calories and 8%
fat per serving).

Protein 26.5 / Fat 2.9 (Saturated Fat 0.5) / Carbohydrate 42.8
Fiber 0.8 / Cholesterol 82 / Sodium 462

Oyster-Spinach Casserole

Vegetable cooking spray
1 cup sliced fresh mushrooms
¼ cup minced green onions
1 clove garlic, minced
2 (10-ounce) packages frozen chopped
   spinach
1 tablespoon reduced-calorie margarine
2 tablespoons all-purpose flour
1 cup skim milk
1 teaspoon lemon juice
¼ teaspoon ground nutmeg
Dash of ground white pepper
2 (12-ounce) containers Select oysters,
   drained and rinsed
¼ cup fine, dry breadcrumbs
2 tablespoons grated Parmesan cheese
Pimiento strips (optional)

Coat a large nonstick skillet with cooking spray; place over medium-high heat until hot. Add mushrooms, green onions, and garlic; sauté until tender. Drain and set aside.

Cook spinach according to package directions, omitting salt; drain and press dry between paper towels. Set aside.

Melt margarine in a medium saucepan over low heat; add flour, stirring until smooth. Cook 1 minute, stirring constantly. Gradually add milk; cook over medium heat, stirring constantly, until thickened and bubbly. Stir in lemon juice, nutmeg, and pepper.

Remove sauce from heat; add sautéed vegetables and spinach, stirring well. Spoon mixture into a 10- x 6- x 2-inch baking dish coated with cooking spray. Arrange oysters over spinach mixture, and sprinkle with breadcrumbs and Parmesan cheese.

Bake, uncovered, at 350° for 35 to 40 minutes or until oyster edges curl. Garnish with pimiento strips, if desired. Serve immediately. Yield: 6 servings (149 calories and 29% fat per serving).

Protein 12.3 / Fat 4.8 (Saturated Fat 1.3) / Carbohydrate 15.3
Fiber 3.5 / Cholesterol 50 / Sodium 281

Scallops Sauté

Vegetable cooking spray
2 tablespoons reduced-calorie margarine
1 pound fresh sugar snap peas
2½ cups diagonally sliced celery
1 pound fresh sea scallops
¼ cup Chablis or other dry white wine
3 tablespoons lemon juice
½ teaspoon dried whole dillweed
½ teaspoon freshly ground pepper
2 tablespoons chopped fresh parsley

Coat a large nonstick skillet with cooking spray; add margarine. Place over medium-high heat until margarine melts. Add peas and celery; sauté 3 to 4 minutes or until crisp-tender. Remove vegetables from skillet, using a slotted spoon; set aside.

Add scallops and next 4 ingredients to skillet; bring to a boil. Cover, reduce heat, and simmer 5 to 6 minutes or until scallops are opaque. Add vegetables, and cook just until thoroughly heated. Sprinkle with chopped parsley, and serve with a slotted spoon. Yield: 4 servings (191 calories and 23% fat per serving).

Protein 22.6 / Fat 4.9 (Saturated Fat 0.7) / Carbohydrate 14.9
Fiber 4.2 / Cholesterol 37 / Sodium 306

Scallops Sauté brings a distinct contrast of textures and flavors to a one-dish meal that's easy to prepare.

Barbecued Shrimp

Vegetable cooking spray
¼ cup diced onion
½ cup reduced-calorie catsup
1 tablespoon chopped fresh rosemary
1 tablespoon brown sugar
1 tablespoon dry mustard
1 tablespoon vinegar
¼ teaspoon garlic powder
Dash of hot sauce
24 jumbo fresh shrimp (about 1 pound),
   peeled and deveined
1 lemon, cut into wedges
¼ cup finely chopped green pepper
2 cups cooked long-grain rice (cooked
   without salt or fat)
Fresh rosemary sprigs (optional)
Lemon slices (optional)

Coat a large nonstick skillet with cooking spray; place over medium-high heat until hot. Add onion; sauté until tender. Remove from heat; add catsup and next 6 ingredients, stirring until mixture is well blended. Cover and let stand at room temperature 2 to 3 hours.

Place shrimp in a shallow dish. Pour catsup mixture over shrimp, turning to coat. Cover and marinate in refrigerator 1 hour.

Thread shrimp on 4 (10-inch) skewers. Coat grill rack with cooking spray; place on grill over medium-hot coals. Place kabobs on rack; cook 12 to 15 minutes or until done, turning once. Squeeze lemon over shrimp.

Coat a large nonstick skillet with cooking spray; place over medium-high heat until hot. Add green pepper; sauté 3 minutes or until crisp-tender. Stir in cooked rice. Transfer rice mixture to a serving platter; arrange kabobs over rice. If desired, garnish with fresh rosemary sprigs and lemon slices. Yield: 4 servings (261 calories and 8% fat per serving).

Protein 21.4 / Fat 2.4 (Saturated Fat 0.3) / Carbohydrate 37.6
Fiber 1.2 / Cholesterol 166 / Sodium 203

Oriental Shrimp Stir-Fry

1 pound fresh asparagus spears
2 tablespoons Chablis or other dry
    white wine
1 tablespoon white wine vinegar
1 tablespoon low-sodium soy sauce
Vegetable cooking spray
2 teaspoons vegetable oil
⅔ cup minced green onions
2 tablespoons peeled, minced gingerroot
1 teaspoon minced garlic
2 pounds medium-size fresh shrimp, peeled
    and deveined
3 cups chopped Chinese cabbage
1 tablespoon cornstarch
1 tablespoon water

Snap off tough ends of asparagus. Remove scales from stalks with a knife or vegetable peeler, if desired. Cut asparagus diagonally into 1-inch pieces. Set aside.

Combine wine, vinegar, and soy sauce in a small bowl, stirring well; set aside.

Coat a wok or large nonstick skillet with cooking spray; add oil. Place over medium-high heat (375°) until hot. Add minced green onions, gingerroot, and minced garlic; stir-fry 1 minute. Add shrimp and asparagus, and stir-fry 5 minutes. Add wine mixture and cabbage; stir-fry mixture 5 minutes.

Combine cornstarch and water in a small bowl, stirring until smooth. Add to shrimp mixture. Cook, stirring constantly, until mixture is thickened. Yield: 6 servings (164 calories and 21% fat per serving).

Protein 25.3 / Fat 3.8 (Saturated Fat 0.7) / Carbohydrate 6.6
Fiber 1.7 / Cholesterol 172 / Sodium 248

Seafood-Stuffed Peppers

4½ cups water
1½ pounds medium-size fresh unpeeled
    shrimp
8 medium-size green peppers
Vegetable cooking spray
1 teaspoon reduced-calorie margarine
½ cup chopped green onions
⅓ cup chopped celery
1 clove garlic, minced
¾ pound fresh lump crabmeat, drained
1 cup cooked long-grain rice (cooked
    without salt or fat)
½ cup (2 ounces) shredded part-skim
    mozzarella cheese
¼ cup grated Parmesan cheese
2 tablespoons chopped fresh parsley
⅛ teaspoon pepper
Dash of hot sauce

Bring water to a boil; add shrimp, and cook 3 to 5 minutes or until shrimp turn pink. Drain; rinse with cold water. Peel, devein, and coarsely chop shrimp; set aside.

Cut tops off peppers; discard tops. Remove and discard seeds. Cook peppers in boiling water to cover 5 minutes. Drain peppers, and set aside.

Coat a large nonstick skillet with cooking spray; add margarine. Place over medium-high heat until margarine melts. Add green onions, celery, and garlic; sauté 5 minutes or until vegetables are tender. Remove from heat; add shrimp, crabmeat, and remaining ingredients, stirring well.

Spoon shrimp mixture evenly into peppers. Place peppers in a 13- x 9- x 2-inch baking dish. Add water to a depth of 1 inch. Bake at 350° for 25 to 30 minutes or until thoroughly heated. Yield: 8 servings (192 calories and 20% fat per serving).

Protein 23.3 / Fat 4.3 (Saturated Fat 1.6) / Carbohydrate 15.0
Fiber 2.5 / Cholesterol 142 / Sodium 323

Spice up your next cookout with the robust flavor of Barbecued Shrimp. Served on a bed of tender rice, the shrimp kabobs make an attractive presentation.

Creamy Seafood Casserole

6 cups water
1½ pounds medium-size fresh unpeeled
  shrimp
½ pound fresh lump crabmeat, drained
3 tablespoons dry sherry
Vegetable cooking spray
1 (4-ounce) can sliced mushrooms, drained
3 tablespoons sliced green onions
2 cups skim milk
½ cup instant nonfat dry milk powder
3 tablespoons margarine, melted
¼ cup all-purpose flour
2 teaspoons low-sodium Worcestershire
  sauce
¼ teaspoon ground white pepper
⅛ teaspoon garlic powder
¼ cup frozen egg substitute, thawed
2 cups cooked vermicelli or thin spaghetti
  (cooked without salt or fat)
2 tablespoons grated Parmesan cheese
Green onion fans (optional)

Bring water to a boil; add shrimp, and cook 3 to 5 minutes or until shrimp turn pink. Drain; rinse with cold water. Peel and devein shrimp. Combine shrimp, crabmeat, and sherry in a medium bowl; cover and chill 30 minutes.

Coat a nonstick skillet with cooking spray; place over medium-high heat until hot. Add mushrooms and green onions; sauté until tender. Set aside.

Combine skim milk and dry milk powder, stirring to dissolve powder; set aside. Melt margarine in a small saucepan over medium heat; add flour, stirring until smooth. Cook 1 minute, stirring constantly. Gradually add milk mixture; cook, stirring constantly, until thickened and bubbly. Stir in Worcestershire sauce, pepper, and garlic powder.

Remove from heat. Gradually stir about one-fourth of hot mixture into egg substitute; add to remaining hot mixture, stirring constantly. Stir in seafood mixture, mushroom mixture, and cooked vermicelli; spoon into a shallow 2-quart casserole coated with vegetable cooking spray.

Bake at 350° for 20 to 25 minutes or until thoroughly heated. Sprinkle with Parmesan cheese, and bake an additional 5 minutes. Garnish with green onion fans, if desired. Yield: 6 servings (316 calories and 23% fat per serving).

Protein 30.8 / Fat 8.2 (Saturated Fat 0.8) / Carbohydrate 28.4
Fiber 1.0 / Cholesterol 153 / Sodium 449

Full of garden vegetables and fresh herbs, Bow Tie Pasta Primavera (page 150) makes a perfect accompaniment for almost any entrée.

Barley and Mushroom Bake

Vegetable cooking spray
2 teaspoons reduced-calorie margarine
2 cups thinly sliced fresh mushrooms
1 cup chopped onion
1 cup pearl barley, uncooked
2½ cups hot water
1½ teaspoons beef-flavored bouillon
   granules
¼ teaspoon salt
⅛ teaspoon pepper
2 tablespoons chopped fresh parsley
Fresh parsley sprigs (optional)

Coat a large nonstick skillet with cooking spray; add margarine. Place over medium heat until margarine melts. Add mushrooms and onion; sauté until tender. Add barley, and sauté 4 to 5 minutes or until barley is lightly browned. Remove from heat.

Transfer barley mixture to a 1½-quart baking dish coated with cooking spray. Stir in water, bouillon granules, salt, and pepper. Cover and bake at 350° for 1 hour and 15 minutes or until barley is tender and liquid is absorbed, stirring every 15 minutes. Remove from oven, and gently stir in chopped parsley. Garnish with fresh parsley sprigs, if desired. Yield: 8 servings (100 calories and 12% fat per ½-cup serving).

Protein 2.8 / Fat 1.3 (Saturated Fat 0.4) / Carbohydrate 20.0
Fiber 4.1 / Cholesterol 0 / Sodium 263

Herbed Bulgur Pilaf

Vegetable cooking spray
2 teaspoons vegetable oil
½ cup coarsely shredded carrot
¼ cup thinly sliced green onions
1 large clove garlic, minced
1 cup hot water
½ cup bulgur wheat, uncooked
2 teaspoons honey
½ teaspoon chicken-flavored bouillon
   granules
½ teaspoon dried mint flakes
½ teaspoon dried whole basil

Coat a large nonstick skillet with cooking spray; add oil. Place over medium-high heat until hot. Add carrot, green onions, and garlic; sauté 1 minute. Add water and remaining ingredients; stir well. Bring to a boil; cover, reduce heat, and simmer 12 to 15 minutes or until bulgur is tender and liquid is absorbed.

Fluff bulgur with a fork, and transfer to a serving bowl. Yield: 4 servings (122 calories and 19% fat per ½-cup serving).

Protein 3.1 / Fat 2.6 (Saturated Fat 0.4) / Carbohydrate 21.7
Fiber 1.5 / Cholesterol 0 / Sodium 113

Couscous Toss

1 cup canned no-salt-added chicken broth,
   undiluted
1 teaspoon dried whole basil
1 small clove garlic, minced
¾ cup couscous, uncooked
1 tablespoon white wine vinegar
1½ teaspoons olive oil
¼ teaspoon pepper
⅛ teaspoon salt
1 cup seeded, chopped tomato

Combine chicken broth, basil, and garlic in a medium saucepan, stirring well; bring to a boil. Remove from heat. Add couscous; cover and let stand 5 minutes or until couscous is tender and liquid is absorbed. Fluff couscous with a fork.

Combine vinegar, olive oil, pepper, and salt in a small bowl, stirring well with a wire whisk. Add vinegar mixture and tomato to couscous, tossing mixture well.

Transfer couscous mixture to a serving bowl. Yield: 6 servings (80 calories and 18% fat per ½-cup serving).

Protein 2.6 / Fat 1.6 (Saturated Fat 0.2) / Carbohydrate 13.6
Fiber 0.7 / Cholesterol 0 / Sodium 76

Barley and Mushroom Bake is not only high in fiber but also high in flavor.

Calico Wild Rice, a medley of wild rice, apple, carrot, celery, and green pepper, tastes delicious warm or cold.

Calico Wild Rice

2 tablespoons raisins
¼ cup hot water
½ cup wild rice, uncooked
3 cups water, divided
Vegetable cooking spray
2 cups chopped apple
¾ cup shredded carrot
¼ cup chopped celery
¼ cup chopped green pepper
1½ teaspoons chicken-flavored bouillon
  granules
¼ teaspoon dried whole sage
⅛ teaspoon pepper
¾ cup converted rice, uncooked
Fresh sage sprig (optional)

Combine raisins and ¼ cup hot water; let stand 5 minutes. Drain and set aside.

Rinse wild rice in 3 changes of hot water; drain. Combine wild rice and 1½ cups water in a medium saucepan. Bring to a boil; cover, reduce heat, and simmer 50 minutes or until rice is tender and liquid is absorbed. Remove from heat, and set aside.

Coat a large nonstick skillet with cooking spray; place over medium-high heat until hot. Add apple and next 3 ingredients; sauté until crisp-tender. Set aside.

Combine remaining 1½ cups water, bouillon granules, sage, and pepper in a large saucepan; bring to a boil. Stir in converted rice. Cover, reduce heat, and simmer 20 minutes or until rice is tender and liquid is absorbed. Remove from heat; stir in reserved raisins, wild rice, and apple mixture. Cover and let stand 5 minutes.

Transfer to a serving bowl. Garnish with a fresh sage sprig, if desired. Yield: 12 servings (91 calories and 4% fat per ½-cup serving).

Protein 2.3 / Fat 0.4 (Saturated Fat 0) / Carbohydrate 20.5
Fiber 1.4 / Cholesterol 0 / Sodium 109

Wild Rice with Artichokes

¼ cup wild rice, uncooked
Vegetable cooking spray
½ cup converted rice, uncooked
1 (9-ounce) package frozen artichoke
   hearts, thawed and chopped
1½ cups sliced fresh mushrooms
⅓ cup chopped onion
1½ teaspoons chicken-flavored bouillon
   granules
1 teaspoon fines herbes
1 clove garlic, minced
1¼ cups water
¾ cup Chablis or other dry white wine

Rinse wild rice in 3 changes of hot water; drain. Coat a large nonstick skillet with cooking spray; place over medium heat until hot. Add wild and converted rice; sauté until rice is lightly browned. Stir in artichoke hearts and remaining ingredients; remove from heat.

Spoon rice mixture into a 1½-quart baking dish coated with cooking spray. Cover and bake at 350° for 1 hour or until rice is tender and liquid is absorbed. Yield: 9 servings (73 calories and 6% fat per ½-cup serving).

Protein 2.6 / Fat 0.5 (Saturated Fat 0.1) / Carbohydrate 15.5
Fiber 0.8 / Cholesterol 0 / Sodium 154

Curried Three-Grain Pilaf

2 cups water
1 teaspoon curry powder
½ teaspoon salt
1 bay leaf
½ cup chopped onion
½ cup chopped celery
½ cup chopped sweet red pepper
¼ cup brown rice, uncooked
¼ cup bulgur, uncooked
¼ cup pearl barley, uncooked
¼ cup chopped fresh parsley

Combine first 4 ingredients in a medium saucepan; bring to a boil. Stir in onion, celery, pepper, and grains. Cover, reduce heat, and simmer 1 hour or until grains are tender and liquid is absorbed.

Remove rice mixture from heat. Remove and discard bay leaf. Add chopped parsley, stirring well to combine. Yield: 6 servings (107 calories and 5% fat per ½-cup serving).

Protein 3.0 / Fat 0.6 (Saturated Fat 0.1) / Carbohydrate 22.7
Fiber 2.9 / Cholesterol 0 / Sodium 210

Spicy Black Beans and Tomatoes

Vegetable cooking spray
1 teaspoon olive oil
½ cup chopped onion
2 cloves garlic, minced
2 (14½-ounce) cans no-salt-added whole
   tomatoes, drained and chopped
2 tablespoons canned chopped green chiles
2 (15-ounce) cans black beans,
   rinsed and drained
1 tablespoon chopped fresh cilantro
½ teaspoon ground cumin
½ teaspoon ground red pepper
¼ teaspoon chili powder

Coat a large nonstick skillet with cooking spray; add oil. Place over medium-high heat until hot. Add chopped onion and garlic; sauté until tender. Add chopped tomato and green chiles; reduce heat, and cook, uncovered, 6 to 8 minutes or until mixture is slightly thickened, stirring occasionally.

Stir in beans and remaining ingredients. Cover and cook 5 minutes or until thoroughly heated. Yield: 8 servings (105 calories and 9% fat per ½-cup serving).

Protein 6.1 / Fat 1.1 (Saturated Fat 0.2) / Carbohydrate 18.8
Fiber 2.8 / Cholesterol 0 / Sodium 187

Mediterranean Linguine

Vegetable cooking spray
1 cup sliced fresh mushrooms
1 medium-size green pepper, seeded and cut into thin strips
1 medium-size sweet red pepper, seeded and cut into thin strips
1 clove garlic, minced
1 (14-ounce) can artichoke hearts, drained and quartered
½ cup commercial reduced-calorie Italian dressing
3 tablespoons sliced, pitted ripe olives
1 tablespoon chopped fresh parsley
6 ounces linguine, uncooked
½ cup (2 ounces) shredded part-skim mozzarella cheese

Coat a large nonstick skillet with cooking spray; place over medium-high heat until hot. Add mushrooms and next 3 ingredients; sauté until vegetables are crisp-tender. Add artichokes, Italian dressing, olives, and parsley; cook 3 minutes or until thoroughly heated, stirring occasionally.

Cook linguine according to package directions, omitting salt and fat; drain well. Combine linguine and vegetable mixture; toss well. Transfer mixture to a serving dish; sprinkle with cheese, and serve immediately. Yield: 11 servings (105 calories and 28% fat per ½-cup serving).

Protein 4.4 / Fat 3.3 (Saturated Fat 0.7) / Carbohydrate 15.7
Fiber 2.5 / Cholesterol 3 / Sodium 189

Mediterranean Linguine, a versatile pasta side dish, adds an international dimension to any menu.

Linguine Florentine

2 pounds fresh spinach
3 cups cooked linguine (cooked without
   salt or fat)
2 teaspoons olive oil
½ cup grated Parmesan cheese
¼ teaspoon pepper
1 tablespoon chopped walnuts, toasted

Remove and discard stems from spinach; wash leaves thoroughly. Place spinach in a large Dutch oven (do not add water); cover and cook over medium heat about 4 minutes or until wilted. Drain spinach well, and squeeze between paper towels until barely moist. Finely chop spinach, and set aside.

Combine linguine and olive oil in a large bowl, tossing gently. Add chopped spinach, cheese, and pepper; toss gently. Transfer mixture to a serving bowl; sprinkle with walnuts. Yield: 6 servings (191 calories and 27% fat per 1-cup serving).

Protein 9.1 / Fat 5.7 (Saturated Fat 2.2) / Carbohydrate 25.7
Fiber 2.6 / Cholesterol 7 / Sodium 199

Siesta Pasta

6 ounces spaghetti, uncooked
Vegetable cooking spray
1 cup fresh broccoli flowerets
1 cup thinly sliced carrot
1 cup sliced zucchini
¼ cup sliced onion
1 small sweet yellow pepper, seeded
   and cut into julienne strips
⅓ cup chopped green pepper
10 cherry tomatoes, halved
2 tablespoons commercial oil-free
   Italian dressing
¼ cup grated Parmesan cheese
1 tablespoon minced fresh parsley
¼ teaspoon sweet red pepper flakes

Cook spaghetti according to package directions, omitting salt and fat. Drain; set aside.

Coat a large nonstick skillet with cooking spray; place over medium-high heat until hot. Add broccoli and next 3 ingredients; sauté 4 minutes. Add yellow pepper and green pepper; sauté 4 minutes. Add spaghetti, tomatoes, and Italian dressing; cook until thoroughly heated, tossing gently to combine.

Transfer to a serving bowl. Sprinkle with cheese, parsley, and pepper flakes; toss gently to combine. Serve immediately. Yield: 8 servings (123 calories and 13% fat per 1-cup serving).

Protein 5.3 / Fat 1.8 (Saturated Fat 0.8) / Carbohydrate 22.0
Fiber 2.2 / Cholesterol 3 / Sodium 119

Vermicelli with Tomato-Basil Sauce

8 ounces vermicelli, uncooked
Vegetable cooking spray
1 medium onion, thinly sliced
2 cloves garlic, minced
5 cups peeled, chopped tomato (about 5
   medium tomatoes)
1 (8-ounce) can no-salt-added tomato sauce
¼ cup minced fresh basil
⅛ teaspoon pepper
2 tablespoons grated Parmesan cheese

Cook vermicelli according to package directions, omitting salt and fat. Drain well, and set aside.

Coat a Dutch oven with cooking spray; place over medium heat until hot. Add onion and garlic; sauté 5 minutes or until onion is tender. Stir in tomato, tomato sauce, basil, and pepper. Bring to a boil; reduce heat, and simmer 15 minutes, stirring occasionally. Add vermicelli; cook, uncovered, until thoroughly heated, stirring occasionally. Transfer mixture to a large platter; sprinkle with Parmesan cheese. Yield: 8 servings (155 calories and 8% fat per 1-cup serving).

Protein 5.8 / Fat 1.4 (Saturated Fat 0.4) / Carbohydrate 30.8
Fiber 2.5 / Cholesterol 1 / Sodium 47

Bow Tie Pasta Primavera

½ pound fresh asparagus spears
1½ cups fresh broccoli flowerets
1 large carrot, scraped and diagonally sliced
1 cup sliced yellow squash
Olive oil-flavored vegetable cooking spray
1 teaspoon olive oil
1 cup sliced fresh mushrooms
½ cup chopped onion
½ cup chopped sweet red pepper
1 clove garlic, minced
8 ounces bow tie pasta, uncooked
1 tablespoon margarine
1 tablespoon all-purpose flour
¾ cup skim milk
¼ cup canned no-salt-added chicken broth,
    undiluted
¼ cup plus 1 tablespoon freshly grated
    Parmesan cheese, divided
1 tablespoon chopped fresh parsley
1 tablespoon chopped fresh basil
¼ teaspoon salt
¼ teaspoon freshly ground pepper

Snap off tough ends of asparagus. Remove scales from stalks with a knife or vegetable peeler, if desired. Cut spears diagonally into 1-inch pieces.

Arrange asparagus, broccoli, and carrot in a vegetable steamer over boiling water. Cover and steam 5 minutes. Add squash; cover and steam an additional 5 minutes or until vegetables are crisp-tender. Set aside.

Coat a large nonstick skillet with cooking spray; add oil. Place over medium heat until hot. Add mushrooms, onion, sweet red pepper, and garlic; sauté 3 to 5 minutes or until vegetables are tender. Set aside.

Cook pasta according to package directions, omitting salt and fat. Drain well, and set aside.

Melt margarine in a small, heavy saucepan over low heat; add flour, stirring until smooth. Cook 1 minute, stirring constantly. Gradually add milk and chicken broth to mixture, stirring constantly. Cook over medium heat, stirring constantly, until thickened and bubbly.

Combine steamed vegetables, mushroom mixture, and pasta in a large bowl. Add sauce, ¼ cup Parmesan cheese, and remaining ingredients; toss well. Transfer to a large serving bowl, and sprinkle with remaining 1 tablespoon Parmesan cheese. Serve warm. Yield: 8 servings (177 calories and 20% fat per 1-cup serving).

Protein 7.8 / Fat 4.0 (Saturated Fat 1.2) / Carbohydrate 28.1
Fiber 2.3 / Cholesterol 3 / Sodium 189

An abundance of color and flavor is yours to enjoy with Spicy Bean Enchiladas (page 154). Each low-fat serving is topped with a zesty tomato sauce, Cheddar cheese, sour cream, and green onions.

Cuban Black Beans and Rice

1 pound dried black beans
Vegetable cooking spray
2 teaspoons olive oil
1 cup chopped onion
½ cup chopped sweet red pepper
½ cup chopped green pepper
5 cloves garlic, minced
5 cups water
1 (6-ounce) can no-salt-added tomato paste
1 (4-ounce) jar diced pimiento, undrained
2 tablespoons seeded, minced jalapeño pepper
1 tablespoon vinegar
1 teaspoon ground cumin
1 teaspoon hot sauce
¾ teaspoon salt
¼ teaspoon pepper
4½ cups cooked long-grain rice (cooked without salt or fat)

Sort and wash beans; place in a Dutch oven. Cover with water to a depth of 2 inches above beans; let soak 8 hours. Drain and rinse beans. Return beans to pan, and set aside.

Coat a large nonstick skillet with cooking spray; add oil. Place skillet over medium-high heat until hot. Add onion, sweet red pepper, green pepper, and garlic; sauté 4 to 5 minutes or until tender.

Add onion mixture, 5 cups water, and next 8 ingredients to beans; bring to a boil. Cover, reduce heat, and simmer 2 hours or until beans are tender, stirring occasionally.

To serve, place ½ cup cooked rice in each individual serving bowl; spoon 1 cup bean mixture over each serving. Yield: 9 servings (342 calories and 6% fat per serving).

Protein 14.9 / Fat 2.3 (Saturated Fat 0.4) / Carbohydrate 67.1
Fiber 7.8 / Cholesterol 0 / Sodium 216

Kidney Bean Casserole

Vegetable cooking spray
¾ cup chopped onion
⅓ cup chopped green pepper
⅓ cup chopped celery
2 large cloves garlic, minced
2 (16-ounce) cans red kidney beans, drained
1 cup peeled, chopped tomato
¼ cup water
½ teaspoon chili powder
¼ teaspoon pepper
3 dashes of hot sauce
2 cups cooked long-grain rice (cooked without salt or fat)
½ cup (2 ounces) shredded reduced-fat sharp Cheddar cheese

Coat a large nonstick skillet with cooking spray; place over medium-high heat until hot. Add onion, green pepper, celery, and garlic; sauté 5 minutes or until tender. Add beans and next 5 ingredients; stir well. Cover and cook 8 to 10 minutes or until thoroughly heated, stirring often.

Spoon rice into bottom of a 1½-quart casserole coated with cooking spray. Spoon bean mixture evenly over rice; sprinkle with cheese. Cover and let stand 5 minutes before serving. Yield: 4 servings (372 calories and 10% fat per serving).

Protein 19.5 / Fat 4.1 (Saturated Fat 1.8) / Carbohydrate 65.1
Fiber 7.0 / Cholesterol 10 / Sodium 127

Packed with a robust mixture of tomatoes, beans, and spices, Chili-Stuffed Baked Potatoes are hearty and satisfying, yet low in fat.

Chili-Stuffed Baked Potatoes

8 (8-ounce) baking potatoes
Vegetable cooking spray
1⅓ cups sliced fresh mushrooms
½ cup chopped onion
⅓ cup chopped green pepper
1 clove garlic, minced
1 (16-ounce) can red kidney beans, drained
   and rinsed
1 (14½-ounce) can no-salt-added stewed
   tomatoes, drained
¼ teaspoon ground cumin
⅛ teaspoon dried whole oregano
⅛ teaspoon ground red pepper
⅛ teaspoon pepper
⅛ teaspoon hot sauce
½ cup (2 ounces) shredded reduced-fat
   Monterey Jack cheese
2 tablespoons sliced green onions
Fresh oregano sprigs (optional)

Scrub potatoes; prick several times with a fork. Bake at 400° for 1 hour or until soft.

Coat a large saucepan with cooking spray; place over medium-high heat until hot. Add mushrooms, onion, green pepper, and garlic; sauté until tender. Stir in beans and next 6 ingredients; cook over medium-low heat just until thoroughly heated, stirring occasionally.

Cut a lengthwise slit in each potato; fluff pulp with a fork. Arrange in a 13- x 9- x 2-inch baking dish. Spoon chili mixture evenly over potatoes, lightly packing mixture into potatoes; sprinkle evenly with cheese. Bake at 400° for 5 to 7 minutes or until cheese melts. Top with green onions. Garnish with fresh oregano sprigs, if desired. Yield: 8 servings (336 calories and 5% fat per serving).

Protein 11.1 / Fat 1.9 (Saturated Fat 0.9) / Carbohydrate 70.4
Fiber 5.8 / Cholesterol 5 / Sodium 132

Three-Cheese Lasagna Rolls arranged over colorful tomato sauce will make an impressive entrée any night of the week.

Cheese Tortellini with Herbed Tomato Sauce

Vegetable cooking spray
½ cup minced onion
½ cup diced celery
½ cup diced carrot
2 cloves garlic, minced
1 (14½-ounce) can no-salt-added whole tomatoes, undrained and finely chopped
2 tablespoons minced fresh oregano
2 tablespoons minced fresh basil
2 (9-ounce) packages fresh cheese tortellini, uncooked
Fresh basil sprigs (optional)

Coat a nonstick skillet with cooking spray; place over medium-high heat until hot. Add onion, celery, carrot, and garlic; sauté 5 minutes or until onion is tender. Add tomato, oregano, and basil; reduce heat, and simmer, uncovered, 20 minutes or until thickened.

Cook tortellini according to package directions, omitting salt and fat; drain well.

For each serving, top ¾ cup tortellini with ⅔ cup sauce. Garnish with basil, if desired. Yield: 6 servings (301 calories and 19% fat per serving).

Protein 14.5 / Fat 6.2 (Saturated Fat 2.0) / Carbohydrate 48.4
Fiber 0.7 / Cholesterol 40 / Sodium 347

Three-Cheese Lasagna Rolls

9 lasagna noodles, uncooked
2 (10-ounce) packages frozen chopped spinach, thawed
Vegetable cooking spray
½ cup chopped onion
½ cup chopped fresh mushrooms
2 cloves garlic, minced
3 tablespoons dry white vermouth
½ cup freshly grated Parmesan cheese
½ cup (2 ounces) shredded part-skim mozzarella cheese
½ cup lite ricotta cheese
½ cup frozen egg substitute, thawed
1 teaspoon dried whole basil
⅛ teaspoon pepper
Chunky Tomato Sauce
Fresh basil sprigs (optional)

Cook noodles according to package directions, omitting salt and fat. Drain well, and set aside. Drain spinach; press between paper towels to remove excess moisture. Set spinach aside.

Coat a large nonstick skillet with cooking spray; place over medium-high heat until hot. Add onion, mushrooms, garlic, and vermouth; sauté until tender. Transfer to a bowl; add spinach, Parmesan cheese, and next 5 ingredients.

Spread spinach mixture evenly over lasagna noodles, leaving a ¼-inch border around edges of each noodle. Roll each noodle up, jellyroll fashion, beginning at narrow end. Arrange rolls, seam side down, in an 11- x 7- x 2-inch baking dish coated with cooking spray. Cover and bake at 350° for 30 minutes or until thoroughly heated.

To serve, cut rolls in half. Spoon ¼ cup Chunky Tomato Sauce on each individual plate, and place 3 rolls on top of sauce. Garnish with fresh basil sprigs, if desired. Yield: 6 servings (280 calories and 18% fat per serving).

Chunky Tomato Sauce

Vegetable cooking spray
¼ cup plus 2 tablespoons finely chopped sweet red pepper
¼ cup plus 2 tablespoons shredded carrot
2 cloves garlic, minced
¾ teaspoon dried whole basil
¼ teaspoon dried marjoram
¼ teaspoon freshly ground pepper
1½ cups no-salt-added tomato sauce
3 tablespoons water

Coat a nonstick skillet with cooking spray; place over medium-high heat until hot. Add sweet red pepper and next 5 ingredients; sauté 5 minutes or until vegetables are tender. Stir in tomato sauce and water; bring to a boil. Cover, reduce heat, and simmer 5 minutes or until mixture is thickened. Yield: 1½ cups.

Protein 17.9 / Fat 5.5 (Saturated Fat 2.8) / Carbohydrate 41.1
Fiber 4.8 / Cholesterol 14 / Sodium 303

Vegetable Lasagna

1 (10-ounce) package frozen chopped
  spinach, thawed
1 (12-ounce) carton 1% low-fat cottage
  cheese
¼ cup frozen egg substitute, thawed
Vegetable cooking spray
1 teaspoon olive oil
¾ cup minced onion
1 cup sliced fresh mushrooms
2 cloves garlic, minced
2 (14½-ounce) cans no-salt-added whole
  tomatoes, drained and chopped
¼ cup minced fresh parsley
¼ cup no-salt-added tomato paste
3 tablespoons Burgundy or other dry
  red wine
2 teaspoons dried whole basil
1½ teaspoons dried whole oregano
1 teaspoon brown sugar
½ teaspoon pepper
6 lasagna noodles, uncooked and divided
3 cups shredded zucchini, divided
1¼ cups (5 ounces) finely shredded part-
  skim mozzarella cheese, divided
2 tablespoons grated Parmesan cheese

Drain spinach; press between paper towels
to remove excess moisture. Combine spinach,
cottage cheese, and egg substitute in a medium
bowl; stir well, and set aside.

Coat a large nonaluminum saucepan with
cooking spray; add oil. Place over medium-high
heat until hot. Add onion; sauté 3 minutes.
Add mushrooms and garlic; sauté 2 minutes or
until mushrooms are tender. Stir in tomato and
next 7 ingredients. Reduce heat, and simmer,
uncovered, 20 minutes, or until thickened,
stirring occasionally.

Spoon one-third of tomato mixture into an
11- x 7- x 2-inch baking dish coated with
cooking spray. Arrange 3 noodles lengthwise in
a single layer over tomato mixture; top with 1
cup spinach mixture. Layer 1½ cups zucchini
over spinach mixture, and sprinkle with ½ cup
mozzarella cheese. Repeat layers; top with
remaining tomato mixture. Cover and refrigerate
8 hours.

Bake, covered, at 350° for 1½ hours or until
thoroughly heated. Sprinkle with remaining ¼
cup mozzarella cheese and Parmesan cheese.
Bake, uncovered, an additional 5 minutes or
until cheeses melt. Let stand 5 minutes before
serving. Yield: 6 servings (283 calories and 21%
fat per serving).

Protein 22.3 / Fat 6.7 (Saturated Fat 3.3) / Carbohydrate 35.7
Fiber 3.6 / Cholesterol 17 / Sodium 446

Spinach-Ricotta Stuffed Shells

Vegetable cooking spray
1 cup chopped onion
7 cups chopped fresh spinach
1 cup minced cabbage
2 tablespoons Chablis or other dry
  white wine
⅔ cup lite ricotta cheese
2 tablespoons minced fresh parsley
⅛ teaspoon pepper
15 cooked jumbo macaroni shells (cooked
  without salt or fat)
1 (10½-ounce) can low-sodium chicken
  broth, undiluted
1 (6-ounce) can no-salt-added tomato paste
¼ teaspoon salt
¼ teaspoon ground nutmeg
⅛ teaspoon pepper

Coat a Dutch oven with cooking spray;
place over medium-high heat until hot. Add
onion; sauté until tender. Add spinach,
cabbage, and wine; sauté 4 minutes. Stir in
ricotta cheese, parsley, and ⅛ teaspoon pepper;
cook an additional 2 minutes, stirring frequently.

Spoon 2½ tablespoons spinach mixture into
each macaroni shell. Arrange shells in an 11- x
7- x 2-inch baking dish coated with cooking
spray; set aside.

Combine broth and remaining ingredients
in a small bowl, stirring well; spoon sauce over
shells. Cover and bake at 350° for 30 minutes
or until thoroughly heated. Yield: 5 servings
(246 calories and 12% fat per serving).

Protein 14.2 / Fat 3.4 (Saturated Fat 0.2) / Carbohydrate 40
Fiber 4.1 / Cholesterol 10.7 / Sodium 224

Italian Zucchini Casserole

2 pounds zucchini, thinly sliced lengthwise
Vegetable cooking spray
1 cup 1% low-fat cottage cheese
½ cup frozen egg substitute, thawed
¼ cup grated Parmesan cheese, divided
2 tablespoons skim milk
½ teaspoon pepper
¾ cup (3 ounces) shredded part-skim
  mozzarella cheese, divided
1 (14½-ounce) can no-salt-added whole
  tomatoes, undrained and chopped
¼ cup chopped green onions
1 clove garlic, minced
½ teaspoon dried whole basil

Arrange zucchini on rack of a broiler pan coated with cooking spray. Broil 3 inches from heat until browned, turning after 2 minutes.

Combine cottage cheese, egg substitute, 2 tablespoons Parmesan cheese, milk, and pepper in container of an electric blender; top with cover, and process until smooth.

Arrange one-third of zucchini in bottom of an 11- x 7- x 2-inch baking dish coated with cooking spray. Top with half of cottage cheese mixture and ½ cup mozzarella cheese.

Top with half of remaining zucchini, remaining cottage cheese mixture, and remaining ¼ cup mozzarella cheese. Arrange remaining zucchini over layers, and sprinkle with remaining 2 tablespoons Parmesan cheese. Bake at 375° for 30 minutes or until mixture is set and top is golden.

Combine tomato, green onions, garlic, and basil in a small saucepan; bring to a boil. Reduce heat, and simmer, uncovered, 10 minutes. Serve sauce with casserole. Yield: 6 servings (129 calories and 29% fat per serving).

Protein 14.1 / Fat 4.1 (Saturated Fat 2.4) / Carbohydrate 10.2
Fiber 0.9 / Cholesterol 12 / Sodium 328

Broccoli-Cheese Calzones

1 package dry yeast
1 cup warm water (105° to 115°), divided
¼ cup honey
¼ cup margarine, melted
¼ cup frozen egg substitute, thawed
2½ cups all-purpose flour, divided
1½ cups whole wheat flour
¾ teaspoon salt
2 tablespoons whole wheat flour
Vegetable cooking spray
Broccoli-Cheese Filling

Dissolve yeast in ¼ cup warm water in a large bowl; let stand 5 minutes. Combine remaining ¾ cup warm water, honey, margarine, and egg substitute; add to yeast mixture. Stir in 1 cup all-purpose flour, 1½ cups whole wheat flour, and salt. Stir in enough of the remaining 1½ cups all-purpose flour to make a soft dough.

Sprinkle remaining 2 tablespoons whole wheat flour over work surface. Turn dough out onto floured surface; knead until smooth and elastic (about 8 to 10 minutes). Place dough in a bowl coated with cooking spray; turn to coat top. Cover and let rise in a warm place (85°), free from drafts, 1 hour or until doubled in bulk.

Punch dough down; divide into 10 equal portions. Roll each portion into a 6-inch circle. Spoon ⅓ cup Broccoli-Cheese Filling onto half of each circle, leaving a ½-inch border. Moisten edges; fold plain halves over filling. Crimp edges to seal. Place on baking sheets coated with cooking spray. Bake at 400° for 15 minutes or until golden. Yield: 10 servings (312 calories and 25% fat per serving).

Broccoli-Cheese Filling

1 (10-ounce) package frozen chopped
  broccoli, thawed
1 (15-ounce) carton lite ricotta cheese
½ cup (2 ounces) shredded part-skim
  mozzarella cheese
¼ cup grated Parmesan cheese
½ teaspoon dried whole oregano

Cook broccoli according to package directions, omitting salt and fat. Drain; press between paper towels. Combine broccoli and remaining ingredients; stir well. Yield: 3⅓ cups.

Protein 14.1 / Fat 8.5 (Saturated Fat 2.9) / Carbohydrate 46
Fiber 4.2 / Cholesterol 12.4 / Sodium 341

Chile-Cheese Casserole

1½ cups lite ricotta cheese
1 cup (4 ounces) shredded reduced-fat
    Monterey Jack cheese
1 (4-ounce) can chopped green chiles,
    drained
½ cup frozen egg substitute, thawed
¼ cup chopped green onions
4 (6-inch) corn tortillas
Vegetable cooking spray
¼ cup chopped green pepper
1 clove garlic, minced
2 (16-ounce) cans red kidney beans,
    drained
1 (14½-ounce) can no-salt-added whole
    tomatoes, undrained and chopped
1 (8-ounce) can no-salt-added tomato
    sauce
2 teaspoons chili powder
½ cup (2 ounces) shredded reduced-fat
    sharp Cheddar cheese
2 tablespoons chopped green onions

Combine first 5 ingredients in a medium
bowl; stir well, and set aside.

Cut each tortilla into 8 wedges; place on an
ungreased baking sheet. Bake at 350° for 10
minutes or until crisp. Set aside.

Coat a nonstick skillet with cooking spray;
place over medium-high heat until hot. Add
green pepper and garlic; sauté until tender. Stir
in beans, tomato, tomato sauce, and chili
powder; bring to a boil. Reduce heat; simmer,
uncovered, 15 minutes, stirring occasionally.

Spread half of cheese mixture in a
2-quart casserole coated with cooking spray;
arrange 8 tortilla wedges over cheese mixture.
Spread half of bean mixture evenly over wedges.
Repeat layers with remaining cheese mixture, 8
tortilla wedges, and remaining bean mixture.

Cover and bake at 350° for 30 minutes or
until thoroughly heated. Sprinkle with
Cheddar cheese; bake, uncovered, an additional
5 minutes or until cheese melts. Top with 2
tablespoons green onions. Serve with remaining
tortilla wedges. Yield: 8 servings (259 calories and
24% fat per serving).

Protein 20.5 / Fat 6.8 (Saturated Fat 3.5) / Carbohydrate 30.5
Fiber 3.8 / Cholesterol 22 / Sodium 359

Corn Frittata

Vegetable cooking spray
1¼ cups fresh corn cut from cob (about 3 ears)
¼ cup chopped green onions
1½ cups frozen egg substitute, thawed
⅓ cup skim milk
1½ teaspoons minced fresh basil
⅛ teaspoon salt
⅛ teaspoon pepper
2 small tomatoes, cut into 12 wedges
1 cup (4 ounces) shredded reduced-fat
    Cheddar cheese
Fresh basil sprigs (optional)

Coat a medium nonstick skillet with
cooking spray; place over medium-high heat

until hot. Add corn and green onions; sauté
until tender. Combine egg substitute and next 4
ingredients; stir well.

Pour egg mixture over vegetables in skillet.
Cover and cook over medium-low heat 15
minutes or until mixture is almost set.

Arrange tomato wedges near center of egg
mixture, and sprinkle with Cheddar cheese.
Cover and cook an additional 5 minutes or
until cheese melts. Cut frittata into 6 wedges.
Garnish with fresh basil sprigs, if desired. Serve
immediately. Yield: 6 servings (133 calories and
29% fat per serving).

Protein 13.7 / Fat 4.3 (Saturated Fat 2.2) / Carbohydrate 11.2
Fiber 1.9 / Cholesterol 12 / Sodium 295

*Corn Frittata showcases summer vegetables
in a cheesy, no-fuss dish that is surprisingly
low in calories.*

Artichoke-Cheddar Strata

Vegetable cooking spray
1 teaspoon margarine
½ cup chopped green onions
3 slices whole wheat bread, cubed
¾ cup (3 ounces) shredded reduced-fat
    Cheddar cheese
1 (14-ounce) can artichoke hearts, drained
    and quartered
1 (4-ounce) jar sliced pimientos, drained
¾ cup frozen egg substitute, thawed
1 (12-ounce) can evaporated skimmed milk
½ teaspoon dry mustard
⅛ teaspoon ground red pepper

    Coat a small nonstick skillet with cooking spray; add margarine. Place over medium heat until margarine melts. Add chopped green onions; sauté 3 to 4 minutes or until tender. Remove from heat, and set aside.

    Arrange half of bread cubes in a 9-inch quiche dish coated with cooking spray. Top with half of cheese, half of artichokes, half of green onions, and half of pimiento. Repeat layers with remaining bread cubes, cheese, artichokes, green onions, and pimiento.

    Combine egg substitute and remaining ingredients; stir well. Pour over mixture in quiche dish. Cover and chill at least 3 hours.

    Let stand at room temperature 30 minutes. Bake, uncovered, at 350° for 1 hour or until set. Yield: 6 servings (179 calories and 22% fat per serving).

Protein 15.0 / Fat 4.3 (Saturated Fat 1.9) / Carbohydrate 21.4
Fiber 1.2 / Cholesterol 12 / Sodium 445

Open-Faced Breakfast Sandwiches

Vegetable cooking spray
½ cup sliced fresh mushrooms
2 tablespoons chopped green pepper
1½ cups frozen egg substitute, thawed
2 tablespoons skim milk
¼ teaspoon onion powder
⅛ teaspoon salt
8 tomato slices (½ inch thick)
4 (2-ounce) English muffins, split
    and toasted
1 cup (4 ounces) shredded reduced-fat
    sharp Cheddar cheese
⅛ teaspoon pepper

    Coat a medium nonstick skillet with cooking spray; place over medium-high heat until hot. Add mushrooms and green pepper; sauté until tender.

    Combine egg substitute and next 3 ingredients; stir well. Pour over mixture in skillet; cook over medium heat, stirring frequently, until egg substitute is firm but still moist. Remove from heat.

    Place a tomato slice on each muffin half; top each with 2 tablespoons egg mixture and 2 tablespoons cheese. Sprinkle with pepper.

    Place muffin halves on a baking sheet. Broil 5½ inches from heat 1 minute or until cheese melts. Yield: 8 servings (166 calories and 20% fat per serving).

Protein 11.9 / Fat 3.6 (Saturated Fat 1.8) / Carbohydrate 21.3
Fiber 0.7 / Cholesterol 10 / Sodium 379

The distinctive flavor and dramatic presentation of Garlic-Ginger Crown Roast of Pork (page 175) will make it the star of your next dinner party.

Beef Tenderloin in Phyllo Bundles

Vegetable cooking spray
1 cup chopped zucchini
1 cup chopped mushrooms
½ cup chopped onion
1 clove garlic, minced
¼ teaspoon salt
8 (4-ounce) beef tenderloin steaks
2 tablespoons cracked pepper
16 sheets commercial frozen phyllo pastry,
   thawed

Coat a large nonstick skillet with cooking spray; place over medium-high heat until hot. Add zucchini and next 4 ingredients; sauté until vegetables are tender. Remove zucchini mixture from skillet, and set aside.

Sprinkle both sides of each steak with pepper. Coat skillet with cooking spray; place over high heat until hot. Add steaks, and cook 1½ to 2 minutes on each side or until lightly browned. Remove steaks from skillet; drain and pat dry with paper towels. Set aside.

Place 1 sheet of phyllo pastry on wax paper (keep remaining phyllo covered). Coat phyllo with cooking spray. Fold phyllo in half lengthwise; place 1 steak 3 inches from one end. Spoon 2 tablespoons zucchini mixture over steak; fold narrow end of phyllo over stuffing. Fold sides of phyllo over steak; roll up.

Place a second sheet of phyllo on wax paper; cut to a 12-inch square, and coat with cooking spray. Place wrapped steak, stuffing side up, in center of phyllo square. Bring ends to the middle, gently pressing together in center; pull ends up and out to resemble a package.

Coat bundle with cooking spray, and place on an ungreased baking sheet. Repeat procedure with remaining phyllo pastry, steaks, and zucchini mixture.

Bake at 375° for 15 minutes for rare or to desired degree of doneness. Yield: 8 servings (313 calories and 25% fat per serving).

Protein 28.4 / Fat 8.7 (Saturated Fat 3.1) / Carbohydrate 29.3
Fiber 0.8 / Cholesterol 70 / Sodium 137

Herbed Pot Roast

1 (4½-pound) lean boneless rump roast
½ cup Burgundy or other dry red wine
½ cup no-salt-added tomato sauce
¼ cup vinegar
1 tablespoon spicy hot mustard
1 teaspoon dried whole thyme
¼ teaspoon dried whole oregano
¼ teaspoon ground red pepper
2 shallots, minced
1 bay leaf

Trim fat from roast; place in a large zip-top heavy-duty plastic bag. Combine wine and next 7 ingredients in a small bowl, stirring well. Pour mixture over roast; add bay leaf. Seal bag, and marinate in refrigerator up to 8 hours, turning occasionally.

Transfer roast, marinade, and bay leaf to a Dutch oven. Cover and bake at 350° for 2½ hours or until roast is tender.

Transfer roast to a serving platter; let stand 10 minutes before slicing. Discard marinade and bay leaf. Yield: 15 servings (188 calories and 26% fat per serving).

Protein 31.2 / Fat 5.5 (Saturated Fat 2.0) / Carbohydrate 1.2
Fiber 0 / Cholesterol 78 / Sodium 83

Team hearty Roast Beef and Swiss Sandwiches with Rosemary-Roasted Potato Wedges (page 239) for a casual Sunday supper.

Roast Beef and Swiss Sandwiches

¼ cup commercial oil-free Italian
    dressing
2 tablespoons water
½ teaspoon beef-flavored bouillon
    granules
1 small green pepper, seeded and cut
    into rings
1 small sweet yellow pepper, seeded and
    cut into rings
1 medium onion, thinly sliced and
    separated into rings
2 teaspoons cornstarch
½ cup water
2 teaspoons low-sodium Worcestershire
    sauce
12 (¾-ounce) slices reduced-calorie
    Italian bread, toasted and divided
¾ pound thinly sliced cooked roast beef
6 tomato slices
6 (½-ounce) slices reduced-fat Swiss cheese

Combine first 3 ingredients in a large nonstick skillet; bring to a boil. Add pepper rings and onion rings. Cover, reduce heat, and simmer 5 minutes or until vegetables are tender, stirring occasionally.

Combine cornstarch, water, and Worcestershire sauce; stir well. Add to pepper mixture; bring to a boil. Cook, stirring frequently, until thickened.

Place 6 bread slices on a large baking sheet, and top bread slices evenly with roast beef. Spoon pepper mixture evenly over beef. Top each sandwich with 1 tomato slice and 1 cheese slice.

Broil 5½ inches from heat 2 to 3 minutes or until cheese melts. Top with remaining bread slices. Serve immediately. Yield: 6 servings (266 calories and 21% fat per serving).

Protein 27.6 / Fat 6.3 (Saturated Fat 2.7) / Carbohydrate 26.0
Fiber 1.4 / Cholesterol 56 / Sodium 434

Smothered Steak and Onions

4 (4-ounce) lean, cubed sirloin steaks
½ teaspoon salt-free lemon-herb seasoning
Vegetable cooking spray
1 medium onion, sliced and separated
    into rings
1 teaspoon beef-flavored bouillon granules
1 cup hot water
1 tablespoon cornstarch
¼ cup water
2 cups cooked long-grain rice (cooked
    without salt or fat)
Fresh parsley sprigs (optional)

Sprinkle steak with lemon-herb seasoning. Coat a large nonstick skillet with cooking spray; place over medium heat until hot. Add steak, and cook 2 minutes on each side to sear. Arrange onion rings over steak.

Combine bouillon granules and hot water, stirring well; add to skillet. Bring to a boil; cover, reduce heat, and simmer 12 to 15 minutes or until onion is tender. Remove steak and onion from skillet; keep warm.

Combine cornstarch and ¼ cup water; add to mixture in skillet. Cook over medium heat, stirring constantly, until thickened and bubbly. Serve steak and gravy over rice. Garnish with fresh parsley sprigs, if desired. Yield: 4 servings (305 calories and 19% fat per serving).

Protein 27.1 / Fat 6.4 (Saturated Fat 2.2) / Carbohydrate 32.0
Fiber 1.1 / Cholesterol 69 / Sodium 317

Grilled Beef Kabobs

1 (1½-pound) lean boneless beef
    sirloin steak
½ cup commercial reduced-calorie
    Italian dressing
¼ cup Burgundy or other dry red wine
12 boiling onions
12 large mushrooms
2 large sweet red peppers, seeded and cut
    into 1½-inch pieces
2 medium zucchini, cut into 1-inch pieces
Vegetable cooking spray

Trim fat from steak; cut into 1-inch pieces, and place in a zip-top heavy-duty plastic bag.

Combine Italian dressing and wine; pour over steak. Seal bag, and marinate in refrigerator 8 hours, turning bag occasionally.

Cook onions in boiling water to cover 3 minutes; drain well, and set aside.

Remove steak from marinade. Place marinade in a small saucepan; bring to a boil. Reduce heat, and simmer 5 minutes. Set aside.

Thread steak, onions, mushrooms, peppers, and zucchini alternately on 12 (12-inch) skewers. Coat grill rack with cooking spray, and place on grill over medium-hot coals. Place kabobs on rack, and cook 12 minutes or to desired degree of doneness, turning and basting frequently with marinade. Yield: 6 servings (294 calories and 26% fat per serving).

Protein 30.8 / Fat 8.5 (Saturated Fat 3.3) / Carbohydrate 23.9
Fiber 2.1 / Cholesterol 80 / Sodium 301

Beef Stroganoff

1 (1-pound) lean boneless beef sirloin steak
Vegetable cooking spray
2 cups sliced fresh mushrooms
1 cup chopped onion
1½ tablespoons reduced-calorie margarine
1½ tablespoons all-purpose flour
1 cup water
1 teaspoon beef-flavored bouillon granules
½ cup plain nonfat yogurt
¼ cup low-fat sour cream
¼ cup Burgundy or other dry red wine
¼ teaspoon salt
¾ teaspoon pepper
3 cups cooked medium noodles made
    without egg yolks (cooked without
    salt or fat)

Trim fat from steak; cut into thin strips. Coat a Dutch oven with cooking spray; place over medium-high heat until hot. Add steak, mushrooms, and onion; sauté 10 minutes or until steak is browned and vegetables are tender. Remove from heat; drain and pat dry with paper towels.

Melt margarine in a heavy saucepan over low heat; add flour, stirring until smooth. Cook 1 minute, stirring constantly. Gradually add water and bouillon granules; cook over medium heat until thickened and bubbly, stirring constantly.

Combine yogurt (at room temperature) and next 4 ingredients, stirring well; add yogurt mixture and steak mixture to skillet. Cook over low heat 5 minutes or until thoroughly heated, stirring frequently. (Do not boil.) Serve steak mixture over cooked noodles. Yield: 6 servings (305 calories and 30% fat per serving).

Protein 26.2 / Fat 10.2 (Saturated Fat 3.4) / Carbohydrate 26.7
Fiber 0.9 / Cholesterol 62 / Sodium 374

Beef Teriyaki

1 (1½-pound) lean boneless beef sirloin
   steak
¼ cup water
¼ cup low-sodium soy sauce
2 tablespoons molasses
½ teaspoon ground ginger
2 cloves garlic, minced
Vegetable cooking spray
1 teaspoon vegetable oil
1 medium-size sweet red pepper, seeded
   and cut into strips
1 medium-size green pepper, seeded and
   cut into strips
½ cup sliced onion
1 cup sliced fresh mushrooms
1½ teaspoons cornstarch
4 cups cooked long-grain rice (cooked
   without salt or fat)

Partially freeze steak; trim fat from steak. Slice steak diagonally across grain into ¼-inch strips. Combine water and next 4 ingredients in a shallow dish; add steak to soy sauce mixture. Cover and marinate in refrigerator at least 1 hour. Drain, reserving marinade.

Coat a wok or large nonstick skillet with cooking spray; add oil. Place over medium-high heat (375°) until hot. Add steak, peppers, and onion; stir-fry 5 minutes. Add mushrooms, and stir-fry 5 minutes.

Combine cornstarch and reserved marinade, stirring well; add to steak mixture. Cook, stirring constantly, until mixture is thickened and thoroughly heated. Serve steak mixture over cooked rice. Yield: 8 servings (285 calories and 17% fat per serving).

Protein 21.5 / Fat 5.4 (Saturated Fat 1.8) / Carbohydrate 35.3
Fiber 1.5 / Cholesterol 52 / Sodium 249

Gingered Beef and Asparagus Stir-Fry

1 pound lean boneless top round
   steak
3 tablespoons dry sherry
2 tablespoons low-sodium soy
   sauce
1 teaspoon peeled, minced gingerroot
2 cloves garlic, minced
¾ pound fresh asparagus spears
Vegetable cooking spray
2 teaspoons vegetable oil, divided
1 small carrot, scraped and cut into
   julienne strips
1 celery stalk, cut into julienne strips
½ small onion, sliced and separated
   into rings
1½ teaspoons cornstarch
2 cups cooked long-grain rice (cooked
   without salt or fat)

Partially freeze steak; trim fat from steak. Slice steak diagonally across grain into ¼-inch strips. Combine steak and next 4 ingredients in a large shallow dish, stirring well. Cover and marinate in refrigerator 2 to 4 hours, stirring occasionally.

Remove steak from marinade, reserving marinade. Set aside.

Snap off tough ends of asparagus. Remove scales from stalks with a knife or vegetable peeler, if desired. Cut spears into 1-inch pieces, and set aside.

Coat a wok or large nonstick skillet with vegetable cooking spray; add 1 teaspoon oil. Place over high heat (400°) until hot. Add asparagus, carrot, celery, and onion; stir-fry 3 minutes. Remove vegetables from wok, and set aside.

Add remaining 1 teaspoon oil to wok, and place over high heat until hot. Add steak; stir-fry 2 minutes.

Combine cornstarch and reserved marinade, stirring well. Add marinade mixture and vegetables to wok; cook 1 minute or until mixture is thickened and thoroughly heated. Serve beef mixture over rice. Yield: 4 servings (337 calories and 20% fat per serving).

Protein 30.9 / Fat 7.4 (Saturated Fat 2.2) / Carbohydrate 34.4
Fiber 2.4 / Cholesterol 65 / Sodium 275

Beef Fajitas with Chunky Guacamole

1½ pounds lean boneless round steak
2 tablespoons lime juice
½ teaspoon salt
⅛ teaspoon pepper
4 cloves garlic, minced
½ cup chopped fresh cilantro
½ cup chopped tomato
¼ cup chopped onion
12 (6-inch) flour tortillas
Vegetable cooking spray
1½ cups shredded iceberg lettuce
Chunky Guacamole
¾ cup nonfat sour cream

Partially freeze steak; trim fat from steak. Slice steak diagonally across grain into ¼-inch strips. Combine steak and next 4 ingredients in a shallow dish; cover and marinate steak in refrigerator 6 to 8 hours, stirring occasionally.

Combine cilantro, tomato, and onion in a small bowl; stir well. Cover mixture, and chill at least 1 hour.

Wrap tortillas in aluminum foil. Bake at 325° for 15 minutes. Coat a large nonstick skillet with cooking spray; place over medium-high heat until hot. Add steak; cook 5 to 6 minutes or until steak is browned, stirring frequently. Remove steak from skillet using a slotted spoon, and divide evenly among tortillas; roll up tortillas.

To serve, arrange fajitas on a serving platter; top evenly with lettuce, tomato mixture, and Chunky Guacamole. Top each serving with 1 tablespoon sour cream. Yield: 12 servings (225 calories and 27% fat per serving).

Chunky Guacamole

¼ cup plus 1 tablespoon finely chopped tomato
1 tablespoon chopped green onion
½ small jalapeño pepper, seeded and finely chopped
1 clove garlic, minced
½ teaspoon lime juice
⅛ teaspoon salt
½ medium avocado, peeled and cut into ½-inch cubes

Combine first 6 ingredients in a small bowl; stir well. Add avocado, and toss gently. Serve immediately. Yield: ¾ cup.

Protein 16.4 / Fat 6.8 (Saturated Fat 2.0) / Carbohydrate 25.8
Fiber 1.5 / Cholesterol 36 / Sodium 165

Marinated Flank Steak

1 (1½-pound) lean flank steak
½ cup sliced green onions
1 tablespoon sugar
2 tablespoons peeled, grated gingerroot
2 tablespoons low-sodium soy sauce
2 tablespoons dry sherry
2 cloves garlic, minced
Vegetable cooking spray

Trim fat from steak. Score steak on both sides. Combine green onions and next 5 ingredients in a shallow dish; add steak, turning to coat with marinade. Cover and marinate in refrigerator 8 hours; turn occasionally.

Remove steak from marinade, and scrape off seasonings. Discard marinade. Place steak on rack of a broiler pan coated with cooking spray. Broil 5½ inches from heat 5 to 7 minutes on each side or to desired degree of doneness.

Slice steak diagonally across grain into ¼-inch slices. Yield: 6 servings (204 calories and 53% fat per serving).

Protein 20.4 / Fat 12.1 (Saturated Fat 5.1) / Carbohydrate 1.5
Fiber 0 / Cholesterol 56 / Sodium 154

Topped with fresh vegetables and nonfat sour cream, each serving of Beef Fajitas with Chunky Guacamole is lower in sodium and fat than its traditional counterpart.

Pork Medaillons
With Sweet Peppers

¼ cup all-purpose flour
¼ teaspoon dried whole basil
⅛ teaspoon salt
⅛ teaspoon pepper
1 pound pork medaillons
Vegetable cooking spray
1 teaspoon vegetable oil
1 small sweet red pepper, seeded and cut
  into julienne strips
1 small sweet yellow pepper, seeded and cut
  into julienne strips
1 small green pepper, seeded and cut into
  julienne strips
2 teaspoons minced shallot
3 tablespoons dry white vermouth
3 tablespoons water
¼ teaspoon chicken-flavored bouillon
  granules
1 teaspoon cornstarch
½ teaspoon dried whole sage
Fresh basil sprigs (optional)

Combine first 4 ingredients in a small bowl; stir well. Dredge pork medaillons in flour mixture.

Coat a large nonstick skillet with vegetable cooking spray; add oil. Place over medium-high heat until hot. Add medaillons; cook 4 to 5 minutes on each side or until done. Remove medaillons from skillet. Drain and pat dry with paper towels; set medaillons aside, and keep warm. Wipe drippings from skillet with a paper towel.

Coat skillet with cooking spray; place over medium-high heat until hot. Add peppers and shallot; sauté 5 to 7 minutes or until peppers are crisp-tender.

Combine vermouth, water, bouillon granules, cornstarch, and sage, stirring well; add to skillet. Bring to a boil; reduce heat, and cook until thickened, stirring constantly.

Spoon pepper mixture onto a large serving platter; arrange medaillons over peppers. Garnish with fresh basil sprigs, if desired. Yield: 4 servings (217 calories and 26% fat per serving).

Protein 27.3 / Fat 6.3 (Saturated Fat 1.8) / Carbohydrate 11.6
Fiber 1.6 / Cholesterol 83 / Sodium 218

Sweet-and-Sour Pork

1½ pounds lean boneless pork loin
Vegetable cooking spray
1 (8-ounce) can no-salt-added tomato sauce
¼ cup cider vinegar
2 tablespoons brown sugar
2 teaspoons low-sodium soy sauce
⅛ teaspoon garlic powder
⅛ teaspoon pepper
1 (20-ounce) can pineapple chunks in juice,
  undrained
1 medium-size green pepper, seeded and cut
  into 1-inch pieces
1 small onion, thinly sliced
2 tablespoons cornstarch
3 cups cooked long-grain rice (cooked
  without salt or fat)

Trim fat from pork; cut into ½-inch pieces. Coat a large nonstick skillet with cooking spray; place over medium-high heat until hot. Add pork; cook 10 minutes or until browned, stirring frequently. Remove pork from skillet; drain and pat dry with paper towels. Wipe drippings from skillet with a paper towel.

Combine pork, tomato sauce, and next 5 ingredients in skillet; bring to a boil. Cover, reduce heat, and simmer 15 to 20 minutes or until pork is tender.

Drain pineapple, reserving juice; add enough water to juice to equal 1 cup. Set aside. Add pineapple, green pepper, and onion to skillet; cover and simmer 5 to 7 minutes or until vegetables are crisp-tender.

Combine cornstarch and reserved pineapple juice mixture; stir into pork mixture. Cook, stirring constantly, until thickened and bubbly. Serve pork mixture over rice. Yield: 6 servings (411 calories and 25% fat per serving).

Protein 26.7 / Fat 11.2 (Saturated Fat 3.0) / Carbohydrate 48.7
Fiber 1.0 / Cholesterol 74 / Sodium 114

Serve Sweet-and-Sour Pork on a bed of rice for a filling one-dish meal that will please the entire family.

Oven-Fried Pork Chops

4 (6-ounce) lean center-cut loin pork chops
1 egg white, lightly beaten
2 tablespoons unsweetened pineapple juice
1 tablespoon low-sodium soy sauce
¼ teaspoon ground ginger
⅛ teaspoon garlic powder
⅓ cup fine, dry breadcrumbs
¼ teaspoon Italian seasoning
¼ teaspoon paprika
Dash of garlic powder
Vegetable cooking spray

Trim fat from pork chops, and set aside. Combine egg white and next 4 ingredients; stir well. Combine breadcrumbs, Italian seasoning, paprika, and dash of garlic powder; stir well. Dip chops in egg white mixture; dredge in breadcrumb mixture.

Place chops on a rack in a roasting pan coated with cooking spray. Bake chops at 350° for 25 minutes; turn and bake an additional 25 minutes or until tender. Yield: 4 servings (227 calories and 35% fat per serving).

Protein 27 / Fat 8.8 (Saturated Fat 2.7) / Carbohydrate 7.6
Fiber 0.4 / Cholesterol 72 / Sodium 248

Sesame Pork Sandwiches

2 (4-ounce) lean boneless center-cut loin
    pork chops
1 clove garlic, minced
1 teaspoon sesame seeds
Vegetable cooking spray
1 cup sliced fresh mushrooms
½ cup thinly sliced onion
2 tablespoons commercial chutney
2 teaspoons Dijon mustard
1 whole wheat English muffin, split and
    toasted

Trim fat from chops. Place chops between 2 sheets of heavy-duty plastic wrap, and flatten to ¼-inch thickness using a meat mallet or rolling pin. Rub garlic over both sides of chops; sprinkle both sides evenly with sesame seeds.

Coat a medium nonstick skillet with cooking spray; place over medium heat until hot. Add chops, and cook 4 minutes on each side or until done. Remove chops from skillet;

drain and pat dry with paper towels. Set aside, and keep warm. Wipe drippings from skillet with a paper towel.

Coat skillet with cooking spray; place over medium-high heat until hot. Add mushrooms and onion; sauté until tender. Stir in chutney and mustard; cook just until thoroughly heated.

Place one chop on each muffin half; top evenly with mushroom mixture. Serve immediately. Yield: 2 servings (386 calories and 32% fat per serving).

Protein 29.0 / Fat 13.9 (Saturated Fat 3.3) / Carbohydrate 35.5
Fiber 1.6 / Cholesterol 77 / Sodium 412

Honey-Glazed Ham Slices

¼ cup firmly packed brown sugar
¼ cup honey
¼ teaspoon dry mustard
3 whole cloves
4 (3-ounce) slices lean, lower-salt cooked
    ham (about ¼ inch thick)
Vegetable cooking spray
4 slices canned pineapple in juice, drained

Combine first 4 ingredients in a small saucepan; stir well. Bring to a boil over medium heat; boil 2 minutes, stirring brown sugar mixture occasionally. Remove and discard cloves, using a slotted spoon.

Arrange ham slices in an 11- x 7- x 2-inch baking dish coated with cooking spray. Place 1 pineapple slice on each ham slice; spoon brown sugar mixture evenly over pineapple slices. Bake at 325° for 15 minutes or until thoroughly heated. Yield: 4 servings (242 calories and 16% fat per serving).

Protein 15.4 / Fat 4.4 (Saturated Fat 1.4) / Carbohydrate 37.4
Fiber 0 / Cholesterol 42 / Sodium 667

Guests will be delighted when you serve Cornish Hens with Cranberry-Orange Sauce (page 190). Lemon Baby Carrots (page 235) and a dinner roll round out the menu.

Chicken and Vegetable Pot Pies

3 (6-ounce) skinned chicken breast halves
2½ cups water
2 medium baking potatoes, peeled and cut
  into ½-inch cubes
½ cup chopped celery
1 teaspoon chicken-flavored bouillon
  granules
1 (10-ounce) package frozen mixed
  vegetables
2 tablespoons unsalted margarine
2 tablespoons all-purpose flour
1 cup skim milk
1 teaspoon poultry seasoning
1 (4-ounce) can sliced mushrooms, drained
Vegetable cooking spray
1 cup all-purpose flour
1 teaspoon baking powder
¼ teaspoon salt
1½ tablespoons unsalted margarine
½ cup nonfat buttermilk
Celery leaves (optional)

Combine chicken and water in a large saucepan. Bring to a boil; cover, reduce heat, and simmer 30 minutes or until chicken is tender. Remove chicken from broth. Bone chicken, and cut into bite-size pieces; set aside. Skim and discard fat from broth.

Add potato, chopped celery, and bouillon granules to broth. Bring to a boil; cover, reduce heat, and simmer 15 to 20 minutes or until potato is tender. Stir in mixed vegetables; remove from heat, and set aside.

Melt 2 tablespoons margarine in a heavy saucepan over medium heat; add 2 tablespoons flour, stirring until smooth. Cook 1 minute, stirring constantly. Gradually add milk, stirring constantly. Cook, stirring constantly, until mixture is thickened and bubbly. Remove from heat, and stir in poultry seasoning.

Add chicken, vegetable mixture, sauce, and mushrooms to saucepan. Spoon chicken mixture into each of 6 (1-cup) baking dishes coated with cooking spray.

Combine 1 cup flour, baking powder, and salt in a small bowl. Cut in 1½ tablespoons margarine with a pastry blender until mixture resembles coarse meal. Add buttermilk, stirring just until dry ingredients are moistened. Drop dough evenly by spoonfuls onto chicken mixture. Bake at 350° for 45 minutes or until crusts are golden. Garnish with celery leaves, if desired. Yield: 6 servings (316 calories and 26% fat per serving).

Protein 20.2 / Fat 9.1 (Saturated Fat 1.9) / Carbohydrate 38.1
Fiber 3.5 / Cholesterol 35 / Sodium 391

Indian-Style Chicken Breasts

4 (4-ounce) skinned, boned chicken breast
  halves
1 (8-ounce) carton plain nonfat yogurt
½ teaspoon curry powder
½ teaspoon paprika
½ teaspoon peeled, grated gingerroot
⅛ teaspoon ground cardamom
Vegetable cooking spray
2 tablespoons commercial chutney

Place chicken in a shallow baking dish. Combine yogurt and next 4 ingredients; pour over chicken, turning to coat chicken. Cover and marinate in refrigerator 8 hours, turning occasionally.

Remove chicken from marinade, discarding marinade. Arrange chicken on rack of a broiler pan coated with cooking spray. Broil 5½ inches from heat 4 minutes on each side or until done.

Transfer chicken to a serving platter, and top evenly with chutney. Yield: 4 servings (188 calories and 16% fat per serving).

Protein 29 / Fat 3.3 (Saturated Fat 0.9) / Carbohydrate 8.8
Fiber 0.1 / Cholesterol 73 / Sodium 113

Lend warmth to a chilly winter evening by serving hearty Chicken and Vegetable Pot Pies.

Chicken Breast Fricassee tastes rich and creamy but is low in saturated fat and cholesterol.

Chicken Breast Fricassee

4 (4-ounce) skinned, boned chicken breast
   halves
⅛ teaspoon pepper
Vegetable cooking spray
1⅓ cups diagonally sliced carrot
1 cup coarsely chopped onion
1 cup frozen whole kernel corn
½ pound sliced fresh mushrooms
1½ cups water
¼ cup Chablis or other dry white wine
½ teaspoon chicken-flavored bouillon
   granules
½ teaspoon dried whole tarragon
½ teaspoon dried whole thyme
1 bay leaf
2 tablespoons cornstarch
½ cup evaporated skimmed milk
1 teaspoon lemon juice
Fresh tarragon sprigs (optional)

Sprinkle chicken with pepper; set aside. Coat a Dutch oven with cooking spray; place over medium-high heat until hot. Add chicken, and cook 2 minutes on each side or until browned. Add carrot and next 9 ingredients; bring to a boil. Cover, reduce heat, and simmer 15 minutes or until chicken is tender. Remove chicken from pan; transfer to a serving platter.

Combine cornstarch and milk, and add to vegetable mixture, stirring constantly. Bring to a boil; reduce heat, and simmer until thickened and bubbly, stirring constantly. Remove from heat; stir in lemon juice. Discard bay leaf.

Spoon vegetable mixture around chicken on platter. Garnish with fresh tarragon sprigs, if desired. Yield: 4 servings (251 calories and 8% fat per serving).

Protein 32 / Fat 2.2 (Saturated Fat 0.5) / Carbohydrate 26.6
Fiber 4.2 / Cholesterol 67 / Sodium 235

Lemon-Dijon Chicken Breasts

½ cup fine, dry breadcrumbs
2 teaspoons grated lemon rind
3 tablespoons lemon juice
2 tablespoons country-style Dijon mustard
1 tablespoon lime juice
6 (4-ounce) skinned, boned chicken breast
  halves
Vegetable cooking spray
Lemon slices (optional)

Combine breadcrumbs and lemon rind, stirring well. Combine lemon juice, mustard, and lime juice; brush mixture over both sides of chicken. Dredge chicken in breadcrumb mixture. Place chicken in a 13- x 9- x 2-inch baking dish coated with cooking spray; sprinkle with any remaining breadcrumb mixture.

Bake, uncovered, at 375° for 15 minutes. Turn chicken, and bake an additional 15 minutes or until done. Garnish with lemon slices, if desired. Yield: 6 servings (167 calories and 12% fat per serving).

Protein 27.3 / Fat 2.2 (Saturated Fat 0.5) / Carbohydrate 7.4
Fiber 0.4 / Cholesterol 66 / Sodium 284

Caribbean Chicken Paillards

4 (4-ounce) skinned, boned chicken breast
  halves
1½ tablespoons brown sugar
3 tablespoons lime juice
2 tablespoons rum
2 tablespoons low-sodium soy sauce
1 tablespoon low-sodium Worcestershire
  sauce
1 tablespoon vegetable oil
⅛ teaspoon pepper
Vegetable cooking spray
1 tablespoon minced fresh parsley
1 lime, cut into 4 wedges

Place chicken between 2 sheets of heavy-duty plastic wrap, and flatten to ¼-inch thickness, using a meat mallet or rolling pin. Place chicken in a shallow dish.

Combine brown sugar and next 6 ingredients; pour over chicken. Cover and marinate in refrigerator at least 30 minutes, turning twice.

Remove chicken from marinade, discarding marinade. Coat a large nonstick skillet with cooking spray; place over medium-high heat until hot. Add chicken, and cook 5 to 6 minutes on each side or until chicken is tender. Remove chicken from skillet; transfer to a serving platter. Sprinkle with parsley; squeeze 1 lime wedge over each serving. Yield: 4 servings (153 calories and 22% fat per serving).

Protein 26.4 / Fat 3.8 (Saturated Fat 1.0) / Carbohydrate 1.6
Fiber 0 / Cholesterol 72 / Sodium 99

Parmesan Chicken

4 (4-ounce) skinned, boned chicken breast
  halves
⅓ cup fine, dry breadcrumbs
½ teaspoon Italian seasoning
¼ teaspoon dried whole basil
⅛ teaspoon garlic powder
3 tablespoons frozen egg substitute, thawed
Vegetable cooking spray
1 (8-ounce) can no-salt-added tomato sauce
¼ teaspoon garlic powder
¼ teaspoon dried whole basil
¼ cup grated Parmesan cheese
¼ cup (1 ounce) shredded part-skim
  mozzarella cheese

Place chicken between 2 sheets of heavy-duty plastic wrap; flatten to ¼-inch thickness, using a meat mallet or rolling pin. Combine breadcrumbs and next 3 ingredients. Dip chicken in egg substitute; dredge in breadcrumb mixture.

Coat a large nonstick skillet with cooking spray; place over medium-high heat until hot. Add chicken, and cook 2 minutes on each side or until lightly browned. Place chicken in an 11- x 7- x 2-inch baking dish.

Combine tomato sauce, ¼ teaspoon garlic powder, and ¼ teaspoon basil; pour over chicken. Sprinkle with Parmesan cheese. Cover and bake at 350° for 30 minutes or until thoroughly heated; sprinkle with mozzarella cheese. Bake, uncovered, an additional 5 minutes or until cheese melts. Yield: 4 servings (227 calories and 18% fat per serving).

Protein 32.8 / Fat 4.6 (Saturated Fat 2.1) / Carbohydrate 11.7
Fiber 0.4 / Cholesterol 74 / Sodium 290

Spinach-Stuffed Turkey Breast

Vegetable cooking spray
1 cup finely chopped onion
½ cup chopped fresh mushrooms
1 clove garlic, minced
1 (10-ounce) package frozen chopped
  spinach
1 cup soft whole wheat breadcrumbs
2 tablespoons grated Parmesan cheese
¼ cup frozen egg substitute, thawed
½ teaspoon dried whole thyme
½ teaspoon pepper
1 (3½-pound) boneless turkey breast,
  skinned
¾ teaspoon rubbed sage
¼ teaspoon salt
¼ teaspoon ground white pepper
¼ teaspoon paprika
Fresh thyme sprigs (optional)

Coat a large nonstick skillet with cooking spray; place over medium-high heat until hot. Add onion, mushrooms, and garlic; sauté until tender. Set aside.

Cook spinach according to package directions, omitting salt. Drain well, and press between paper towels until barely moist. Combine spinach, onion mixture, breadcrumbs, and next 4 ingredients in a medium bowl; stir well, and set aside.

Trim fat from turkey; remove tendons. Place turkey breast, boned side up, on heavy-duty plastic wrap. From center, slice horizontally through thickest part of each side of breast almost to outer edge; flip each cut piece over to enlarge breast. Place heavy-duty plastic wrap over turkey, and flatten to ½-inch thickness using a meat mallet or rolling pin.

Spoon spinach mixture in center of turkey breast, leaving a 2-inch border at sides; roll up jellyroll fashion, starting with short side. Tie turkey breast securely at 2-inch intervals with string.

Combine sage, salt, white pepper, and paprika in a small bowl, stirring well; rub over surface of turkey.

Place turkey, seam side down, on a rack in a roasting pan coated with cooking spray. Shield turkey with aluminum foil; insert meat thermometer. Bake at 325° for 1 hour; uncover, and bake an additional 30 minutes or until meat thermometer registers 170°.

Transfer turkey to a large serving platter; remove string. Let stand 10 minutes before slicing. Garnish with fresh thyme sprigs, if desired. Yield: 14 servings (142 calories and 8% fat per serving).

Protein 27.2 / Fat 1.2 (Saturated Fat 0.9) / Carbohydrate 4.5
Fiber 1.1 / Cholesterol 70 / Sodium 145

Crispy Turkey Bake

1 (10-ounce) package frozen English peas
2 cups cubed cooked turkey (skinned
  before cooking and cooked without salt)
½ cup (2 ounces) shredded reduced-fat
  sharp Cheddar cheese
½ cup chopped green onions
⅓ cup fat-free mayonnaise
½ teaspoon Dijon mustard
⅛ teaspoon salt
⅛ teaspoon pepper
Vegetable cooking spray
1 medium tomato, cut into 6 slices
1 cup corn flakes cereal, crushed
1 teaspoon reduced-calorie margarine,
  melted

Cook peas according to package directions, omitting salt and fat; drain. Combine peas and next 3 ingredients in a medium bowl. Combine mayonnaise, mustard, salt, and pepper; add to turkey mixture, stirring well.

Spoon mixture into an 11- x 7- x 2-inch baking dish coated with cooking spray; arrange tomato slices on top. Combine crushed cereal and margarine; sprinkle over casserole. Bake at 350° for 20 to 25 minutes or until thoroughly heated. Yield: 6 servings (200 calories and 13% fat per serving).

Protein 20.8 / Fat 2.9 (Saturated Fat 1.6) / Carbohydrate 21
Fiber 2.8 / Cholesterol 46 / Sodium 371

Skewered with red potatoes, yellow squash, and chunks of turkey, Barbecued Turkey Kabobs offer a low-fat alternative to the traditional beef kabob.

Barbecued Turkey Kabobs

2 (½-pound) turkey tenderloins
1 (8-ounce) can no-salt-added tomato
   sauce
3 tablespoons cider vinegar
2 tablespoons water
2 tablespoons molasses
1½ tablespoons low-sodium Worcestershire
   sauce
½ teaspoon dry mustard
¼ teaspoon salt
⅛ teaspoon celery seeds
⅛ teaspoon onion powder
⅛ teaspoon ground red pepper
12 small round red potatoes, halved
4 medium-size yellow squash (about 1
   pound), each cut into 8 pieces
Vegetable cooking spray

Trim fat from turkey tenderloins; remove tendons. Cut tenderloins into 1-inch pieces.

Combine tomato sauce and next 9 ingredients in a large shallow baking dish; stir well. Add turkey, stirring to coat well. Cover and marinate in refrigerator 3 hours, stirring occasionally.

Cook potatoes in boiling water to cover 10 minutes or until tender. Drain and let cool.

Remove turkey from marinade. Place marinade in a small saucepan; bring to a boil. Reduce heat, and simmer 5 minutes. Thread turkey and vegetables alternately on 8 (10-inch) skewers.

Coat grill rack with cooking spray; place on grill over medium-hot coals. Place kabobs on rack, and cook 15 to 17 minutes or until turkey is done, turning and basting frequently with marinade. Yield: 4 servings (283 calories and 5% fat per serving).

Protein 29.5 / Fat 1.5 (Saturated Fat 0.8) / Carbohydrate 38.4
Fiber 3.8 / Cholesterol 70 / Sodium 235

Turkey Loaf with Dill Sauce

2 pounds freshly ground raw turkey
2 cups soft whole wheat breadcrumbs
½ cup shredded carrot
½ cup frozen egg substitute, thawed
¼ cup finely chopped onion
1 tablespoon minced fresh parsley
1½ teaspoons dry mustard
½ teaspoon pepper
Vegetable cooking spray
Dill Sauce
Fresh dillweed sprigs (optional)

Combine first 8 ingredients in a large bowl; stir well. (Mixture will be slightly soft.) Shape mixture into an 8- x 4-inch loaf. Place loaf on a rack in a roasting pan coated with cooking spray.

Bake at 350° for 1 hour and 10 minutes or until meat is no longer pink. Let stand 10 minutes; transfer loaf to a serving platter. Serve with Dill Sauce; garnish with fresh dillweed sprigs, if desired. Yield: 10 servings (174 calories and 21% fat per serving).

Dill Sauce

½ cup fat-free mayonnaise
¼ cup plus 2 tablespoons nonfat sour cream
3 tablespoons water
2 tablespoons lemon juice
1½ tablespoons Dijon mustard
1 teaspoon dried whole dillweed

Combine all ingredients in a saucepan; stir well. Cook over low heat until thoroughly heated, stirring constantly. Yield: 1⅓ cups.

Protein 23.1 / Fat 4.0 (Saturated Fat 1.2) / Carbohydrate 10
Fiber 0.7 / Cholesterol 53 / Sodium 352

Turkey Tostadas

6 (6-inch) flour tortillas
Vegetable cooking spray
¾ pound freshly ground raw turkey
¼ cup minced onion
2 cloves garlic, minced
1 jalapeño pepper, seeded and minced
1 (8-ounce) can no-salt-added tomato sauce
¾ cup chopped tomato
1 teaspoon dried whole oregano
½ teaspoon dried whole thyme
Dash of hot sauce
⅓ cup (1.3 ounces) shredded reduced-fat
  sharp Cheddar cheese
¼ cup plus 2 tablespoons nonfat sour cream
Sliced jalapeño pepper (optional)
Fresh cilantro sprigs (optional)

Place tortillas on a large baking sheet; bake at 350° for 7 to 10 minutes or until crisp. Set tortillas aside.

Coat a large nonstick skillet with cooking spray; place over medium-high heat until hot. Add turkey and next 3 ingredients; cook until meat is browned, stirring to crumble meat. Drain; wipe drippings from skillet with a paper towel.

Combine turkey mixture, tomato sauce, tomato, oregano, thyme, and hot sauce in skillet. Bring to a boil; reduce heat, and simmer 10 minutes or until thickened, stirring occasionally.

Spoon turkey mixture evenly over tortillas; sprinkle evenly with cheese. Broil 5½ inches from heat until cheese melts. Top each tostada with 1 tablespoon sour cream. If desired, garnish with jalapeño pepper slices and fresh cilantro sprigs. Yield: 6 servings (232 calories and 21% fat per serving).

Protein 18.4 / Fat 5.3 (Saturated Fat 1.1) / Carbohydrate 28.8
Fiber 1.4 / Cholesterol 41 / Sodium 105

Impress dinner guests with a stunning display of elegant Shrimp and Asparagus Salad (page 203).

SALADS & SALAD DRESSINGS

Congealed Triple Apple Salad

1 envelope unflavored gelatin
1 cup unsweetened apple juice
1 tablespoon sugar
1 cup unsweetened applesauce
¼ teaspoon almond extract
1 cup diced apple
1 teaspoon lemon juice
Vegetable cooking spray
Apple wedges (optional)
Fresh mint sprigs (optional)

Sprinkle gelatin over apple juice in a small saucepan; let stand 1 minute. Add sugar; cook over low heat, stirring constantly, until gelatin and sugar dissolve. Remove from heat; stir in applesauce and almond extract. Chill until the consistency of unbeaten egg white.

Combine diced apple and lemon juice, tossing well; fold apple into gelatin mixture. Spoon into a 3-cup mold coated with cooking spray. Cover and chill until firm.

Unmold salad onto a serving plate. If desired, garnish with apple wedges and fresh mint sprigs. Yield: 5 servings (76 calories and 4% fat per ½-cup serving).

Protein 1.4 / Fat 0.3 (Saturated Fat 0) / Carbohydrate 18.0
Fiber 1.7 / Cholesterol 0 / Sodium 4

Holiday Cranberry Salad

1 envelope unflavored gelatin
½ cup cold water
1½ teaspoons grated orange rind
1 (16-ounce) can jellied whole-berry
  cranberry sauce
1 (8-ounce) can crushed pineapple in juice,
  undrained
¾ cup diced celery
Vegetable cooking spray
Green leaf lettuce (optional)

Sprinkle gelatin over cold water in a saucepan; let stand 1 minute. Cook over low heat, stirring constantly until gelatin dissolves. Remove from heat; stir in orange rind. Chill until the consistency of unbeaten egg white.

Combine cranberry sauce, pineapple, and celery in a bowl; gently fold into gelatin mixture.

Spoon mixture into a 1-quart mold coated with cooking spray. Cover and chill until firm.

Unmold salad onto a lettuce-lined serving plate, if desired. Yield: 8 servings (108 calories and 1% fat per ½-cup serving).

Protein 1.1 / Fat 0.1 (Saturated Fat 0) / Carbohydrate 27.0
Fiber 0.5 / Cholesterol 0 / Sodium 26

Mixed Berries with Raspberry Vinaigrette

1 cup fresh blackberries
1 cup fresh blueberries
1 cup fresh raspberries
1 cup fresh strawberries, halved
½ cup strawberry nectar
2 tablespoons raspberry vinegar
2 teaspoons vegetable oil

Combine first 4 ingredients in a medium bowl, and toss gently. Combine strawberry nectar, vinegar, and oil; stir well. Pour over berries; toss gently. Cover and chill at least 1 hour. Yield: 8 servings (54 calories and 23% fat per ½-cup serving).

Protein 0.5 / Fat 1.4 (Saturated Fat 0.2) / Carbohydrate 10.7
Fiber 3.9 / Cholesterol 0 / Sodium 1

Cantaloupe-Blueberry Salad

1 (8-ounce) carton vanilla low-fat yogurt
1 tablespoon lemon juice
1½ teaspoons poppy seeds
1 teaspoon grated orange rind
1 medium cantaloupe, peeled and seeded
24 Boston lettuce leaves
2 cups fresh blueberries

Combine first 4 ingredients; stir well. Cover and chill thoroughly.

Cut cantaloupe lengthwise into 32 slices. Arrange 4 slices on each of 8 lettuce-lined serving plates; top each with ¼ cup blueberries. Spoon yogurt mixture over salads. Yield: 8 servings (83 calories and 11% fat per serving).

Protein 2.7 / Fat 1.0 (Saturated Fat 0.4) / Carbohydrate 17.7
Fiber 2.8 / Cholesterol 1 / Sodium 30

Drizzled with a lemon-poppy seed dressing, Cantaloupe-Blueberry Salad makes a cool addition to a summer luncheon.

Leave time for Fresh Mushroom Salad to chill before serving so that the numerous flavors can blend.

Fresh Mushroom Salad

¼ cup canned no-salt-added chicken broth,
   undiluted
1 tablespoon minced fresh parsley
1 tablespoon minced fresh basil
3 tablespoons lemon juice
1 teaspoon olive oil
½ teaspoon salt
½ teaspoon ground cumin
¼ teaspoon freshly ground pepper
1 clove garlic, minced
1½ pounds fresh mushrooms, quartered
Fresh basil sprigs (optional)

Combine first 9 ingredients in a large bowl. Add mushrooms; toss gently. Cover and chill at least 2 hours, tossing occasionally. Garnish with fresh basil sprigs, if desired. Yield: 12 servings (20 calories and 32% fat per ½-cup serving).

Protein 1.3 / Fat 0.7 (Saturated Fat 0.1) / Carbohydrate 3.2
Fiber 0.8 / Cholesterol 0 / Sodium 103

Roasted Pepper, Onion, And Broccoli Salad

1 tablespoon water
1 tablespoon rice wine vinegar
1 tablespoon balsamic vinegar
1½ teaspoons olive oil
⅛ teaspoon salt
⅛ teaspoon pepper
1 clove garlic, minced
1 large sweet red pepper
1 large sweet yellow pepper
12 small pearl onions, peeled
½ cup water
2 cups fresh broccoli flowerets

Combine first 7 ingredients in a small bowl; stir well, and set aside.

Cut peppers in half lengthwise; remove and discard seeds and membrane. Place peppers, skin side up, on a baking sheet; flatten with palm of hand. Broil 5½ inches from heat 15 to 20 minutes or until charred. Remove peppers from baking sheet; place peppers in a medium bowl, and cover with plastic wrap. Let peppers cool completely; peel and discard skins. Cut peppers into ½-inch strips; set aside.

Combine onions and ½ cup water in a small saucepan; bring to a boil. Reduce heat, and cook, uncovered, 15 minutes or until tender; drain. Place onions in ice water 5 minutes; drain and set aside.

Cook broccoli in boiling water 30 seconds or until crisp-tender; drain. Rinse broccoli under cold water until cool; drain well.

Arrange pepper strips, onions, and broccoli on 4 individual salad plates. Drizzle vinegar mixture evenly over salads. Yield: 4 servings (63 calories and 33% fat per serving).

Protein 2.5 / Fat 2.3 (Saturated Fat 0.3) / Carbohydrate 9.9
Fiber 2.2 / Cholesterol 0 / Sodium 87

Zesty Potato Salad

2 pounds small round red potatoes
⅓ cup chopped green onions
¼ cup chopped fresh parsley
1 (10½-ounce) can low-sodium chicken
   broth, undiluted
¼ cup cider vinegar
2 tablespoons vegetable oil
1 tablespoon coarse-grained mustard
1 teaspoon sugar
¼ teaspoon salt
¼ teaspoon freshly ground pepper

Wash potatoes. Cook in boiling water to cover 15 minutes or until tender; drain and cool slightly. Slice potatoes, and place in a large bowl. Add green onions and parsley.

Combine chicken broth and remaining ingredients in a small saucepan; bring to a boil. Pour broth mixture over potato mixture; toss gently. Cover and refrigerate at least 8 hours. Serve with a slotted spoon. Yield: 12 servings (83 calories and 26% fat per ½-cup serving).

Protein 1.9 / Fat 2.4 (Saturated Fat 0.4) / Carbohydrate 13.8
Fiber 1.5 / Cholesterol 0 / Sodium 73

Tangy Tomato, Cucumber, And Onion Salad

3 medium tomatoes, cut into wedges
1 large cucumber, scored and sliced
1 small purple onion, sliced and separated
   into rings
6 Boston lettuce leaves
⅔ cup red wine vinegar
2 tablespoons sugar
2 tablespoons finely chopped fresh basil
2 tablespoons low-sodium Worcestershire
   sauce
1 teaspoon finely chopped fresh thyme
½ teaspoon coarsely ground pepper

Arrange tomato, cucumber, and onion on individual lettuce-lined salad plates.

Combine vinegar and remaining ingredients in a small jar; cover tightly, and shake vigorously. Drizzle over each serving. Yield: 6 servings (60 calories and 6% fat per serving).

Protein 1.5 / Fat 0.4 (Saturated Fat 0.1) / Carbohydrate 13.0
Fiber 2.3 / Cholesterol 0 / Sodium 32

Marinated Vegetable Salad

½ pound fresh snow pea pods
8 cherry tomatoes, halved
1 medium zucchini, cut diagonally into
   ¼-inch slices (about 1¼ cups)
1 cup diagonally sliced carrot
¼ cup vinegar
1 tablespoon sugar
1 tablespoon vegetable oil
⅛ teaspoon celery seeds
⅛ teaspoon dry mustard
⅛ teaspoon paprika
2 tablespoons crumbled feta cheese

Arrange snow peas in a vegetable steamer over boiling water. Cover and steam 3 to 5 minutes or until crisp-tender. Remove from steamer; cover and chill thoroughly.

Combine tomatoes, zucchini, and carrot in a 13- x 9- x 2-inch baking dish. Combine vinegar and next 5 ingredients in a jar; cover tightly, and shake vigorously. Pour over vegetables; cover and marinate in refrigerator at least 8 hours.

Arrange snow peas on a serving platter. Spoon vegetables over snow peas, using a slotted spoon; sprinkle with feta cheese. Yield: 4 servings (123 calories and 34% fat per serving).

Protein 4.4 / Fat 4.6 (Saturated Fat 1.2) / Carbohydrate 17.7
Fiber 4.3 / Cholesterol 3 / Sodium 59

Chicken-Pasta Italiano

2 quarts water
½ cup Chablis or other dry white wine
4 (4-ounce) skinned, boned chicken breast
   halves
4 cloves garlic
3 tablespoons chopped fresh basil
2 tablespoons lemon juice
⅛ teaspoon salt
⅛ teaspoon pepper
4 ounces penne or rigatoni pasta, uncooked
1 tablespoon olive oil
1 medium-size sweet red pepper, cut into
   1-inch pieces
4 ripe olives, thinly sliced
Romaine lettuce leaves (optional)
1 tablespoon grated Parmesan cheese

Bring water to a boil in a large saucepan. Add wine, chicken, and garlic; reduce heat, and simmer, uncovered, 15 minutes or until chicken is tender.

Remove chicken and garlic from broth, reserving garlic and broth. Let chicken cool. Cut chicken into ½-inch pieces; set aside. Skim and discard fat from broth; set aside.

Crush garlic in a small bowl. Add basil, lemon juice, salt, and pepper; set aside.

Bring broth to a boil; add pasta. Return to a boil, and cook 12 minutes or until tender; drain. Rinse under cold, running water; drain.

Transfer pasta to a large bowl; add olive oil, and toss gently. Add chicken, reserved garlic mixture, red pepper, and olives; toss gently. Cover and chill at least 1 hour.

Spoon chicken mixture onto a lettuce-lined serving platter, if desired; sprinkle with Parmesan cheese. Yield: 4 servings (298 calories and 23% fat per 1¼-cup serving).

Protein 30.3 / Fat 7.7 (Saturated Fat 1.7) / Carbohydrate 24.5
Fiber 1.4 / Cholesterol 71 / Sodium 193

Chinese Chicken Salad

4 cups shredded Chinese cabbage
2 cups chopped cooked chicken breast
   (skinned before cooking and cooked
   without salt)
½ cup raisins
3 green onions, cut into 1-inch pieces
2½ tablespoons water
2½ tablespoons low-sodium soy sauce
2 tablespoons white wine vinegar
2 teaspoons sesame oil
¼ teaspoon pepper

Combine first 4 ingredients in a large bowl; toss gently.

Combine water and remaining ingredients, stirring with a wire whisk until well blended; pour over chicken mixture, and toss well. Serve immediately. Yield: 4 servings (226 calories and 20% fat per 1½-cup serving).

Protein 24.7 / Fat 5.1 (Saturated Fat 1.1) / Carbohydrate 19.8
Fiber 2.9 / Cholesterol 63 / Sodium 315

Curried Chicken And Mango Salad

¾ cup plain nonfat yogurt
1 tablespoon lime juice
1 tablespoon honey
1 teaspoon curry powder
⅛ teaspoon salt
⅛ teaspoon pepper
2 cups cubed, cooked chicken breast
   (skinned before cooking and cooked
   without salt)
1 cup peeled, cubed mango
Boston lettuce leaves (optional)

Combine first 6 ingredients in a large bowl; stir well. Add chicken and mango; toss gently to coat.

Arrange lettuce leaves on each of 4 individual salad plates, if desired. Spoon chicken mixture evenly onto each lettuce-lined plate. Yield: 4 servings (218 calories and 14% fat per ¾-cup serving).

Protein 29.2 / Fat 3.3 (Saturated Fat 0.9) / Carbohydrate 17.4
Fiber 1.0 / Cholesterol 73 / Sodium 170

Shrimp and Asparagus Salad

½ pound baby carrots with tops
12 small round red potatoes, sliced
1 pound fresh asparagus spears
½ cup white wine vinegar
2 tablespoons water
1½ tablespoons olive oil
2 teaspoons sugar
1 teaspoon dried whole basil
½ teaspoon chicken-flavored
   bouillon granules
½ teaspoon dry mustard
¼ teaspoon salt
¼ teaspoon pepper
⅛ teaspoon hot sauce
1 small clove garlic, crushed
1½ pounds medium-size fresh shrimp,
   cooked, peeled, and deveined
Green leaf lettuce (optional)
2 medium tomatoes, cut into wedges

Scrape baby carrots, leaving 1 inch of green top. Arrange carrots in a vegetable steamer over boiling water. Cover and steam 10 minutes or until tender. Remove carrots, and set aside.

Arrange potato slices in vegetable steamer over boiling water. Cover and steam 10 minutes or until tender. Remove potato; set aside.

Snap off tough ends of asparagus. Remove scales from stalks with a knife or vegetable peeler, if desired. Arrange asparagus in vegetable steamer over boiling water. Cover and steam 5 minutes or until crisp-tender. Remove asparagus; set aside.

Combine vinegar and next 10 ingredients in a small bowl, stirring well with a wire whisk. Place carrot, potato, asparagus, shrimp, and tomato wedges in a 13- x 9- x 2-inch baking dish; pour vinegar mixture over vegetables and shrimp, tossing gently to coat. Cover and marinate in refrigerator 2 hours.

Remove vegetables and shrimp from marinade, reserving marinade. Arrange marinated vegetables and shrimp on a large lettuce-lined serving platter, if desired. Drizzle reserved marinade over salad. Yield: 6 servings (196 calories and 21% fat per serving).

Protein 18.0 / Fat 4.7 (Saturated Fat 0.7) / Carbohydrate 21.7
Fiber 4.7 / Cholesterol 124 / Sodium 336

Southwestern Crabmeat Salad

6 (6-inch) corn tortillas
¾ pound fresh lump crabmeat, drained
½ cup chopped tomato
½ cup chopped green pepper
¼ cup chopped onion
2 tablespoons chopped fresh cilantro
2 tablespoons lime juice
1 tablespoon white wine vinegar
1 small clove garlic, minced
1 teaspoon minced jalapeño pepper
⅛ teaspoon salt
Dash of pepper
1½ cups shredded curly leaf lettuce
Fresh cilantro sprigs (optional)

Place tortillas on a large baking sheet. Bake at 350° for 15 minutes or until crisp. Set aside.

Combine crabmeat, tomato, green pepper, onion, and cilantro in a medium bowl; stir well.

Combine lime juice, vinegar, garlic, jalapeño pepper, salt, and pepper in a small bowl. Add to crabmeat mixture, stirring well.

Place tortillas on each of 6 individual salad plates. Top each tortilla with ¼ cup shredded lettuce and ½ cup crabmeat mixture. Garnish with fresh cilantro sprigs, if desired. Yield: 6 servings (128 calories and 15% fat per serving).

Protein 13.8 / Fat 2.1 (Saturated Fat 0.3) / Carbohydrate 13.9
Fiber 2.1 / Cholesterol 57 / Sodium 255

Warm Scallop Salad

1½ pounds fresh sea scallops
2 tablespoons Chablis or other dry white
    wine
¼ cup canned no-salt-added chicken broth,
    undiluted
¼ cup white wine vinegar
1 tablespoon olive oil
2 teaspoons sugar
½ teaspoon dry mustard
¼ teaspoon salt
⅛ teaspoon pepper
1 clove garlic, crushed
2 cups torn red leaf lettuce
2 cups torn Bibb lettuce
1 cup arugula, trimmed
1 small sweet red pepper, cut into
    julienne strips
1 small sweet yellow pepper, cut into
    julienne strips
¼ cup chopped green onions

Combine scallops and wine in a large bowl, tossing gently; let stand 15 minutes. Place scallops on a steaming rack over boiling water. Cover and steam 5 minutes or until opaque. Remove from heat; set aside, and keep warm.

Combine chicken broth and next 7 ingredients in a medium saucepan; cook over medium heat, stirring occasionally, until thoroughly heated. Remove from heat, and keep warm.

Combine leaf lettuce, Bibb lettuce, arugula, sweet peppers, and green onions in a large bowl; toss well. Pour warm broth mixture over greens, and toss well. Place 1 cup wilted greens on each of 6 individual salad plates. Spoon scallops evenly over greens. Serve immediately. Yield: 6 servings (123 calories and 25% fat per serving).

Protein 15.8 / Fat 3.3 (Saturated Fat 0.4) / Carbohydrate 6.8
Fiber 1.0 / Cholesterol 29 / Sodium 252

Grilled Tuna and Bean Salad

¾ cup dried navy beans
½ cup diced purple onion
3 tablespoons chopped fresh parsley
2 tablespoons white wine vinegar
1 tablespoon olive oil
¼ teaspoon salt
⅛ teaspoon pepper
1 (½-pound) yellowfin tuna steak
    (¾ inch thick)
2 tablespoons lemon juice
¾ teaspoon minced fresh thyme
2 cloves garlic, sliced
Vegetable cooking spray
Red leaf lettuce (optional)

Sort and wash beans; place in a medium saucepan. Cover with water to a depth of 2 inches above beans; bring to a boil, and cook 2 minutes. Remove from heat; cover and let stand 1 hour. Drain and rinse beans.

Return beans to saucepan, and cover with water to a depth of 2 inches above beans; bring to a boil. Cover, reduce heat, and simmer 1 hour or until tender. Drain and rinse beans; let cool completely.

Combine beans, onion, and parsley in a medium bowl; toss gently. Combine vinegar and next 3 ingredients; add to bean mixture, tossing gently. Cover and chill thoroughly.

Place tuna in a shallow baking dish; sprinkle with lemon juice, thyme, and garlic. Cover and marinate in refrigerator 2 hours. Remove tuna from marinade, discarding marinade and garlic.

Coat grill rack with cooking spray; place on grill over medium-hot coals. Place tuna on rack, and cook 5 to 7 minutes on each side or until fish flakes easily when tested with a fork.

Spoon bean mixture onto a lettuce-lined serving platter, if desired. Using a fork, flake tuna into large pieces, and arrange on top of bean mixture. Yield: 4 servings (253 calories and 24% fat per serving).

Protein 22.1 / Fat 6.8 (Saturated Fat 1.3) / Carbohydrate 26.1
Fiber 4.2 / Cholesterol 22 / Sodium 176

Fresh cilantro, jalapeño pepper, and lime juice lend an authentic flavor to Southwestern Crabmeat Salad.

Creamy Pepper Dressing

½ cup plus 3 tablespoons plain nonfat
  yogurt
¼ cup fat-free mayonnaise
1 tablespoon grated Parmesan cheese
1 tablespoon minced green onions
1 to 1½ teaspoons freshly ground pepper
1½ teaspoons cider vinegar
1 teaspoon lemon juice
½ teaspoon low-sodium Worcestershire
  sauce

Combine all ingredients in a small bowl; stir well. Cover and chill thoroughly. Serve with salad greens. Yield: 1 cup (11 calories and 8% fat per tablespoon).

Protein 0.7 / Fat 0.1 (Saturated Fat 0.1) / Carbohydrate 1.8
Fiber 0.1 / Cholesterol 0 / Sodium 62

Herbed Tomato Dressing

1 (14½-ounce) can no-salt-added whole
  tomatoes, undrained
1 (5½-ounce) can no-salt-added vegetable
  juice cocktail
¼ cup red wine vinegar
2 tablespoons powdered pectin
1 tablespoon chopped fresh parsley
2 tablespoons lemon juice
1 teaspoon dried whole oregano
½ teaspoon dried whole basil
½ teaspoon dried whole tarragon
½ teaspoon garlic powder
½ teaspoon onion powder
½ teaspoon pepper

Combine all ingredients in container of an electric blender; top with cover, and process until smooth. Cover and chill thoroughly. Serve with salad greens or cold pasta. Yield: 3 cups (4 calories and 0% fat per tablespoon).

Protein 0.2 / Fat 0 (Saturated Fat 0) / Carbohydrate 1.0
Fiber 0.1 / Cholesterol 0 / Sodium 2

Thousand Island Dressing

1 cup fat-free mayonnaise
½ cup reduced-calorie chili sauce
¼ cup plus 2 tablespoons skim milk
2 tablespoons finely chopped celery
2 tablespoons finely chopped green pepper
1 tablespoon sweet pickle relish
1 tablespoon grated onion
1 teaspoon paprika
¼ teaspoon salt

Combine all ingredients in a medium bowl; stir well. Cover and chill thoroughly. Serve with salad greens. Yield: 2 cups (11 calories and 0% fat per tablespoon).

Protein 0.1 / Fat 0 (Saturated Fat 0) / Carbohydrate 2.5
Fiber 0 / Cholesterol 0 / Sodium 122

Poppy Seed Dressing

1 tablespoon cornstarch
1 teaspoon sugar
½ teaspoon dry mustard
1 cup water
2½ tablespoons vinegar
2½ tablespoons honey
2 teaspoons poppy seeds

Combine first 3 ingredients in a small saucepan; stir in water, vinegar, and honey. Bring to a boil; reduce heat to medium, and cook, stirring constantly, until thickened and bubbly. Remove from heat, and cool slightly. Stir in poppy seeds. Cover and chill thoroughly. Serve with fresh fruit. Yield: 1¼ cups (12 calories and 8% fat per tablespoon).

Protein 0.1 / Fat 0.1 (Saturated Fat 0) / Carbohydrate 2.9
Fiber 0 / Cholesterol 0 / Sodium 0

Accent your holiday menus with Cranberry Conserve and Pear and Apple Chutney (page 212). These fruit-filled condiments enhance the flavor of both pork and poultry.

Lemon Curd

½ cup sugar
¼ cup cornstarch
¼ teaspoon salt
2 cups skim milk
¼ cup frozen egg substitute, thawed
1 tablespoon grated lemon rind
¼ cup plus 1 tablespoon fresh lemon juice

Combine sugar, cornstarch, and salt in a medium saucepan. Gradually stir in milk. Cook over medium heat, stirring constantly, until thickened. Remove from heat.

Gradually stir about one-fourth of hot mixture into egg substitute; add to remaining hot mixture, stirring constantly with a wire whisk. Cook over medium-low heat 2 minutes, stirring constantly. Remove from heat, and let cool slightly.

Stir in lemon rind and lemon juice. Let cool completely; chill at least 2 hours. Serve over fresh fruit or angel food cake. Yield: 2¾ cups (16 calories and 0% fat per tablespoon).

Protein 0.5 / Fat 0 (Saturated Fat 0) / Carbohydrate 3.6
Fiber 0 / Cholesterol 0 / Sodium 21

Blueberry Syrup

¼ cup sugar
1½ tablespoons cornstarch
1 cup boiling water
1 (16-ounce) package frozen unsweetened
  blueberries, thawed and drained
1 tablespoon lemon juice

Combine sugar and cornstarch in a medium saucepan. Gradually stir in water. Cook over medium heat, stirring constantly, until mixture comes to a boil. Reduce heat, and simmer 1 minute, stirring constantly. Remove from heat; stir in blueberries and lemon juice. Serve warm or chilled over pancakes or waffles. Yield: 2 cups (15 calories and 6% fat per tablespoon).

Protein 0.1 / Fat 0.1 (Saturated Fat 0) / Carbohydrate 3.7
Fiber 0.5 / Cholesterol 0 / Sodium 0

Tangy Barbecue Sauce

Vegetable cooking spray
1¼ cups minced onion
½ cup minced celery
1 cup reduced-calorie catsup
2 tablespoons vinegar
2 tablespoons lemon juice
1 tablespoon low-sodium
  Worcestershire sauce
1 tablespoon honey
1 teaspoon dry mustard
¼ teaspoon pepper

Coat a medium saucepan with cooking spray; place over medium-high heat until hot. Add onion and celery; sauté until tender.

Stir in catsup and remaining ingredients. Reduce heat to low, and cook 20 minutes, stirring occasionally. Use for basting meat or poultry while cooking. Yield: 1½ cups (10 calories and 9% fat per tablespoon).

Protein 0.1 / Fat 0.1 (Saturated Fat 0) / Carbohydrate 2.1
Fiber 0.1 / Cholesterol 0 / Sodium 7

Texas Mopping Sauce

½ cup reduced-calorie catsup
3 tablespoons dark corn syrup
2 tablespoons lemon juice
2 tablespoons low-sodium
  Worcestershire sauce
2 teaspoons instant coffee granules
2 teaspoons liquid smoke

Combine all ingredients in a small bowl; stir well. Use for basting meat or poultry while cooking. Yield: ¾ cup plus 2 tablespoons (20 calories and 0% fat per tablespoon).

Protein 0 / Fat 0 (Saturated Fat 0) / Carbohydrate 4.6
Fiber 0 / Cholesterol 0 / Sodium 13

Seafood Cocktail Sauce

1 cup reduced-calorie catsup
1 tablespoon lemon juice
2½ teaspoons prepared horseradish
1 teaspoon red wine vinegar
⅛ teaspoon pepper

Combine all ingredients in a small bowl; stir well. Cover and chill at least 30 minutes. Serve with shellfish. Yield: 1 cup (8 calories and 0% fat per tablespoon).

Protein 0 / Fat 0 (Saturated Fat 0) / Carbohydrate 1.4
Fiber 0 / Cholesterol 0 / Sodium 4

Mushroom-Dill Sauce

½ teaspoon beef-flavored bouillon granules
½ cup hot water
Vegetable cooking spray
1 teaspoon reduced-calorie margarine
1 cup sliced fresh mushrooms
¼ cup chopped shallot
1 tablespoon all-purpose flour
½ teaspoon dried whole dillweed
½ cup plain nonfat yogurt

Dissolve bouillon granules in hot water, and set aside.

Coat a medium nonstick skillet with cooking spray; add margarine. Place over medium heat until margarine melts. Add mushrooms and shallot to skillet; sauté until tender. Add flour and dillweed; cook 1 minute, stirring constantly.

Gradually add bouillon mixture, stirring constantly. Cook, stirring constantly, until thickened and bubbly. Remove from heat; add yogurt (at room temperature), stirring until smooth. Serve with beef or fish. Yield: 1¼ cups (9 calories and 20% fat per tablespoon).

Protein 0.5 / Fat 0.2 (Saturated Fat 0) / Carbohydrate 1.3
Fiber 0.1 / Cholesterol 0 / Sodium 30

Sweet Pepper Sauce

1½ cups chopped green pepper
3 medium-size sweet red peppers
¼ teaspoon salt
⅛ teaspoon ground red pepper

Cook green pepper in boiling water to cover 5 minutes; drain well, and set aside.

Place sweet red peppers on a baking sheet. Broil 5½ inches from heat, turning with tongs as sweet red peppers blister and turn dark on all sides. Place roasted peppers in a paper bag; seal and let stand 10 minutes to loosen skins. Peel roasted peppers over a bowl, collecting juice; discard skins. Remove and discard seeds.

Place roasted peppers and juice in container of an electric blender; add salt and ground red pepper. Top with cover, and process until smooth; stir in green pepper. Cover and chill thoroughly. Serve sauce with poached or grilled fish. Yield: 1¾ cups (7 calories and 13% fat per tablespoon).

Protein 0.2 / Fat 0.1 (Saturated Fat 0) / Carbohydrate 1.4
Fiber 0.4 / Cholesterol 0 / Sodium 22

Calories Count in Condiments

Watch out for the calories in your favorite commercial sauces and condiments. The following totals are based on a serving of 1 tablespoon.

Condiment	Calories
Mayonnaise	99
Tartar sauce	72
Sour cream	31
Catsup	18
Chili sauce	18
Corn relish	18
Spicy mustard	16
Prepared mustard	12
Barbecue sauce	12
Steak sauce	12
Worcestershire sauce	12
Soy sauce	10
Horseradish	6
Picante sauce	5
Taco sauce	5
Salsa	4
Dill pickle relish	3

Chock-full of fresh ingredients, Vegetable Salsa teams nicely with grilled chicken or unsalted tortilla chips.

Low-Calorie Medium White Sauce

½ cup instant nonfat dry milk powder
1½ tablespoons all-purpose flour
1 cup water
¼ teaspoon salt
⅛ teaspoon butter flavoring
Dash of ground white pepper

Combine first 3 ingredients in a small saucepan; stir until smooth. Cook over medium heat, stirring constantly, until mixture is thickened and bubbly. Remove from heat, and stir in salt, butter flavoring, and pepper. Yield: 1 cup plus 2 tablespoons (14 calories and 0% fat per tablespoon).

Protein 1.3 / Fat 0 (Saturated Fat 0) / Carbohydrate 2.2
Fiber 0 / Cholesterol 1 / Sodium 50

Thin White Sauce: Decrease flour in Low-Calorie Medium White Sauce to 1 tablespoon. Yield: 1 cup plus 2 tablespoons (14 calories and 0% fat per tablespoon).

Protein 1.2 / Fat 0 (Saturated Fat 0) / Carbohydrate 2.0
Fiber 0 / Cholesterol 1 / Sodium 50

Thick White Sauce: Increase flour in Low-Calorie Medium White Sauce to 2 tablespoons. Yield: 1 cup plus 2 tablespoons (15 calories and 0% fat per tablespoon).

Protein 1.3 / Fat 0 (Saturated Fat 0) / Carbohydrate 2.3
Fiber 0 / Cholesterol 1 / Sodium 50

Cheese Sauce: Add ⅓ cup (1.3 ounces) shredded 40% less-fat Cheddar cheese and ⅛ teaspoon dry mustard to Low-Calorie Medium White Sauce, stirring until cheese melts. Serve with cooked vegetables or pasta. Yield: 1¼ cups plus 2 tablespoons (16 calories and 17% fat per tablespoon).

Protein 1.3 / Fat 0.3 (Saturated Fat 0.2) / Carbohydrate 2.2
Fiber 0 / Cholesterol 2 / Sodium 53

Curry Sauce: Add ½ teaspoon curry powder to Low-Calorie Medium White Sauce. Serve with chicken or fish. Yield: 1 cup plus 2 tablespoons (14 calories and 0% fat per tablespoon).

Protein 1.3 / Fat 0 (Saturated Fat 0) / Carbohydrate 2.2
Fiber 0 / Cholesterol 1 / Sodium 50

Herb Sauce: Add 2 tablespoons chopped fresh chives, 2 teaspoons minced fresh parsley, and ½ teaspoon chopped fresh thyme to Low-Calorie Medium White Sauce. Serve with poultry or seafood. Yield: 1 cup plus 3 tablespoons (14 calories and 0% fat per tablespoon).

Protein 1.2 / Fat 0 (Saturated Fat 0) / Carbohydrate 2.1
Fiber 0 / Cholesterol 1 / Sodium 48

Horseradish Sauce: Add 2½ tablespoons prepared horseradish to Low-Calorie Medium White Sauce. Serve with beef. Yield: 1¼ cups (18 calories and 0% fat per tablespoon).

Protein 1.2 / Fat 0 (Saturated Fat 0.1) / Carbohydrate 2.2
Fiber 0 / Cholesterol 1 / Sodium 47

Wine and Cheese Sauce: Add ⅓ cup (1.3 ounces) shredded 40% less-fat Cheddar cheese, 2 tablespoons sherry, ¼ teaspoon dry mustard, dash of ground nutmeg, and dash of ground red pepper to Low-Calorie Medium White Sauce, stirring until cheese melts. Serve with cooked pasta or poultry. Yield: 1½ cups (15 calories and 18% fat per tablespoon).

Protein 1.2 / Fat 0.3 (Saturated Fat 0) / Carbohydrate 2.0
Fiber 0 / Cholesterol 2 / Sodium 49

Vegetable Salsa

1 (14½-ounce) can no-salt-added stewed tomatoes, undrained and chopped
1 (8¾-ounce) can no-salt-added whole kernel corn, drained
½ cup shredded jicama
¼ cup minced fresh cilantro
¼ cup minced onion
1 tablespoon minced fresh chives
1 tablespoon vinegar
1 teaspoon sugar
1½ teaspoons vegetable oil
1 jalapeño pepper, seeded and minced
1 clove garlic, minced

Combine all ingredients; stir well. Cover and chill at least 1 hour. Serve with grilled chicken or unsalted tortilla chips. Yield: 3 cups (7 calories and 26% fat per tablespoon).

Protein 0.2 / Fat 0.2 (Saturated Fat 0) / Carbohydrate 1.3
Fiber 0.1 / Cholesterol 0 / Sodium 2

Italian Caponata

Vegetable cooking spray
1 teaspoon olive oil
3½ cups diced eggplant (about 1 pound)
2 cups peeled, seeded, and finely chopped
   tomato
1 cup minced celery
1 cup minced onion
½ cup minced sweet red pepper
½ cup minced green pepper
2 tablespoons red wine vinegar
2 cloves garlic, minced
1½ teaspoons dried whole basil
1½ teaspoons dried whole oregano

Coat a Dutch oven with cooking spray; add oil. Place over medium-high heat until hot. Add eggplant and next 5 ingredients; sauté 5 minutes or until vegetables are crisp-tender.

Stir in vinegar, garlic, basil, and oregano; cook an additional 20 minutes, stirring occasionally. Let cool to room temperature; cover and chill at least 4 hours. Serve with grilled pork or poultry. Yield: 3½ cups (6 calories and 15% fat per tablespoon).

Protein 0.2 / Fat 0.1 (Saturated Fat 0) / Carbohydrate 1.2
Fiber 0.3 / Cholesterol 0 / Sodium 3

Spicy Pear Relish

2¼ cups peeled, shredded pear
¾ cup plus 2 tablespoons peeled,
   shredded apple
¼ cup cider vinegar
2 tablespoons golden raisins
2 tablespoons sugar
1½ tablespoons minced green onions
¼ teaspoon pumpkin pie spice
⅛ teaspoon salt
⅛ teaspoon dried whole thyme

Combine all ingredients in a medium nonaluminum saucepan; stir well. Bring to a boil; reduce heat to medium, and simmer 10 minutes, stirring occasionally. Serve warm or at room temperature with pork. Yield: 2 cups (16 calories and 6% fat per tablespoon).

Protein 0.1 / Fat 0.1 (Saturated Fat 0) / Carbohydrate 4.2
Fiber 0.5 / Cholesterol 0 / Sodium 9

Harvest Gold Relish

1½ cups frozen whole kernel corn
⅔ cup chopped tomato
½ cup chopped green pepper
¼ cup finely chopped green onions
¼ cup Dilled Vinegar
2 tablespoons brown sugar
½ jalapeño pepper, seeded and minced
¼ teaspoon salt
1 tablespoon minced fresh dillweed

Combine first 7 ingredients in a nonaluminum saucepan; bring to a boil. Reduce heat to medium, and simmer, uncovered, 20 to 25 minutes or until liquid has evaporated, stirring frequently. Remove from heat; cool 5 minutes. Stir in salt and dillweed. Let cool to room temperature; cover and chill thoroughly. Serve with grilled beef or pork. Yield: 2 cups (10 calories and 9% fat per tablespoon).

Dilled Vinegar

1 cup minced fresh dillweed
2 cups cider vinegar

Place dillweed in a wide-mouth quart glass jar. Place vinegar in a medium nonaluminum saucepan; bring to a boil. Pour hot vinegar over dillweed; cover. Let mixture stand 30 minutes. Strain vinegar, discarding dillweed. Return vinegar to jar; seal jar with an airtight lid. Yield: 2 cups (2 calories and 0% fat per tablespoon).

Protein 0.3 / Fat 0.1 (Saturated Fat 0) / Carbohydrate 2.5
Fiber 0.3 / Cholesterol 0 / Sodium 19

Ladle up bowlfuls of nourishing Chunky Chicken Noodle Soup (page 224) for a simple, yet satisfying meal.

Berry Soup

2 cups fresh raspberries
1 cup sliced fresh strawberries
1 (8-ounce) carton vanilla low-fat yogurt
1 cup unsweetened orange juice
¼ cup rosé wine
2 tablespoons powdered sugar
1 teaspoon grated orange rind

Place raspberries and strawberries in container of an electric blender or food processor; top with cover, and process until smooth. Strain fruit mixture, and discard seeds.

Place strained fruit mixture in container of blender. Add yogurt, orange juice, wine, powdered sugar, and orange rind; top with cover, and process until smooth. Pour mixture into a bowl. Cover and chill thoroughly. Yield: 4 cups (139 calories and 8% fat per 1-cup serving).

Protein 4.0 / Fat 1.2 (Saturated Fat 0.5) / Carbohydrate 27.7
Fiber 5.3 / Cholesterol 3 / Sodium 39

Refreshing Melon Soup

4 cups cubed ripe cantaloupe, divided
½ cup unsweetened orange juice
2 cups cubed ripe honeydew
¼ cup vanilla low-fat yogurt
1½ tablespoons powdered sugar
Fresh mint sprigs (optional)

Place 3 cups cantaloupe in container of an electric blender; top with cover, and process until smooth. With blender running, add orange juice; process until well blended. Transfer cantaloupe mixture to a bowl.

Place remaining 1 cup cantaloupe and honeydew in container of blender; top with cover, and process until smooth. Add yogurt and powdered sugar; process until well blended. Combine cantaloupe mixtures; stir well. Cover and chill thoroughly.

Ladle soup into individual bowls. Garnish with fresh mint sprigs, if desired. Yield: 1½ quarts (85 calories and 5% fat per 1-cup serving).

Protein 1.9 / Fat 0.5 (Saturated Fat 0.3) / Carbohydrate 20.3
Fiber 1.9 / Cholesterol 0 / Sodium 23

Kiwifruit-Apple Soup

9 kiwifruit, peeled and cubed
1 cup unsweetened apple juice
½ cup vanilla low-fat yogurt
1½ tablespoons sugar

Position knife blade in food processor bowl. Add kiwifruit; process 1 minute or until smooth. Transfer pureed fruit to a bowl, and add remaining ingredients to fruit, stirring well. Cover and chill thoroughly. Yield: 4 cups (163 calories and 8% fat per 1-cup serving).

Protein 3.5 / Fat 1.4 (Saturated Fat 0.4) / Carbohydrate 34.3
Fiber 5.5 / Cholesterol 1 / Sodium 21

Savory Carrot Soup

Vegetable cooking spray
1 teaspoon vegetable oil
½ cup chopped onion
1 clove garlic, minced
2½ cups thinly sliced carrot
⅛ teaspoon pepper
1 tablespoon all-purpose flour
4 cups water
2 teaspoons chicken-flavored
    bouillon granules
Fresh dillweed sprigs (optional)

Coat a nonstick skillet with cooking spray; add oil. Place over medium-high heat until hot. Add onion and garlic; sauté until tender. Add carrot and pepper; cover and cook over medium heat 15 minutes or until carrot is tender.

Add flour; cook 1 minute, stirring constantly. Gradually add water and bouillon granules; bring to a boil, stirring constantly. Reduce heat, and simmer, uncovered, 5 to 10 minutes, stirring occasionally.

Pour carrot mixture into container of an electric blender or food processor; top with cover, and process until smooth. Transfer mixture to a bowl; cover and chill thoroughly.

Ladle soup into individual bowls. Garnish with fresh dillweed sprigs, if desired. Yield: 4½ cups (47 calories and 25% fat per ¾-cup serving).

Protein 1.1 / Fat 1.3 (Saturated Fat 0.3) / Carbohydrate 8.5
Fiber 2.2 / Cholesterol 0 / Sodium 295

Fruit soups such as (clockwise from top) Kiwifruit-Apple Soup, Refreshing Melon Soup, and Berry Soup are ideal for summer meals.

Cool Gazpacho

3¼ cups no-salt-added tomato juice
2 cups peeled, seeded, and diced tomato
2 cups chopped cucumber
¾ cup diced green pepper
¼ cup diced onion
¼ cup diced celery
¼ cup sliced green onions
2 tablespoons chopped fresh parsley
3 tablespoons red wine vinegar
1 teaspoon chopped fresh cilantro
½ teaspoon salt
⅛ teaspoon freshly ground pepper
3 cloves garlic, minced
Dash of hot sauce

Combine all ingredients in a large bowl, stirring well. Cover and refrigerate at least 8 hours. Yield: 2 quarts (44 calories and 6% fat per 1-cup serving).

Protein 2.0 / Fat 0.3 (Saturated Fat 0.1) / Carbohydrate 10.3
Fiber 1.5 / Cholesterol 0 / Sodium 168

Fresh Tomato Soup with Basil

Vegetable cooking spray
4½ cups peeled, seeded, and chopped tomato
¾ cup chopped onion
½ cup chopped celery
1 cup water
1 teaspoon chicken-flavored bouillon granules
½ teaspoon sugar
¼ teaspoon freshly ground pepper
⅓ cup finely chopped fresh basil
Fresh basil sprigs (optional)

Coat a Dutch oven with cooking spray; place over medium heat until hot. Add tomato, onion, and celery; sauté 5 minutes or until onion is tender.

Add water and next 3 ingredients; bring to a boil. Cover, reduce heat, and simmer 30 minutes, stirring occasionally.

Transfer mixture in batches to container of an electric blender or food processor; top with cover, and process until smooth. Pour into a bowl; stir in chopped basil. Cover and chill.

Ladle soup into individual bowls. Garnish with fresh basil sprigs, if desired. Yield: 5 cups (55 calories and 16% fat per 1-cup serving).

Protein 2.1 / Fat 1.0 (Saturated Fat 0.1) / Carbohydrate 11.7
Fiber 3.1 / Cholesterol 0 / Sodium 191

Asparagus Vichyssoise

2 pounds fresh asparagus spears
1 medium leek
2 cups peeled, diced potato
3 cups water
2 teaspoons chicken-flavored bouillon granules
1¼ cups skim milk
¼ teaspoon salt
⅛ teaspoon ground white pepper
⅛ teaspoon hot sauce
Lemon rind strips (optional)

Snap off tough ends of asparagus. Remove scales from stalks with a knife or vegetable peeler, if desired. Cut asparagus into 1-inch pieces, reserving tips. Cook asparagus tips in a small amount of boiling water 3 to 4 minutes or until tender. Drain well, and chill thoroughly.

Cut white part of leek into ¼-inch-thick slices, and set aside. Reserve green top for another use.

Combine uncooked asparagus pieces, leek slices, potato, water, and bouillon granules in a large saucepan; bring to a boil. Cover, reduce heat, and simmer 25 minutes or until vegetables are tender. Place mixture in container of an electric blender or food processor; top with cover, and process until smooth. Pour mixture into a large bowl; stir in milk and next 3 ingredients. Cover and chill thoroughly.

Ladle soup into individual bowls; arrange reserved asparagus tips over each serving. Garnish with lemon rind strips, if desired. Yield: 2 quarts (82 calories and 7% fat per 1-cup serving).

Protein 4.4 / Fat 0.6 (Saturated Fat 0.2) / Carbohydrate 16.1
Fiber 1.7 / Cholesterol 1 / Sodium 309

Broccoli-Cheddar Soup

1 quart water
6 cups fresh broccoli flowerets
Vegetable cooking spray
1 cup chopped onion
1 clove garlic, minced
1 cup plain nonfat yogurt
⅓ cup all-purpose flour
2 (10½-ounce) cans low-sodium chicken
   broth, undiluted
¾ cup water
¼ teaspoon salt
⅛ teaspoon ground red pepper
⅛ teaspoon pepper
1 cup (4 ounces) shredded reduced-fat
   sharp Cheddar cheese, divided

Bring 1 quart water to a boil in a Dutch oven; add broccoli, and cook 7 minutes or until tender. Drain well, and set aside.

Coat a large nonstick skillet with cooking spray; place over medium-high heat until hot. Add onion and garlic; sauté until tender.

Position knife blade in food processor bowl; add broccoli and onion mixture. Process until smooth, scraping sides of bowl occasionally. Set mixture aside.

Combine yogurt and flour in a large saucepan, stirring well with a wire whisk. Add broth and next 4 ingredients; stir well. Cook over medium heat 20 minutes or until thickened and bubbly, stirring constantly. Add broccoli mixture and ¾ cup cheese, stirring until cheese melts. Ladle soup into individual bowls, and top evenly with remaining cheese. Yield: 7 cups (126 calories and 26% fat per 1-cup serving).

Protein 9.8 / Fat 3.6 (Saturated Fat 1.9) / Carbohydrate 13.9
Fiber 2.8 / Cholesterol 12 / Sodium 247

French Onion Soup

1 cup sliced carrot
4 cups canned no-salt-added beef broth,
   undiluted
1 clove garlic, crushed
Vegetable cooking spray
1 teaspoon reduced-calorie margarine
3 medium-size yellow onions, thinly sliced
4 (½-inch-thick) slices French bread
½ cup (2 ounces) shredded reduced-fat
   Swiss cheese

Combine first 3 ingredients in a Dutch oven; bring to a boil. Cover, reduce heat, and simmer 20 minutes. Strain broth through a double layer of cheesecloth, discarding carrot and garlic. Return broth to pan; set aside.

Coat a large nonstick skillet with vegetable cooking spray; add margarine. Place over medium heat until margarine melts. Add onion slices; reduce heat to medium-low, and cook 25 minutes or until onion slices are tender and lightly browned, stirring occasionally. Add browned onion to beef broth; bring onion mixture to a boil. Cover, reduce heat, and simmer 10 minutes, stirring occasionally.

Place bread slices on a baking sheet. Bake at 350° for 5 minutes or until bread slices are lightly toasted. Sprinkle bread slices with cheese; bake an additional 3 minutes or until cheese melts.

Ladle soup into individual bowls, and top with cheese toast. Serve immediately. Yield: 4 cups (209 calories and 19% fat per 1-cup serving).

Protein 9.6 / Fat 4.4 (Saturated Fat 1.9) / Carbohydrate 30.2
Fiber 2.5 / Cholesterol 10 / Sodium 233

Cuban Black Bean Soup

1 pound dried black beans
9 cups water
2 cloves garlic, crushed
¾ teaspoon salt
1½ cups finely chopped green pepper
1½ cups finely chopped onion
2 tablespoons lemon juice
1½ teaspoons ground cumin
½ teaspoon dried whole oregano
3 cloves garlic, crushed
2 to 4 drops of hot sauce
Marinated Rice

Sort and wash beans; place in a large Dutch oven. Cover with water to a depth of 2 inches above beans; let soak 8 hours.

Drain beans, and return to pan. Add 9 cups water, 2 cloves garlic, and salt; bring to a boil. Cover partially; reduce heat, and simmer 2 hours or until beans are tender.

Add chopped green pepper and next 6 ingredients to beans; bring to a boil. Reduce heat, and simmer, partially covered, 30 to 45 minutes or until vegetables are tender, stirring occasionally.

Ladle soup into individual bowls. Top each serving with 2 tablespoons Marinated Rice. Yield: 2½ quarts (190 calories and 7% fat per 1-cup serving).

Marinated Rice

⅔ cup cooked brown rice (cooked without salt or fat)
½ cup finely chopped tomato
¼ cup chopped green onions
2 teaspoons lemon juice
1 teaspoon olive oil

Combine all ingredients in a medium bowl, stirring well. Cover and chill at least 3 hours. Yield: 1¼ cups.

Protein 10.8 / Fat 1.4 (Saturated Fat 0.3) / Carbohydrate 35.6
Fiber 7.2 / Cholesterol 0 / Sodium 183

Zesty Pinto Bean Soup

Vegetable cooking spray
½ cup finely chopped green pepper
2 (16-ounce) cans pinto beans, drained and divided
¾ cup water, divided
1 (14½-ounce) can no-salt-added whole tomatoes, undrained and chopped
2 tablespoons canned chopped green chiles
1 jalapeño pepper, seeded and chopped
1 teaspoon ground cumin
¼ teaspoon ground red pepper
⅓ cup thinly sliced green onions

Coat a saucepan with cooking spray; place over medium-high heat until hot. Add green pepper; sauté 2 minutes. Remove from heat. Add 1½ cups pinto beans and ¼ cup water; mash.

Stir in remaining beans, remaining ½ cup water, tomato, and next 4 ingredients; bring to a boil. Reduce heat, and simmer, uncovered, 10 minutes, stirring occasionally. Ladle soup into individual bowls; top with onions. Yield: 5 cups (109 calories and 8% fat per 1-cup serving).

Protein 5.2 / Fat 1.0 (Saturated Fat 0) / Carbohydrate 20.4
Fiber 2.8 / Cholesterol 0 / Sodium 367

A variety of herbs and other seasonings create a fiesta of flavors in Cuban Black Bean Soup (in foreground) and Zesty Pinto Bean Soup.

Chunky Chicken Noodle Soup

8 (6-ounce) skinned chicken breast halves
1 quart water
3 fresh celery leaves
¾ teaspoon poultry seasoning
¼ teaspoon dried whole thyme
2 cups water
2 cups medium noodles made without
  egg yolks, uncooked
½ cup sliced celery
½ cup sliced carrot
⅓ cup sliced green onions
2 tablespoons minced fresh parsley
1½ teaspoons chicken-flavored bouillon
  granules
½ teaspoon coarsely ground pepper
1 bay leaf
Coarsely ground pepper

Combine chicken, 1 quart water, celery leaves, poultry seasoning, and thyme in a large Dutch oven; bring to a boil. Cover, reduce heat, and simmer 45 minutes or until chicken is tender.

Remove chicken from broth, reserving broth. Let chicken cool to touch. Bone and coarsely chop chicken; set aside. Skim fat from broth, and strain broth through a double layer of cheesecloth, discarding celery leaves and herbs.

Combine broth, 2 cups water, and next 8 ingredients in pan; bring to a boil. Cover, reduce heat, and simmer 20 minutes, stirring occasionally.

Add chicken; bring to a boil. Reduce heat, and simmer an additional 5 minutes, stirring occasionally. Remove and discard bay leaf. Ladle soup into individual bowls, and sprinkle with pepper. Yield: 3 quarts (145 calories and 19% fat per 1-cup serving).

Protein 20.9 / Fat 3.1 (Saturated Fat 0.7) / Carbohydrate 6.7
Fiber 0.3 / Cholesterol 52 / Sodium 193

Four-Meat Burgoo

¼ pound lean boneless round steak
¼ pound veal cutlets
¼ pound lean boneless pork shoulder
4 (6-ounce) skinned chicken breast halves
1½ quarts water
1 (14½-ounce) can no-salt-added whole
  tomatoes, undrained and chopped
1 (8¾-ounce) can no-salt-added whole
  kernel corn, drained
1 cup chopped onion
¾ cup shredded cabbage
¾ cup thinly sliced fresh okra
½ cup peeled, cubed round red potato
½ cup frozen lima beans
½ cup chopped green pepper
⅓ cup sliced carrot
¼ cup chopped fresh parsley
2 hot red peppers
2½ teaspoons low-sodium Worcestershire
  sauce
¼ teaspoon salt
⅛ teaspoon ground red pepper

Trim fat from steak, veal, and pork; cut into 1-inch pieces.

Combine steak, veal, pork, chicken, and water in a large Dutch oven; bring to a boil. Cover, reduce heat, and simmer 30 minutes or until meat and chicken are tender.

Remove meat and chicken from broth; reserving broth. Let chicken cool to touch. Bone chicken, and cut into bite-size pieces. Skim and discard fat from reserved broth.

Combine meat, chicken pieces, reserved broth, chopped tomato, and remaining ingredients in pan, stirring well; bring mixture to a boil.

Reduce heat, and simmer, uncovered, 2 to 2½ hours or until mixture is thickened, stirring occasionally. Remove and discard hot red peppers. Ladle soup into individual bowls, and serve warm. Yield: 2 quarts (228 calories and 21% fat per 1-cup serving).

Protein 26.7 / Fat 5.2 (Saturated Fat 1.6) / Carbohydrate 15.8
Fiber 1.3 / Cholesterol 72 / Sodium 172

Chili Con Carne

2¼ pounds lean boneless round steak
Vegetable cooking spray
2 cups chopped onion
4 cloves garlic, minced
2 (14½-ounce) cans no-salt-added whole
   tomatoes, undrained and chopped
2½ cups water
1½ tablespoons ground cumin
¾ teaspoon crushed red pepper
½ teaspoon dried whole oregano
¼ teaspoon salt
1 bay leaf

Trim fat from steak; cut steak into 1-inch pieces. Coat a large Dutch oven with cooking spray; place over medium-high heat until hot.

Add steak; cook until browned on all sides, stirring frequently. Drain well, and pat dry with paper towels. Wipe drippings from pan with a paper towel.

Coat pan with cooking spray; place over medium-high heat until hot. Add onion and garlic; sauté 4 to 5 minutes or until tender.

Stir in steak, tomato, and remaining ingredients; bring to a boil. Reduce heat, and simmer, uncovered, 1 hour and 15 minutes or until meat is tender and mixture is thickened, stirring occasionally. Remove and discard bay leaf. Yield: 7 cups (211 calories and 31% fat per 1-cup serving).

Protein 26.0 / Fat 7.3 (Saturated Fat 2.5) / Carbohydrate 9.9
Fiber 0.9 / Cholesterol 70 / Sodium 158

Vegetarian Chili

Vegetable cooking spray
1 teaspoon olive oil
1½ cups chopped onion
1½ cups chopped green pepper
1 cup chopped celery
2 (16-ounce) cans pinto beans, rinsed and
   drained
2 (14½-ounce) cans no-salt-added whole
   tomatoes, undrained and chopped
1 (6-ounce) can no-salt-added tomato paste
1½ cups water
1 cup chopped fresh mushrooms
1 jalapeño pepper, seeded and chopped
1 tablespoon chili powder
1½ teaspoons ground cumin
1 teaspoon dried whole oregano
½ teaspoon pepper
½ (16-ounce) package firm tofu

Coat a large Dutch oven with cooking spray; add oil. Place over medium-high heat until hot. Add chopped onion, green pepper, and celery; sauté 4 to 5 minutes or until vegetables are crisp-tender.

Add pinto beans and next 9 ingredients; stir well. Bring to a boil; cover, reduce heat, and simmer 30 minutes, stirring occasionally. Wrap tofu in several layers of cheesecloth or paper towels; press lightly to remove excess moisture. Remove cheesecloth; cut tofu into 1½-inch pieces. Gently stir tofu into bean mixture; bring to a boil. Cover, reduce heat, and simmer, stirring occasionally, 10 minutes or until tofu is thoroughly heated. Yield: 2½ quarts (119 calories and 18% fat per 1-cup serving).

Protein 6.3 / Fat 2.4 (Saturated Fat 0.3) / Carbohydrate 20.1
Fiber 3.0 / Cholesterol 0 / Sodium 226

Corn and Pepper Chowder

Vegetable cooking spray
1 teaspoon olive oil
1 cup chopped onion
1 cup diced sweet red pepper
2½ tablespoons all-purpose flour
½ teaspoon ground cumin
⅛ teaspoon ground red pepper
2 cups water
1¼ cups peeled, diced potato
1 teaspoon chicken-flavored bouillon
    granules
2 cups frozen whole kernel corn
2 tablespoons canned chopped green chiles,
    drained
1 cup evaporated skimmed milk
¼ teaspoon pepper

Coat a large Dutch oven with cooking spray; add oil. Place over medium-high heat until hot. Add onion and sweet red pepper; sauté 5 minutes or until vegetables are tender.

Stir in flour, cumin, and ground red pepper; cook 1 minute, stirring constantly. Gradually stir in water; add potato and bouillon granules. Bring mixture to a boil, stirring frequently. Cover, reduce heat, and simmer 10 minutes or until potato is tender and mixture is thickened.

Add corn and remaining ingredients; cook until thoroughly heated, stirring occasionally. Yield: 1½ quarts (138 calories and 11% fat per 1-cup serving).

Protein 6.3 / Fat 1.7 (Saturated Fat 0.3) / Carbohydrate 26.8
Fiber 2.7 / Cholesterol 2 / Sodium 289

Seafood Gumbo

3 (6-ounce) skinned chicken breast halves
2 quarts water
Vegetable cooking spray
1 tablespoon vegetable oil
2 medium onions, sliced
1¼ cups diced green pepper
1 teaspoon minced garlic
2 tablespoons all-purpose flour
6 cups water
2 (14½-ounce) cans no-salt-added whole
    tomatoes, undrained and chopped
1 pound fresh okra, sliced
2 tablespoons chopped fresh parsley
1 teaspoon vinegar
½ teaspoon salt
½ teaspoon pepper
¼ teaspoon crushed red pepper
¼ teaspoon dried whole thyme
1 bay leaf
1 pound fresh crabmeat, drained
1 pound medium-size fresh shrimp, peeled
    and deveined

Combine chicken and 2 quarts water in a large saucepan; bring to a boil. Cover, reduce heat, and simmer 30 minutes or until chicken is tender. Remove chicken from broth; discard broth. Let chicken cool to touch. Bone and chop chicken; set aside.

Coat a large Dutch oven with cooking spray; add oil. Place over medium-high heat until hot. Add sliced onion, green pepper, and minced garlic; sauté 5 minutes or until vegetables are crisp-tender.

Add flour; cook 1 minute, stirring constantly. Gradually stir in 6 cups water; add chicken, chopped tomato, and next 8 ingredients, stirring well. Bring to a boil; reduce heat, and simmer, uncovered, 40 to 45 minutes. Stir in crabmeat and shrimp; cook 8 minutes or until shrimp are done. Remove and discard bay leaf. Yield: 1 gallon (132 calories and 18% fat per 1-cup serving).

Protein 18.6 / Fat 2.7 (Saturated Fat 0.5) / Carbohydrate 7.8
Fiber 0.9 / Cholesterol 80 / Sodium 211

Southwestern Beef Stew

1 pound lean boneless round steak
Vegetable cooking spray
1 (14½-ounce) can no-salt-added whole
    tomatoes, undrained and chopped
1 cup water
1 cup peeled, cubed potato
1 cup sliced carrot
¾ cup chopped onion
¾ cup light beer
¼ cup chopped sweet red pepper
¼ cup chopped fresh cilantro
2 teaspoons dried whole oregano
1½ teaspoons chili powder
1 teaspoon beef-flavored bouillon granules
1 jalapeño pepper, seeded and chopped
1 clove garlic, minced
2 tablespoons all-purpose flour
2 tablespoons water

Trim fat from steak; cut steak into 1-inch pieces.

Coat a Dutch oven with cooking spray; place over medium-high heat until hot. Add steak; cook 10 minutes or until steak is browned on all sides. Drain and pat dry with paper towels. Wipe drippings from pan with a paper towel. Return steak to pan; add tomato and next 12 ingredients. Bring to a boil. Cover, reduce heat, and simmer 1 hour and 15 minutes or until meat is tender.

Combine flour and 2 tablespoons water, stirring until smooth. Add to stew, and stir well. Cook over medium heat until thickened and bubbly, stirring constantly. Yield: 1½ quarts (172 calories and 20% fat per 1-cup serving).

Protein 17.1 / Fat 3.8 (Saturated Fat 1.3) / Carbohydrate 17.4
Fiber 2.3 / Cholesterol 39 / Sodium 225

Hearty Hamburger Stew

Vegetable cooking spray
1 pound ground chuck
1 cup chopped onion
3 cups water
1 (14½-ounce) can no-salt-added whole
    tomatoes, undrained and chopped
½ cup chopped celery
2 teaspoons beef-flavored bouillon granules
2 teaspoons low-sodium Worcestershire
    sauce
⅛ teaspoon pepper
1 bay leaf
1 (10-ounce) package frozen baby lima beans
1 (8¾-ounce) can no-salt-added whole
    kernel corn, drained
4 ounces small shell macaroni, uncooked

Coat a Dutch oven with cooking spray; place over medium heat until hot. Add ground chuck and onion; cook until meat is browned, stirring to crumble meat. Drain meat mixture; pat dry with paper towels. Wipe drippings from pan with a paper towel.

Return meat mixture to pan; add water and next 6 ingredients, stirring well. Bring to a boil; cover, reduce heat, and simmer 30 minutes.

Add lima beans, corn, and macaroni; bring to a boil. Reduce heat, and simmer, uncovered, 20 minutes, stirring occasionally. Remove and discard bay leaf. Yield: 9 cups (217 calories and 32% fat per 1-cup serving).

Protein 13.9 / Fat 7.7 (Saturated Fat 2.8) / Carbohydrate 22.7
Fiber 1.3 / Cholesterol 29 / Sodium 296

You'll find it hard to resist low-fat Burgundy Beef Stew, a savory blend of beef, carrots, onions, and mushrooms.

Burgundy Beef Stew

1½ pounds lean boneless round steak
Vegetable cooking spray
1 teaspoon vegetable oil
½ teaspoon dried whole thyme
2 large cloves garlic, minced
3 cups Burgundy or other dry red wine
¼ cup no-salt-added tomato paste
2 bay leaves
2 (13¾-ounce) cans no-salt-added beef
 broth, undiluted
½ cup plus 3 tablespoons water, divided
1½ pounds round red potatoes, quartered
½ pound fresh mushrooms, quartered
6 medium carrots, scraped and cut into
 1-inch pieces
2 small onions, quartered
3 tablespoons cornstarch
¼ cup chopped fresh parsley
½ teaspoon salt
¼ teaspoon pepper

Trim fat from steak; cut steak into 1-inch pieces. Coat a large Dutch oven with cooking spray; add oil. Place over medium-high heat until hot. Add steak; cook until browned, stirring frequently. Drain well, and pat dry with paper towels. Wipe drippings from pan with a paper towel.

Coat pan with cooking spray; place over medium-high heat until hot. Add steak, thyme and garlic; cook 1 minute, stirring constantly. Stir in wine, tomato paste, and bay leaves; bring to a boil. Cover, reduce heat, and simmer 1½ hours or until steak is tender.

Add beef broth, ½ cup water and next 4 ingredients; bring to a boil. Cover, reduce heat, and simmer 40 minutes or until vegetables are tender. Remove and discard bay leaves.

Combine cornstarch and remaining 3 tablespoons water, stirring well. Add to stew, and stir well. Cook over medium heat until thickened and bubbly, stirring constantly. Stir in parsley, salt, and pepper. Yield: 2½ quarts (213 calories and 17% fat per 1-cup serving).

Protein 20.2 / Fat 4.1 (Saturated Fat 1.3) / Carbohydrate 23.4
Fiber 3.1 / Cholesterol 45 / Sodium 183

Chicken and Okra Stew

2 cups diced cooked chicken breast
 (skinned before cooking and cooked
 without salt)
2 (10½-ounce) cans low-sodium chicken
 broth, undiluted
1 (14½-ounce) can no-salt-added stewed
 tomatoes, undrained and chopped
1 (10-ounce) package frozen sliced okra
1 cup diced onion
¼ teaspoon salt
¼ teaspoon dried whole basil
¼ teaspoon dried whole oregano
¼ teaspoon pepper
¼ teaspoon hot sauce
2 cloves garlic, minced
2 tablespoons all-purpose flour
¼ cup skim milk

Combine first 11 ingredients in a large Dutch oven; stir well. Bring to a boil; cover, reduce heat, and simmer 45 minutes.

Combine flour and milk, stirring until smooth. Add to stew, and stir well. Cook over medium heat until thickened and bubbly, stirring constantly. Yield: 7 cups (130 calories and 12% fat per 1-cup serving).

Protein 16.1 / Fat 1.8 (Saturated Fat 0.5) / Carbohydrate 11.4
Fiber 0.8 / Cholesterol 38 / Sodium 137

Fat-Proof Your Diet

If you want to be healthy and control your weight, eat less fat. We have all heard this advice, but knowing exactly how much less fat and what foods have less fat is not always clear.

Although our bodies need some fat, most of us eat six to eight times more than we need. Fat supplies nine calories per gram—more than twice the calories of either carbohydrate or protein. Therefore, reducing fat is the best way to reduce calories; at the same time you'll lower the risk of heart disease, cancer, and obesity.

Seafood Stew

Vegetable cooking spray
1 teaspoon vegetable oil
¼ cup chopped green pepper
2 tablespoons chopped onion
1 clove garlic, minced
1 (14½-ounce) can no-salt-added whole
tomatoes, undrained and coarsely chopped
1 (8-ounce) can no-salt-added tomato sauce
½ cup Burgundy or other dry red wine
3 tablespoons chopped fresh parsley
¼ teaspoon salt
¼ teaspoon dried whole oregano
¼ teaspoon dried whole basil
½ pound amberjack fillets
½ pound large fresh shrimp, peeled and
deveined
½ pound fresh sea scallops

Coat a large Dutch oven with cooking spray; add oil. Place over medium-high heat until hot. Add green pepper, onion, and garlic; sauté 4 to 5 minutes or until vegetables are tender.

Add chopped tomato and next 6 ingredients; stir well. Bring to a boil; cover, reduce heat, and simmer 10 minutes, stirring occasionally.

Cut amberjack fillets into 1-inch pieces. Add amberjack pieces, shrimp, and scallops to tomato mixture, stirring well. Bring to a boil over medium heat; cover, reduce heat, and simmer 8 to 10 minutes or until shrimp turn pink, and fish flakes easily when tested with a fork. Yield: 5 cups (165 calories and 14% fat per 1-cup serving).

Protein 24.4 / Fat 2.6 (Saturated Fat 0.5) / Carbohydrate 10.4
Fiber 0.3 / Cholesterol 88 / Sodium 301

In English Peas and Pearl Onions (page 238), the addition of mushrooms and pearl onions transforms a simple vegetable into a special dish.

Honey-Mustard Brussels Sprouts

1 pound fresh brussels sprouts
1½ cups water
1 teaspoon chicken-flavored bouillon
  granules
2 tablespoons honey
2 teaspoons Dijon mustard
2 teaspoons lemon juice

Wash brussels sprouts thoroughly, and remove discolored leaves. Cut off stem ends, and cut a shallow X in bottom of each brussels sprout using a sharp knife.

Combine water and bouillon granules in a medium saucepan; bring to a boil. Add brussels sprouts, and return to a boil. Cover, reduce heat, and simmer 10 to 12 minutes or until brussels sprouts are tender. Drain; transfer to a serving bowl, and keep warm.

Combine honey, mustard, and lemon juice. Pour over brussels sprouts, tossing gently to coat. Serve immediately. Yield: 6 servings (52 calories and 9% fat per ½-cup serving).

Protein 2.2 / Fat 0.5 (Saturated Fat 0.1) / Carbohydrate 11.7
Fiber 2.6 / Cholesterol 0 / Sodium 195

Caraway-Cabbage Medley

½ cup water
½ teaspoon chicken-flavored bouillon
  granules
8 cups shredded cabbage (about 1 small
  cabbage)
2 cups sliced fresh mushrooms
1 cup minced onion
1 cup shredded carrot
1 tablespoon caraway seeds
¼ teaspoon salt
Cabbage leaves (optional)

Combine water and bouillon granules in a large Dutch oven; bring to a boil. Add shredded cabbage and next 5 ingredients, stirring well to combine. Cook, uncovered, over medium-high heat 10 minutes or until cabbage is tender, stirring constantly.

Serve in a cabbage leaf-lined bowl, if desired. Yield: 6 servings (58 calories and 9% fat per 1-cup serving).

Protein 2.7 / Fat 0.6 (Saturated Fat 0.1) / Carbohydrate 12.3
Fiber 4.3 / Cholesterol 0 / Sodium 192

Sweet-and-Sour Cabbage with Apples

⅔ cup red wine vinegar
2 tablespoons sugar
¼ teaspoon salt
7½ cups finely chopped red cabbage
  (about 2 pounds)
2 teaspoons reduced-calorie margarine
2 medium apples, peeled and cut into thin
  wedges
½ cup finely chopped onion
1 cup water
3 tablespoons red currant jelly
3 tablespoons Burgundy or other dry red wine
⅛ teaspoon ground cloves
1 bay leaf

Combine first 3 ingredients in a large bowl, stirring mixture well. Add cabbage, tossing well; set aside.

Melt margarine in a large, nonaluminum Dutch oven over medium heat. Add apple and onion; sauté 5 minutes or until onion is tender. Add cabbage mixture, water, jelly, wine, cloves, and bay leaf; bring to a boil. Reduce heat to medium-low, and cook, uncovered, 1 hour or until liquid has evaporated. Remove and discard bay leaf. Yield: 12 servings (57 calories and 9% fat per ½-cup serving).

Protein 0.7 / Fat 0.6 (Saturated Fat 0.1) / Carbohydrate 13.0
Fiber 1.8 / Cholesterol 0 / Sodium 62

Pineapple and ground ginger give carrots a flavor boost in Tropical Carrots.

Lemon Baby Carrots

1 pound fresh baby carrots with tops
2 tablespoons lemon juice
2 teaspoons reduced-calorie margarine, melted
1 teaspoon sugar
Dash of ground white pepper

Scrape and trim baby carrots, leaving ½ inch of green tops, if desired. Arrange carrots in a vegetable steamer over boiling water. Cover and steam 10 minutes or until crisp-tender. Transfer carrots to a serving bowl.

Combine lemon juice and remaining ingredients; stir well. Pour over carrots, and toss gently. Yield: 4 servings (42 calories and 28% fat per serving).

Protein 0.6 / Fat 1.3 (Saturated Fat 0.2) / Carbohydrate 7.8
Fiber 1.9 / Cholesterol 0 / Sodium 40

Tropical Carrots

1¾ cups diagonally sliced carrot
1 (8-ounce) can pineapple tidbits in juice, undrained
2 teaspoons cornstarch
¼ teaspoon ground ginger

Place carrot in a saucepan. Add water to cover; bring to a boil. Cover, reduce heat, and simmer 12 minutes or until crisp-tender; drain.

Combine pineapple with juice, cornstarch, and ginger in a medium saucepan; bring to a boil. Reduce heat to low, and cook, stirring constantly, until thickened. Add carrot, and cook 1 minute or until thoroughly heated, stirring occasionally. Yield: 4 servings (52 calories and 3% fat per ½-cup serving).

Protein 0.9 / Fat 0.2 (Saturated Fat 0) / Carbohydrate 12.6
Fiber 2.4 / Cholesterol 0 / Sodium 24

Orange-Ginger Carrots

Vegetable cooking spray
1 teaspoon reduced-calorie margarine
1 pound carrots, scraped and cut
  into julienne strips
2 tablespoons unsweetened
  orange juice
1 teaspoon brown sugar
¼ teaspoon ground ginger
⅛ teaspoon salt
⅛ teaspoon dry mustard
Dash of pepper
1½ teaspoons sesame seeds, toasted

Coat a large nonstick skillet with cooking spray. Add margarine; place over medium heat until margarine melts. Add carrot; sauté 8 minutes or until crisp-tender.

Add orange juice and next 5 ingredients; cook over medium-low heat 8 to 10 minutes or until carrot is tender, stirring occasionally. Transfer mixture to a serving bowl. Sprinkle with sesame seeds; toss gently. Yield: 4 servings (63 calories and 23% fat per ½-cup serving).

Protein 1.4 / Fat 1.6 (Saturated Fat 0.2) / Carbohydrate 12.0
Fiber 3.3 / Cholesterol 0 / Sodium 119

Spiced Carrot Soufflé

1½ cups sliced carrot
Vegetable cooking spray
⅓ cup firmly packed brown sugar
1 teaspoon vanilla extract
½ teaspoon ground ginger
½ teaspoon ground cinnamon
¼ teaspoon salt
⅛ teaspoon ground mace
2 tablespoons reduced-calorie margarine
2 tablespoons all-purpose flour
¾ cup skim milk
¼ cup frozen egg substitute, thawed
4 egg whites

Place carrot in a medium saucepan; add water to cover. Bring to a boil; reduce heat, and simmer 20 minutes or until carrot is tender. Drain and set aside.

Cut a piece of aluminum foil long enough to fit around a 1½-quart soufflé dish, allowing a 1-inch overlap; fold foil lengthwise in thirds. Coat one side of foil and bottom of dish with cooking spray. Wrap foil around outside of dish, coated side against dish, allowing foil to extend 3 inches above rim to form a collar. Secure foil with string.

Combine carrot, brown sugar, and next 5 ingredients in container of an electric blender; top with cover, and process until smooth. Transfer carrot mixture to a bowl, and set aside.

Melt margarine in a small, heavy saucepan over medium heat. Add flour; stir until smooth. Cook 1 minute, stirring constantly. Gradually add milk, stirring constantly. Cook, stirring constantly, until mixture is thickened and bubbly. Gradually stir about one-fourth of hot mixture into egg substitute; add to remaining hot mixture, stirring constantly. Remove from heat; stir in carrot mixture.

Beat egg whites at high speed of an electric mixer until stiff peaks form. Gently fold egg whites into carrot mixture; spoon into prepared dish. Bake at 350° for 45 to 50 minutes or until puffed and golden. Remove collar from soufflé dish. Serve immediately. Yield: 8 servings (93 calories and 19% fat per serving).

Protein 3.8 / Fat 2.0 (Saturated Fat 0.3) / Carbohydrate 15.2
Fiber 1.1 / Cholesterol 0 / Sodium 165

Cauliflower au Gratin

4 cups fresh cauliflower flowerets
Vegetable cooking spray
1½ tablespoons cornstarch
1½ cups skim milk
½ cup (2 ounces) shredded
  reduced-fat sharp Cheddar cheese
1½ tablespoons grated Parmesan cheese,
  divided
⅛ teaspoon dry mustard
⅛ teaspoon pepper
Dash of ground nutmeg
1 tablespoon fine, dry breadcrumbs

Arrange cauliflower in a vegetable steamer over boiling water. Cover; steam until crisp-tender.

Transfer to an 11- x 7- x 2-inch baking dish coated with cooking spray; set aside.

Combine cornstarch and milk in a small saucepan, stirring well. Cook over medium heat, stirring constantly, until thickened. Stir in Cheddar cheese, 1 tablespoon Parmesan cheese, mustard, pepper, and nutmeg; cook mixture until cheese melts, stirring constantly.

Pour sauce over cauliflower; sprinkle with remaining Parmesan cheese and breadcrumbs. Broil 5½ inches from heat 5 minutes or until lightly browned and bubbly. Yield: 8 servings (71 calories and 27% fat per ½-cup serving).

Protein 5.7 / Fat 2.1 (Saturated Fat 0.9) / Carbohydrate 8.0
Fiber 1.8 / Cholesterol 7 / Sodium 117

Fresh Corn Pudding

Vegetable cooking spray
¾ cup chopped onion
¾ cup chopped green pepper
¾ cup chopped sweet red pepper
3 tablespoons all-purpose flour
½ teaspoon ground cumin
½ teaspoon chili powder
¼ teaspoon salt
⅛ teaspoon pepper
1 (12-ounce) can evaporated skimmed milk
½ cup frozen egg substitute, thawed
4 cups fresh corn cut from cob (about 6 ears)
Green and sweet red pepper rings (optional)

Coat a large nonstick skillet with cooking spray; place over medium-high heat until hot.

Add onion and chopped peppers; sauté 5 minutes or until crisp-tender.

Add flour and next 4 ingredients; cook 1 minute, stirring constantly. Gradually add milk; stir constantly. Cook, stirring constantly, until mixture is thickened and bubbly. Gradually stir about one-fourth of hot mixture into egg substitute; add to remaining hot mixture, stirring constantly. Remove from heat; stir in corn.

Spoon mixture into a 2-quart casserole coated with cooking spray. Bake at 350° for 40 minutes or until set. Garnish with pepper rings, if desired. Yield: 12 servings (87 calories and 9% fat per ½-cup serving).

Protein 5.3 / Fat 0.9 (Saturated Fat 0.2) / Carbohydrate 16.4
Fiber 2.7 / Cholesterol 1 / Sodium 106

Savory Green Beans

½ pound fresh green beans
Vegetable cooking spray
½ cup chopped onion
2 cups peeled, chopped tomato
1 (2-ounce) jar diced pimiento,
  drained
¼ teaspoon salt
¼ teaspoon dried whole savory,
  crushed
⅛ teaspoon freshly ground pepper

Wash beans; trim ends, and remove strings. Cut beans into 2-inch pieces; set aside.

Coat a nonstick skillet with cooking spray; place over medium-high heat until hot. Add onion; sauté until tender. Add beans, tomato, and remaining ingredients. Cover; simmer 25 minutes or just until beans are tender. Yield: 6 servings (37 calories and 10% fat per ½-cup serving).

Protein 1.7 / Fat 0.4 (Saturated Fat 0.1) / Carbohydrate 8.1
Fiber 2.1 / Cholesterol 0 / Sodium 109

Hot and Spicy Green Beans

1 pound fresh green beans
Vegetable cooking spray
2 teaspoons vegetable oil
2 cloves garlic, sliced
½ teaspoon dry mustard
¼ teaspoon crushed red pepper
¼ teaspoon ground turmeric
¼ teaspoon salt
¼ cup water
1 large baking potato (about 10 ounces),
    peeled and cut into ½-inch pieces
1 tablespoon chopped fresh parsley
1 tablespoon lemon juice

Wash beans; trim ends, and remove strings. Cut beans into 1½-inch pieces; set aside.

Coat a large nonstick skillet with cooking spray; add oil. Place over medium-high heat until hot. Add garlic and next 3 ingredients; sauté 1 minute. Add beans and salt; cook 10 minutes, stirring frequently.

Add water and potato; cover, reduce heat, and simmer 10 minutes or until vegetables are tender. Stir in parsley and lemon juice. Yield: 8 servings (51 calories and 25% fat per ½-cup serving).

Protein 2.0 / Fat 1.4 (Saturated Fat 0.2) / Carbohydrate 8.9
Fiber 1.8 / Cholesterol 0 / Sodium 81

Sherried Mushrooms

Vegetable cooking spray
½ cup sliced green onions
1 pound sliced fresh mushrooms
2 tablespoons dry sherry
1 tablespoon low-sodium Worcestershire sauce
¼ teaspoon freshly ground pepper

Coat a large nonstick skillet with cooking spray; place over medium-high heat until hot. Add green onions; sauté until tender.

Stir in mushrooms and remaining ingredients; cover and cook over low heat 10 minutes or until mushrooms are tender. Yield: 6 servings (26 calories and 14% fat per ½-cup serving).

Protein 1.8 / Fat 0.4 (Saturated Fat 0.1) / Carbohydrate 5.0
Fiber 1.2 / Cholesterol 0 / Sodium 15

English Peas and Pearl Onions

2½ cups shelled fresh English peas
16 pearl onions
3 cups water
Vegetable cooking spray
½ pound sliced fresh mushrooms
1 (2-ounce) jar sliced pimiento, drained
¼ teaspoon salt
¼ teaspoon ground savory
⅛ teaspoon freshly ground pepper

Place peas, onions, and water in a saucepan; bring to a boil. Cover, reduce heat, and simmer 15 minutes or until peas are tender; drain well.

Coat a large nonstick skillet with cooking spray; place over medium-high heat until hot. Add mushrooms; sauté 4 minutes or until tender. Stir in peas and onions, pimiento, and remaining ingredients; cook, stirring occasionally, until thoroughly heated. Yield: 8 servings (51 calories and 5% fat per ½-cup serving).

Protein 3.2 / Fat 0.3 (Saturated Fat 0.1) / Carbohydrate 9.5
Fiber 2.0 / Cholesterol 0 / Sodium 79

Fancy English Peas

2 (10-ounce) packages frozen English peas
Vegetable cooking spray
1 tablespoon reduced-calorie margarine
¾ cup finely chopped onion
¼ cup finely chopped green pepper
2 tablespoons minced fresh parsley
1 (2-ounce) jar diced pimiento, drained
½ teaspoon vinegar
¼ teaspoon salt
⅛ teaspoon ground nutmeg

Cook peas according to package directions, omitting salt; drain well, and set aside.

Coat a nonstick skillet with cooking spray; add margarine. Place over medium-high heat until margarine melts. Add onion and next 3 ingredients; sauté until vegetables are tender.

Stir in peas, vinegar, salt, and nutmeg; cook until thoroughly heated, stirring occasionally. Yield: 7 servings (79 calories and 16% fat per ½-cup serving).

Protein 4.4 / Fat 1.4 (Saturated Fat 0.2) / Carbohydrate 13.1
Fiber 3.9 / Cholesterol 0 / Sodium 171

Three-Pepper Sauté

Vegetable cooking spray
2 medium-size green peppers, cut
   into strips
1 medium-size sweet red pepper, cut
   into strips
1 medium-size sweet yellow pepper,
   cut into strips
1 clove garlic, crushed
¼ teaspoon salt
¼ teaspoon dried whole oregano
2 tablespoons vinegar

Coat a large nonstick skillet with cooking spray; place over medium-high heat until hot. Add peppers, garlic, salt, and oregano; sauté 5 to 7 minutes or until crisp-tender. Remove from heat, and stir in vinegar. Yield: 9 servings (21 calories and 17% fat per ½-cup serving).

Protein 0.6 / Fat 0.4 (Saturated Fat 0.1) / Carbohydrate 4.4
Fiber 1.2 / Cholesterol 0 / Sodium 68

American Fries

3 medium-size baking potatoes (about
   1½ pounds)
½ teaspoon onion powder
½ teaspoon paprika
¼ teaspoon garlic powder
¼ teaspoon salt
¼ teaspoon pepper
Vegetable cooking spray

Scrub potatoes; cut into ¼-inch-thick slices. Pat slices dry with paper towels. Combine onion powder and next 4 ingredients in a large zip-top plastic bag; add potato slices, and shake well to coat.

Arrange potato slices in a single layer on a large baking sheet coated with cooking spray. Bake at 425° for 12 to 15 minutes on each side or until lightly browned. Yield: 6 servings (85 calories and 2% fat per ½-cup serving).

Protein 2.5 / Fat 0.2 (Saturated Fat 0.1) / Carbohydrate 18.8
Fiber 1.9 / Cholesterol 0 / Sodium 106

Homestyle Potatoes

4 medium-size baking potatoes (about 2
   pounds), peeled and cubed
⅓ cup skim milk
¼ cup plain nonfat yogurt
2 tablespoons reduced-calorie margarine
¼ teaspoon salt
⅛ teaspoon pepper

Cook potato in boiling water to cover 30 minutes or until tender. Drain potato, and mash. Add milk and remaining ingredients; beat at medium speed of an electric mixer just until mixture is smooth. Yield: 7 servings (111 calories and 18% fat per ½-cup serving).

Protein 3.1 / Fat 2.2 (Saturated Fat 0.3) / Carbohydrate 20.5
Fiber 1.7 / Cholesterol 0 / Sodium 134

Rosemary-Roasted Potato Wedges

3 medium-size baking potatoes (about
   1½ pounds)
1½ tablespoons olive oil
Vegetable cooking spray
½ teaspoon dried whole rosemary, crushed
¼ teaspoon salt
¼ teaspoon pepper
Fresh rosemary sprigs (optional)

Scrub potatoes; cut each potato lengthwise into 6 wedges. Place wedges in a bowl, and cover with cold water. Let stand 30 minutes; drain and pat dry with paper towels.

Toss wedges with olive oil. Place wedges, cut side down, in a single layer on a baking sheet coated with cooking spray. Combine rosemary, salt, and pepper; sprinkle half of mixture evenly over wedges. Bake at 400° for 20 minutes; turn wedges, and sprinkle with remaining rosemary mixture. Bake an additional 25 to 30 minutes or until tender and lightly browned.

Transfer wedges to a serving plate, and garnish with fresh rosemary sprigs, if desired. Yield: 6 servings (129 calories and 25% fat per 3 wedges).

Protein 2.9 / Fat 3.6 (Saturated Fat 0.5) / Carbohydrate 22.1
Fiber 2.2 / Cholesterol 0 / Sodium 107

Spiced Rutabagas

3½ cups peeled, cubed rutabaga
2 cups water
½ teaspoon ground cinnamon
¼ teaspoon ground nutmeg
⅛ teaspoon pepper
1 tablespoon sugar
1 tablespoon chopped fresh parsley

Combine first 5 ingredients in a medium saucepan; bring to a boil. Cover, reduce heat, and simmer 30 minutes, stirring occasionally.

Add sugar, and cook, uncovered, an additional 20 minutes or until rutabaga is tender, stirring occasionally. Transfer to a serving bowl; sprinkle with chopped parsley. Serve immediately. Yield: 6 servings (37 calories and 5% fat per ½-cup serving).

Protein 1.0 / Fat 0.2 (Saturated Fat 0.1) / Carbohydrate 8.7
Fiber 0.9 / Cholesterol 0 / Sodium 16

Broiled Herbed Tomatoes

4 medium tomatoes
Vegetable cooking spray
2 tablespoons fine, dry breadcrumbs
2 tablespoons grated Parmesan cheese
2 tablespoons minced fresh parsley
1 teaspoon dried whole basil
1 teaspoon dried whole oregano
¼ teaspoon freshly ground pepper
⅛ teaspoon salt
2 teaspoons reduced-calorie margarine, melted

Cut tops off tomatoes; discard tops. Arrange tomatoes on rack of a broiler pan coated with cooking spray; set aside.

Combine breadcrumbs and remaining ingredients; stir well. Sprinkle breadcrumb mixture over cut surface of tomatoes. Broil 5½ inches from heat 2 to 3 minutes or until lightly browned. Yield: 8 servings (57 calories and 30% fat per serving).

Protein 2.4 / Fat 1.9 (Saturated Fat 0.5) / Carbohydrate 9.4
Fiber 2.4 / Cholesterol 1 / Sodium 108

Two-Squash Sauté

Vegetable cooking spray
1 teaspoon reduced-calorie margarine
2 medium zucchini, cut into julienne strips
2 medium-size yellow squash, cut into julienne strips
½ teaspoon chicken-flavored bouillon granules
¼ teaspoon dried whole basil
⅛ teaspoon freshly ground pepper

Coat a large nonstick skillet with cooking spray; add margarine. Place over medium-high heat until margarine melts. Add zucchini and remaining ingredients; sauté 5 minutes or until squash is crisp-tender. Yield: 6 servings (19 calories and 33% fat per ½-cup serving).

Protein 1.0 / Fat 0.7 (Saturated Fat 0.1) / Carbohydrate 2.9
Fiber 0.9 / Cholesterol 0 / Sodium 76

Herbed Spaghetti Squash

1 (3-pound) spaghetti squash
1 tablespoon minced fresh parsley
2 teaspoons reduced-calorie margarine
½ teaspoon dried whole basil
¼ teaspoon salt
⅛ teaspoon pepper
Dash of dried whole sage
Fresh basil sprig (optional)

Wash squash; cut in half lengthwise. Remove and discard seeds. Place squash, cut sides down, in a Dutch oven; add water to pan to a depth of 2 inches. Bring to a boil; cover, reduce heat, and simmer 20 to 25 minutes or until squash is tender. Drain squash; let cool.

Using a fork, remove spaghetti-like strands from squash; discard shells. Place strands in a serving bowl; add parsley and next 5 ingredients, and toss gently. Garnish with a fresh basil sprig, if desired. Yield: 8 servings (29 calories and 25% fat per ½-cup serving).

Protein 0.6 / Fat 0.8 (Saturated Fat 0.1) / Carbohydrate 5.2
Fiber 1.1 / Cholesterol 0 / Sodium 97

Serve Herbed Spaghetti Squash (in foreground) or Two-Squash Sauté for a fresh-from-the-garden presentation.

Oven-Fried Zucchini Chips

3 medium zucchini
¼ cup frozen egg substitute, thawed
2 tablespoons commercial reduced-calorie
  Italian dressing
½ cup fine, dry breadcrumbs
2 tablespoons grated Parmesan cheese
⅛ teaspoon freshly ground pepper
Vegetable cooking spray

Cut zucchini into ¼-inch-thick slices; set aside. Combine egg substitute and Italian dressing in a small bowl; stir well. Combine breadcrumbs, Parmesan cheese, and pepper in a small bowl; stir well.

Dip zucchini in egg mixture; dredge in breadcrumb mixture. Place zucchini on a baking sheet coated with cooking spray. Bake at 475° for 5 minutes; turn and bake an additional 5 minutes or until golden. Serve immediately. Yield: 8 servings (58 calories and 14% fat per ½-cup serving).

Protein 3.1 / Fat 0.9 (Saturated Fat 0.3) / Carbohydrate 9.7
Fiber 0.6 / Cholesterol 1 / Sodium 125

Southern Turnip Greens

2 pounds fresh turnip greens
4 cups water
1 cup peeled, diced turnips
¼ pound chopped reduced-fat, lower-salt
  cooked ham
1 tablespoon balsamic vinegar
1 teaspoon sugar
¼ teaspoon hot sauce
⅛ teaspoon pepper

Remove and discard stems from turnip greens. Wash turnip greens thoroughly, and pat dry with paper towels. Tear turnip greens into bite-size pieces.

Place turnip greens in a large Dutch oven; add water. Bring to a boil; cover, reduce heat, and simmer 20 minutes, stirring occasionally.

Stir in turnips and ham; cover and cook an additional 30 minutes or until turnips are tender. Drain well. Add vinegar and remaining ingredients; stir gently. Yield: 6 servings (73 calories and 17% fat per ½-cup serving).

Protein 5.8 / Fat 1.4 (Saturated Fat 0.4) / Carbohydrate 11.3
Fiber 4.0 / Cholesterol 9 / Sodium 225

Wilted Watercress and Tomatoes

Vegetable cooking spray
1 teaspoon olive oil
2 cups torn fresh watercress
1 cup torn arugula
2 medium tomatoes, seeded and
  coarsely chopped
1 tablespoon lemon juice
¼ teaspoon pepper

Coat a nonstick skillet with cooking spray; add oil. Place over medium-high heat until hot. Add watercress and arugula. Sauté until wilted. Add tomatoes, and cook until thoroughly heated. Sprinkle with lemon juice and pepper. Yield: 4 servings (46 calories and 37% fat per serving).

Protein 2.3 / Fat 1.9 (Saturated Fat 0.2) / Carbohydrate 6.8
Fiber 1.9 / Cholesterol 0 / Sodium 28

Summer Garden Medley

Vegetable cooking spray
1 teaspoon vegetable oil
1 cup chopped onion
¾ cup chopped green pepper
3 medium tomatoes, peeled and
   quartered
2 cups sliced fresh okra
¼ teaspoon salt
¼ teaspoon pepper

Coat a large nonstick skillet with cooking spray; add oil. Place over medium-high heat until hot.

Add onion and green pepper; sauté 5 minutes or until tender. Add tomato and remaining ingredients; cover and cook 5 minutes or until thoroughly heated, stirring occasionally. Yield: 7 servings (46 calories and 23% fat per ½-cup serving).

Protein 1.6 / Fat 1.2 (Saturated Fat 0.2) / Carbohydrate 8.5
Fiber 2.0 / Cholesterol 0 / Sodium 95

Vegetable Ragoût

Vegetable cooking spray
1½ cups chopped onion
1 cup chopped green pepper
3 cloves garlic, minced
4 cups peeled, cubed eggplant (about
   1 medium)
2¾ cups sliced yellow squash
2 cups chopped tomato
½ cup chopped fresh mushrooms
½ teaspoon salt
½ teaspoon dried Italian seasoning
¼ teaspoon pepper
1 cup sliced fresh okra

Coat a large Dutch oven with cooking spray; place over medium-high heat until hot. Add onion, green pepper, and garlic; sauté 3 minutes or until crisp-tender.

Stir in eggplant and next 6 ingredients; cook 5 minutes, stirring frequently. Add okra; cook an additional 5 minutes or until thoroughly heated, stirring frequently. Yield: 6 servings (68 calories and 9% fat per 1-cup serving).

Protein 2.9 / Fat 0.7 (Saturated Fat 0.1) / Carbohydrate 14.8
Fiber 3.7 / Cholesterol 0 / Sodium 207

RECIPE INDEX

SUBJECT INDEX

Acknowledgments and Credits

Source of Nutritional Data:

Computrition, Inc., Chatsworth, California. Primarily comprised of *The Composition of Foods: Raw, Processed, Prepared.* Handbooks - 8 series. United States Department of Agriculture, Human Nutrition Information Service, 1976-1990.

Oxmoor House wishes to thank the following individuals and merchants:

Carl Adams Antiques, Tuscaloosa, AL
Annieglass, Santa Cruz, CA
Bromberg's, Birmingham, AL
Michelle Matsos Calvin, Birmingham, AL
Cassis & Co., New York, NY
Chris Childs, Birmingham, AL
Christine's, Birmingham, AL
Dande-Lion, Birmingham, AL
Deruta of Italy, New York, NY
Barbara Eigen Arts, Jersey City, NJ
Fioriware, Zanesville, OH
Gien, New York, NY
Goldsmith/Corot, New York, NY
Gorham, Smithfield, RI
Haldon, Irving, TX
Leapard's Interiors, Tuscaloosa, AL
M's Fabric Gallery, Birmingham, AL
Macy's, Birmingham, AL
Mesa International, Elkins, NH
Susan Oliver, Birmingham, AL
Porta, Piscataway, NJ
The Potagers, Tuscaloosa, AL
Sasaki, New York, NY
Table Matters, Birmingham, AL
Taitu, Dallas, TX
Vietri, Hillsborough, NC
Wedgwood, Wall, New Jersey
Maralyn Wilson Gallery, Birmingham, AL
Yamazaki Tableware Incorporated, Teterboro, NJ

Photographers

Ralph Anderson: front cover, pages 2, 6, 16, 38, 56, 87, 91, 93, 95, 97, 99, 100, 102, 105, 109, 111, 113, 119, 121, 123, 125, 143, 144, 148, 151, 156, 161, 163, 168, 172, 174, 177, 191, 204, 207, 210, 213, 215, 217, 223, 228

Jim Bathie: back cover, pages 6, 25, 34, 41, 42, 45, 47, 48, 51, 52, 55, 58, 61, 62, 65, 67, 68, 71, 72, 75, 79, 82, 84, 129, 130, 135, 136, 139, 141, 153, 165, 179, 182, 184, 193, 195, 197, 200, 220, 231, 235, 240, 243

Photo Stylists

Kay E. Clarke: front cover, back cover, pages 2, 6, 16, 34, 38, 48, 55, 56, 61, 62, 65, 67, 68, 71, 72, 75, 79, 82, 105, 111, 113, 119, 121, 123, 125, 144, 148, 151, 156, 161, 163, 168, 172, 174, 179, 182, 184, 193

Virginia R. Cravens: pages 6, 41, 42, 45, 47, 51, 52, 58, 84, 87, 91, 93, 95, 97, 99, 100, 102, 109, 129, 130, 135, 136, 139, 141, 143, 153, 165, 177, 191, 195, 197, 200, 204, 207, 210, 213, 215, 217, 220, 223, 228, 231, 235, 240, 243